Crime and Society in England, 1750–1900

Ranging from the middle of the eighteenth through to the end of the nineteenth century, *Crime and Society in England, 1750–1900* explores the developments in policing, the courts and the penal system as England became increasingly industrialised and urbanised. Through a consideration of the difficulty of defining crime, the book presents criminal behaviour as being intrinsically tied to historical context and uses this theory as the basis for its examination of crime within English society during this period.

In this fifth edition Professor Emsley explores the most recent research, including the increased focus on ethnicity, gender and cultural representations of crime, allowing students to gain a broader view of modern English society. Divided thematically, the book's coverage includes:

- the varying perceptions of crime across different social groups
- crime in the workplace
- the concepts of a 'criminal class' and 'professional criminals'
- the developments in the courts, the police and the prosecution of criminals.

Thoroughly updated to address key questions surrounding crime and society in this period, and fully equipped with illustrations, tables and charts to further highlight important aspects, *Crime and Society in England, 1750–1900* is the ideal introduction for students of modern crime.

Clive Emsley is Emeritus Professor of History at the Open University. His books include *Hard Men: Violence in England since 1750* (2005); *Crime Police and Penal Policy: European Experiences 1750–1940* (2007); *The Great British Bobby* (2009); *Crime and Society in Twentieth Century England* (2011); *Soldier, Sailor, Beggarman, Thief: Crime and the British Armed Services since 1914* (2013); *Napoleon* (2014); and *Exporting British Policing during the Second World War* (2017).

THEMES IN BRITISH SOCIAL HISTORY
Edited by John Stevenson

Newspapers and English Society 1696–1855
Hannah Barker

The English Family 1450–1700
R. Houlbrooke

The Professions in Early Modern England, 1450–1800: Servants of the Commonwealth
Rosemary O'Day

Women's Agency in Early Modern Britain and the American Colonies
Rosemary O'Day

Popular Cultures in England 1550–1750
Barry Reay

Crime in Early Modern England 1550–1750 (second edition)
J. A. Sharpe

Gender in English Society 1650–1850: The Emergence of Separate Spheres?
Robert B. Shoemaker

Literature and Society 1650–1850: Ideology, Politics and Culture, 1680–1820
W. A. Speck

Popular Disturbances in England 1700–1832 (second edition)
John Stevenson

The English Town, 1680–1840: Government, Society and Culture
Rosemary Sweet

Sex, Politics and Society: The Regulations of Sexuality Since 1800
(fourth edition)
Jeffrey Weeks

Crime and Society in England, 1750–1900 (fifth edition)
Clive Emsley

Crime and Society in England, 1750–1900

FIFTH EDITION

Clive Emsley

Routledge
Taylor & Francis Group

LONDON AND NEW YORK

This edition published 2018
by Routledge
2 Park Square, Milton Park, Abingdon, Oxon, OX14 4RN

and by Routledge
711 Third Avenue, New York, NY 10017

Routledge is an imprint of the Taylor & Francis Group, an informa business

© 2018 Clive Emsley

First edition published by Pearson Education Ltd 1978
Fourth edition published by Routledge 2010

British Library Cataloguing-in-Publication Data
A catalogue record for this book is available from the British Library

Library of Congress Cataloging-in-Publication Data
Names: Emsley, Clive, author.
Title: Crime and society in England, 1750–1900 / Clive Emsley.
Description: Fifth edition. | Abingdon, Oxon ; New York, NY : Routledge, 2017. |
   Series: Themes in British social history | Includes bibliographical references
   and index.
Identifiers: LCCN 2017024426 | ISBN 9781138941755 (hardback : alk. paper) |
   ISBN 9781138941762 (pbk. : alk. paper) | ISBN 9781315144719 (ebook : alk. paper)
Subjects: LCSH: Crime—England—History—18th century. | Crime—
   England—History—19th century.
Classification: LCC HV6949.E5 E47 2017 | DDC 364.94209/034—dc23
LC record available at https://lccn.loc.gov/2017024426

ISBN: 978-1-138-94175-5 (hbk)
ISBN: 978-1-138-94176-2 (pbk)
ISBN: 978-1-315-14471-9 (ebk)

Typeset in Sabon
by Apex CoVantage, LLC

MIX
Paper from
responsible sources
FSC
www.fsc.org
FSC™ C013985

Printed in the United Kingdom
by Henry Ling Limited

For Jenny

poisoning. The overdose of laudanum which killed her appeared to have been administered by a group of local women, including the wife of one of the overseers of the poor. A wall of silence descended around the case; Mary Kirkbride came from a family notorious for burdening the parish with illegitimate children and for bringing trouble to the community.[14] Six years later the new Metropolitan Police broke up a political demonstration in Calthorpe Street, London; during the fracas P. C. Robert Culley was stabbed and mortally wounded. A significant proportion of artisan London believed that the police had acted in a 'ferocious and brutal' manner quite 'unprovoked by the people'. This attitude was reflected in the verdict of the coroner's jury – 'justifiable homicide' – and the subsequent feting of that jury by the populace.[15] Just over half a century later Captain Thomas Dudley and one of his ship's crew, Edwin Stephens, were tried for murdering cabin boy Richard Parker. Dudley had stabbed Parker in the throat with his penknife and bled him to death over his ship's chronometer case. Dudley, Stephens and another seaman, Ned Brooks, then drank the blood and ate the body over the next five days. The incident is horrific; but so too were the circumstances in which Dudley and his crew found themselves. They had been shipwrecked in the South Atlantic and adrift in an open boat for nineteen days with little food – two tins of turnips and a small turtle caught on the fourth day. Dudley gave a full statement when he was rescued, and was astonished when he and Stephens were arrested; Brooks was a Crown witness. Dudley's defence was that he had observed a custom of the sea; public opinion appears to have acquiesced, though there was disquiet that Dudley and the others had selected the weakest among their unfortunate group rather than drawing lots. Defence counsel argued that Dudley and his crew were outside the jurisdiction of any court as well as of civilised society. The different courts hearing the case over a seven-month period fudged and hedged over the legal and ethical problems. Dudley and Stephens were found guilty and sentenced to death for murder; but, in the event, they were only required to serve a token period of hard labour.[16]

The killings of Kirkbride, Culley and Parker have not been described as 'social crimes' yet, to the extent that each was condoned or excused by different social groups, the label would not be entirely inappropriate. This underlines some of the problems in using the term: if the armed poacher or armed smuggler was a social criminal, why not the killer of P. C. Culley? And if the killer of P. C. Culley, why not the killers of Kirkbride and Parker, save that the former were well-to-do and, apparently, acting with cold-blooded premeditation while their victim was poor and unfortunate; and Parker was not killed in any context of class struggle. The value of the concept of social crime is that it draws attention to the fact that laws were not universally accepted and that some offences, on some occasions, could be legitimised by social groups and communities. But used as a blanket term for certain offences, rather too many lawbreakers are cloaked in the mantle of Robin Hood; as E. P. Thompson, the inspiration behind much of the early research on the history of crime warned, 'there is not "nice" social crime here and "nasty" antisocial crime there'.[17]

Radical criminologists have fulminated about modern legal systems in the Western world which drag hundreds of poor, petty offenders through the courts but which often allow large-scale corporate offences to go unprosecuted.[18] It is clear that considerable sums were embezzled and otherwise fraudulently appropriated in the late Hanoverian and Victorian periods, and that employers sometimes flouted laws or cut metaphorical corners and real costs which cheated their workforce and endangered life. Herbert Spencer believed that fraud was endemic in railway companies a decade after the 'railway mania' of 1844 to 1847. It was not that the company directors were morally lower than the community as a whole but that:

there is the familiar fact that the corporate conscience is ever inferior to the individual conscience – that a body of men will commit as a joint act, that which every individual of them would shrink from did he feel personally responsible.

In addition there was a remoteness from the effects of corruption:

Hence in railway affairs a questionable share transaction, an exorbitant charge, a proceeding which brings great individual advantage without apparently injuring any one, but which, even if analysed in its ultimate results, can but very circuitously affect unknown persons living no one knows where, may be brought home to men who, could the results be embodied before them, would be shocked at the cruel injustices they had committed – men who in their private business where the results can be thus embodied, are sufficiently equitable.[19]

Sixty years later Judge Edward Parry warned how 'knaves' running building societies, investment schemes and similar organisations took money from the poor, but structured their contracts in such a way that they were legally immune from prosecution even when the poor man's savings were squandered or lost. Often it was a matter of class and education:

Fraud is a more complicated offence than larceny, and defrauders sometimes get the better of the law. Cheating is not always a crime, and successful cheating is a question of better education.[20]

Nineteenth-century gentlemen were aware of corporate crime and of legal, but reprehensible, corporate behaviour, yet these kinds of offences did not much vex either theorists of crime or legislators. The law was very slow to act against abuses in the commercial world; and while, for example, the 1844 Company Act required that auditors examine a company's books before it could function legally, there was no requirement that 'auditors' be accountants. It was not until the twentieth century that balance sheets and profit and loss accounts had to be published, and only after the Second World War did investors get any real protection. Legislation against abuses in factories and mines, and against the truck system for paying wages, was passed in the first half of the nineteenth century; but the inspectorate established to enforce the factory legislation had few inspectors and limited powers. Furthermore the inspectors were discouraged from prosecuting offenders. In 1876 Alexander Redgrave looked back over more than thirty years as clerk to the factory inspectorate:

In the inspection of factories it has been my view always that we are not acting as policemen . . . that in enforcing this Factory Act, we do not enforce it as a policeman would check an offence which he is told to detect. We have endeavoured not to enforce the law, if I may use such an expression, but it has been my endeavours . . . that we should be the advisors of all classes, that we should explain the law, and that we should do everything we possibly could do to induce them to observe the law, and that a prosecution should be the very last thing we should take up.[21]

Of course it is unlikely that the rulers of a state will legislate against their own interests or supporters; it might, therefore, be argued that the nineteenth-century state, dependent on a new economic order involving a new level of capitalist investment, a burgeoning factory system and a massive exploitation of coal and iron, would not act against the financiers, owners and employers in this new order except when compelled by the most flagrant abuses. This is not an argument that can be proven or disproved; it depends very much on a predetermined attitude to the state and the society which emerged during the Industrial Revolution. It might better be argued, and with a greater reference to the evidence, that the policy of state intervention in these areas was complex, fluctuating and often tentative. Tightening up on financial fraud is an exceedingly difficult task for legislators and the courts. What, for want of a better term, can be called *laissez-faire* ideology also had a role; there was a fear that too much legislation and too much inspection would inhibit Britain's industrial development. Inspectors and inspections cost money, and no nineteenth-century treasury minister, let alone parliament, would have been prepared to sanction the kind of expenditure necessary to check a significant proportion of abuses on the factory floor or at the coal face. There were other restraints also; in the case of some chemical processes, the unchecked side effects of which destroyed vegetation and harmed the health of the workforce, there was simply insufficient expertise to enable the control of noxious and dangerous vapours until well into the nineteenth century; and the noxious vapours of the alkali industry, like the general pall of smoke which hung over industrial cities and also endangered health, were seen as signs of Britain's progress and a mark of full employment. Such feelings were to be found as much among the workers, whose health was threatened, as among the employers, whose factories and processes did the threatening.[22] Furthermore the illegal use of juvenile labour was connived at by some of the workforce, and safety precautions were resented by workers if they slowed the work process, especially if this might impact on wages. It was even suggested, during the 1890s, that female workers discarded the respirators and protective clothing given by more reputable employers 'because they hide the charms of the wearers'.[23]

The fact that corrupt, dangerous, fraudulent and otherwise reprehensible activities did not become crimes until the law decreed, raises another series of questions about who makes the law, who administers it, and what legislators and agents of the law think they are doing. In the middle of the eighteenth century, Adam Smith could suggest to students at the University of Glasgow that:

when . . . some have great wealth and others nothing, it is necessary that the arm of authority should be continually stretched forth, and permanent laws or regulations made which may protect the property of the rich from the inroads of the poor. . . . Laws and governments may be considered in this and in every case as a combination of the rich to oppress the poor, and preserve to themselves the inequality of the goods which would otherwise be soon destroyed by the attacks of the poor, who if not hindered by the government would soon reduce the others to an equality with themselves by open violence.[24]

Observing England during the early 1830s Alexis de Tocqueville concluded that the law was, indeed, functioning in such a fashion:

The English have left the poor but two rights; that of obeying the same laws as the rich, and that of standing on an equality with them if they can obtain equal wealth. But those two rights are more apparent than real, since it is the rich who make the laws and who create for their own or their children's profit, the chief means of getting wealth.[25]

and increasingly, legislators began to see crime in a national context. Peel's reorganisation of the criminal law during the 1820s was symptomatic of this change. Yet laws passed in the context of perceiving a national problem still had to be implemented. Victims and witnesses had to report offences, local agents on the streets and in the courts had to act on what was presented to them; all and any of these may have had a different perception from that of the majority at Westminster. The law may have been deemed impartial and, increasingly, the product of consensual values by members of the judiciary, by legislators, theorists and others, but the law had to be interpreted and enforced by local agents who had their own assumptions, interests and prejudices. On occasion these groups could be at odds with each other.[38]

Offenders were brought before one of three principal kinds of court during the eighteenth and nineteenth centuries: petty sessions, quarter sessions or assizes. The least serious offences could be dealt with summarily by magistrates sitting alone, or in pairs in petty sessions. The petty sessions became increasingly formal and regularised during the period, with the venue often moving from private accommodation, sometimes an inn or a magistrate's parlour, to a more formal building. The magistrate who presided was, technically, a royal appointment; in practice, in the counties he was selected by the Lord Lieutenant for approval by the Lord Chancellor. He had to be a man of some wealth and social standing to have his name entered on a county's commission of the peace. Then, before he could act, he had to be of sufficient public spirit to take out his *dedimus potestatum*, which involved travelling to the county town, swearing an oath before the clerk of the peace, and paying the appropriate fees. Corporate boroughs also had magisterial benches generally composed of some combination of mayor and aldermen; borough corporations were usually self-perpetuating oligarchies of the principal inhabitants until the Municipal Corporations Act of 1835 established a common system of election for town councils. This Act also sought to separate the executive arm of town administration (the town council) from the judicial arm (the magistrates), and required that borough magistrates be supervised by a recorder, a barrister appointed by the Crown; but throughout the nineteenth century town councillors continued to be selected as borough magistrates. The number of offences which could be tried summarily increased during the eighteenth century and even more markedly during the nineteenth, particularly with the passage of the Juvenile Offenders Acts 1847 and 1850 and the Criminal Justice Acts 1855 and 1879. In the larger towns and cities stipendiary magistrates, acting in what were increasingly referred to as 'police courts', took on more and more of the burdens of summary jurisdiction. The first stipendiaries were appointed in London in 1792. But these paid professionals, like their unpaid associates and predecessors, were gentlemen; after 1835, however, they had to have served a minimum of five years at the bar as a barrister.

The courts of quarter sessions heard more serious offences that were prosecuted on indictment. These courts met four times a year, hence their name. They were established in both counties and corporate towns and, in theory though rarely in practice, all serving magistrates in the respective county or town could attend and hear the cases in a body presided over by a chairman. Again, as the nineteenth century wore on, there was a greater degree of formality in the proceedings and in the buildings, which were increasingly part of, or attached to, the Shire or Town Hall. At the borough sessions the chairmanship of the magistrates' bench was taken over by the supervisory recorder. The verdicts at quarter sessions were decided by juries but the magistrates decided upon the sentence.

The most serious indictable offences were tried before judges and juries at assizes. The judges were drawn from London's experienced legal elite; they were commonly appointed from barristers with, on average, some two decades' practice at the bar. During the eighteenth and early nineteenth centuries there were two assizes each year held in the major county towns of most counties at Lent and during the summer; Northumberland, Cumberland, Westmoreland and Durham were the exceptions, each having only one assize a year. Emergencies, such as serious food riots in Sussex in 1795 and the Luddite disturbances of the early nineteenth century, could lead to special assizes being held. The nineteenth century saw experiments with different numbers of assizes in different counties. The metropolitan equivalent of the assizes was the court meeting at the Old Bailey which was holding eight sessions a year during the 1750s; in 1834 the Old Bailey was enlarged and rehoused in the new Central Criminal Court.

During the eighteenth and early nineteenth centuries the Old Bailey had the nearest thing to a judge specialising in the criminal law in its principal presiding judge, the Recorder of London. The two or three judges who assisted at the Old Bailey, and the judges who, in pairs, rode the six assize circuits in Lent and summer, were all drawn from one of the three principal law courts – King's Bench, Common Pleas or Exchequer – where the work was predominantly civil. Indeed, half of the work at the assizes was civil, and at each assize one of the two judges would deal with the civil cases while the other heard criminal matters. Thus, for much of the period, most of the individual judges who dealt with criminal cases had relatively political context which changed from decade to decade, even from year to year. In some years the context may have provoked a ferocious response to a particular offence, in others the response could have been far more lenient. Over 200 prosecutions for sedition in England have been counted for the years 1792 to 1801. This was probably 200 more than in the preceding decade, and is probably an underestimate of the number of charges laid. It reflects the growth of Painite radicalism in England during the decade of the French Revolution; it also reflects the panic of many men of property and their determination to crush Jacobinism at home as well as abroad.[8] A Mancunian who cursed the King, his chief minister and the latter's policies following the severe impact of the 1784 Fustian Tax may have been cautioned or completely ignored. The same man damning the King, his chief minister and the latter's policies a decade later, as the cost of the Revolutionary Wars demanded more and more sacrifices in men and money, was much more likely to find himself before the courts charged with seditious words. Of course, such a narrow 'political' offence as speaking sedition is only likely to occur in public before an audience which can provide a witness or two. Yet similar variations can be suggested with reference to the prosecution of other crimes. A statistical increase in indictments for petty theft during the years of dearth in the eighteenth and early nineteenth centuries may reflect a genuine increase in theft brought about by necessity. It is equally possible that in periods of economic hardship some farmers and gentlemen preferred prosecutions rather than admonitions, in order to deter potential offenders. Conversely there were some that appear to have been inclined to greater leniency because of the distress. The problem of assessing the reasons for individuals to initiate a prosecution is compounded by Peter King's study of Essex which sets the evidence of Essex indictments together with that of others working on different counties. King points out that if, as seems possible, only one in ten of the crimes committed during the eighteenth and early nineteenth centuries was prosecuted, then a five per cent increase in decisions to prosecute because of a particular panic could result in a fifty per cent increase in the indictments available for the historian to count. Over several counties the statistics reveal an increase in the level of indictments in the late eighteenth century but, King warns, it is impossible to determine whether this 'was caused by a rise in the proportion of property offenders being indicted or by an increase in actual lawbreaking activity'. However, as he also explains, the number of individuals on a gaol calendar for trial was something that contemporaries used to assess the level of crime. It also had an impact on jury and sentencing decisions.[9]

A rapid growth in the number of prosecutions of juveniles for theft in London in the late eighteenth and early nineteenth centuries may have been, in part, the result of the city's rapid growth, and the decline of apprenticeship and living-in service. These processes were not new, however, and changing attitudes among victims, magistrates, police and prison reformers, together with a reduction in capital offences and an increase in financial incentives for prosecutors, were all, probably, equally important. In particular in London in the early nineteenth century there appears to have been a greater preparedness to draw young people into the criminal justice system, to label them as criminal and to identify them as a significant part of a criminal problem.[10]

The fear of increased crime, in itself, may have generated some increase in prosecutions. In November 1765 the printer of the *Chelmsford Chronicle* appears consciously to have used one or two robberies and some reports of robberies both to boost his sales and to assert his newspaper's claim to being the main organ of information in Essex. His emphasis on these offences, in turn, generated arrests on flimsy evidence and rewarded him with yet more copy. The stereotypical bandit gangs described in the newspaper were never apprehended.[11] The London garotting panic of 1862 appears to have prompted an increase in prosecutions for street robbery. Once press, police and private individuals were aware of the offence, they began to see it all around. James Pilkington M.P. was 'garotted' in Pall Mall on 17 July 1862. There had been only fifteen robberies with violence in the metropolis in the first six months of the year but, following the attack on Pilkington, panic developed; *The Times* orchestrated a press attack on philanthropists who, it claimed, were too soft on the kind of 'habitual criminals' who were thought to be the 'garotters'. As a result the number of reported incidents, and prosecutions, increased: in September there were two alleged garottings, in October twelve, in November thirty-two.[12]

Changes in policing could also affect the statistics of crime. In 1828 two parliamentary select committees agreed that most of the apparent increase in crime manifested in the committal figures before them was the result of better enforcement and changes in classification.[13] The establishment of the new police forces from the 1830s produced increases in the numbers of individuals committed for petty public order offences: drunk and disorderly, drunk and incapable, obstructing the highway, vagrancy. These offences took place in public and arrests were relatively easy; police statistics from one large town suggest that a surprisingly large number of men experienced arrest for such offences during the 1840s and 1850s.[14]

the pattern, though naturally not the level, of crime. While admitting that control reactions to some lesser offences might be 'highly unstable, irregular, and even whimsical' he emphasised that:

in respect of the more serious and traditional thefts and acts of violence, the actions of the controllers will be very much more, even if not absolutely, constrained by a long-standing and traditional consensus as to the heinousness of the criminal act and the unquestionable desirability of as direct an action against it as possible, and also by public expectation that the law be evenly and efficiently enforced and that justice appear to be done.[29]

Furthermore, he pointed out, while working-class suspicion of the new police never died out during the nineteenth century, members of the working class were ever more inclined to turn to the police and the law when they were the victims of crime. This, he suggested, in the long term, served to narrow the gap between actual indictable crime and recorded crime. The statistical decline in theft and violence after the 1840s supports his argument since this decline occurred at the very time when police and court activity, and public co-operation with this activity, were increasing. However, once Gatrell's arguments had gained the status of orthodoxy, Howard Taylor forcefully presented a more critical and sceptical approach to the national figures. Taylor emphasised how changes in policing and prosecution, especially when taken over by public agencies, can affect the statistics. He also stressed how a police agenda might encourage police manipulation of the figures and how government funding of the criminal justice system itself may have limited the pursuit of some prosecutions and hence the overall statistics. These latter suggestions have, in turn, prompted a strong counterblast with a challenge for less assumption and more hard evidence that would demonstrate both the police working together as an interest group and the Treasury imposing limitations on costs.[30]

Taking the various forms of raw crime statistics over the whole period from 1750 to 1900 the following pattern emerges: a gradual increase in theft and assault during the second half of the eighteenth century, becoming much steeper in the second decade of the nineteenth century and continuing at a steady rate until the close of the 1840s. For the second half of the nineteenth century the figures show a gradual decline in theft and violence, though housebreaking and burglary remain at a constant, and thus at a proportionately greater level. Within this overall pattern there are marked annual fluctuations, as well as significant peaks and troughs. Second, the statistics suggest that throughout the period the most common crime – well over half and often more than three-quarters – was small-scale theft. Third, the great majority of offenders – generally three in four – were male. There was a strong concentration of young men in their teens and early twenties; and across the eighteenth and nineteenth centuries the number of female offenders – at least those coming before the principal courts – was proportionately in decline.[31] This overall pattern of crime can readily be accommodated within the historical understanding of the development of English society during the period.

The gradual increase in eighteenth-century crime might be accounted for, at least in part, by the increase in population. It might also partly be explained with reference to increasing possessions, urbanisation and the capitalisation of industry. There was more to steal in an expanding town, but also, given the looser ties between urban and capitalist employers and their workforces, the desire to settle offences without recourse to the law may have diminished. Beattie's research on Surrey and Sussex has revealed more indictments in the urban parishes in, and on the fringe of, the metropolis. King's study of Essex presents a similar picture though it also suggests that the convenience of a local court was, of itself, an encouragement to prosecution; those small towns with their own courts had higher levels of crime recorded in their court's proceedings than those towns whose inhabitants had to trek to county quarter sessions to conduct, and thus to leave a record of, a prosecution. As noted in the introduction, the eighteenth century saw an increase in the number of capital statutes, giving rise to the descriptive phrase 'the Bloody Code'; but the great majority of capital prosecutions – ninety-five per cent or more – in the second half of the century were based on statutes enacted before 1742, and many of which went back to the Tudors.[32] The periodic fluctuations in theft during the century have been explained with reference to war and dearth, though not by the simplistic assumptions that dearth automatically led to more theft, and that massive demobilisation also, automatically, led to more theft as former soldiers and sailors, thrown on to the labour market, were compelled to steal for want of money and employment.

Analyses of the statistics, and the content of indictments and surviving depositions, taken together with a variety of other evidence, suggests two things. First, enlistment in time of war removed many of those most commonly indicted for property offences in times of peace, namely young men in their late teens and early twenties. Such young men seem to have been particularly vulnerable to the temptation of criminal activity for a variety of reasons. During the eighteenth century young men in their late teens and early twenties were often living-in apprentices or servants of against the employment of cheap labour.[43] The years up to the middle of the century witnessed cycles of economic booms and slumps. The slump of the late 1830s and early 1840s was the nadir; 1842 was possibly the worst year for unemployment in the entire century with thousands, especially in the urban areas of the northern industrial districts, compelled to sell or pawn their possessions and to rely on charity, soup kitchens or the New Poor Law. On the land the agricultural worker, increasingly distanced from his employer, was in as unfavourable a situation as his urban counterpart in the succession of crises. The decline of protection for, and supervision of, young males which resulted from the repeal of the Statute of Artificers and the continuing decline of living-in conditions for both urban and rural workers, probably strengthened the forces pushing young men into a marginal existence in their early years of adulthood. But the peaks of committals, coinciding with the depths of the economic depressions, suggest that some offenders stole to keep body and soul together. Among those committed in the Black Country during the 1830s and 1840s, David Philips noted an increase in the numbers of adults in their late twenties and thirties in the depression years, which suggests people turning to illegal activity when jobs and money were short.[44] A confession which protested hunger and poverty in mitigation quite probably was an attempt to get more lenient treatment, but it might still have been the truth and the incidence of such confessions is striking. At the Old Bailey in December 1816, for example, sixteen-year-old William Dennison admitted stealing a coat: 'I do not wish to add falsehood to fraud, I own I took the coat, but it was from mere distress.' John Waldon, who worked from time to time for a cabinet maker, admitted stealing a stool which he had been instructed to deliver: 'The distress of my family caused me to act as I did. I was going along with the stool as my master had desired, and the gentleman asked me if I would sell it, and I did.' Twenty years later Sarah Field admitted pawning some of her widowed landlady's possessions: 'It was through distress – I meant to take them out the next day.'[45] In rural Bedfordshire in the spring of 1819, as the worst of the post-war depression came to an end, Thomas Parkins was indicted for stealing two faggots from the property of the Honorable William Waldergrave of Cardington: 'I was in great distress, my Wife near lying in, I went to get a faggot, to make her a bit of fire.' The following year two men and a boy were indicted for stealing fowls, ten bushels of soot, and a bridle from a farmer. 'I was in distress,' protested William King, 'I had neither money nor victuals, and was forced to do something . . . I was going about the country to look for work.' 'I could get no work,' declared fellow offender John Gascoigne, 'nor any victuals and was driven to it . . . we were to have ten pence a bucket for the soot . . . we roasted one of the fowls under a hedge.' In 1822, John Stone of Leicester was prosecuted for stealing a watch:

I am a poor Stocking Weaver in distress. I was travelling into Leicestershire, after having been to London to offer myself for a soldier; but was not tall enough. My parents are in distress, my Father out of employment. I have eight brothers and sisters.

The voluntary statements of two of the three men charged in 1830 with stealing two smock frocks from a Dunstable draper put another slant on the motives of such petty offenders – John Morgan: 'I was very much distressed and I done it for the purpose of being taken up'; James Lilburn: 'I was very much distressed and did it to be taken up.'[46]

   The incidence of such claims by the accused and the known plight of poor labourers in the early nineteenth century prompted George Rudé to suggest that historians divide crime into three main categories for analysis: '(1) *acquisitive* crime; (2) "social" or "survival" crime; and (3) *protest* crime, or protest made in breach of the law'.[47] There are several problems with this. Rudé himself noted the difficulty of fitting '*some* violent crimes' (my italics) into the scheme. But the squalid nature and apparent petty causes of the overwhelming majority of violent crimes raise the question as to whether the scheme is at all applicable to crime against the person with the exception of poaching affrays and other major disorders which could fit under the 'protest' crime category. But even applied solely to property crime the scheme has problems. It has already been suggested that a plea of poverty may have been true; it may also have been false. Can a historian always determine whether a crime is either 'acquisitive' or 'survival' in origin? Is it not possible for an offence to be both? In January 1766 Sarah Plint, otherwise Anne Price, was prosecuted at the Old Bailey by William Thompson, an engraver, for stealing bed linen and other property from the room where she lodged. A single woman living alone in a single lodging room in eighteenth-century London was likely to be on the margin of existence, but Plint/Price was noted in court for having a string of aliases and for having been twice tried for similar offences; she was found guilty and sentenced to seven years' transportation. In January 1801 John Brand was prosecuted at the Old Bailey by John Gregory, his master a potato merchant, for stealing sixty-three pounds of potatoes. Brand protested:

I have a large family, and every necessary of life is excessively dear; and it is in the habit of the trade to allow men potatoes for their family's use; I was taking these home for that purpose.

Gregory responded: 'I paid him sixteen shillings a week, besides potatoes for his family's use, whenever he asked for them.' On the occasion of the theft Brand made no such request; the jury accepted Gregory's word. Rudé himself gives several examples of men and women accused of petty thefts – thefts which, at first glance, might appear to have been 'survival crimes' – who, when they were apprehended, had pockets full of pawn tickets; of course 'survival' may have prompted their action but this suggests that for some petty offenders the practice of stealing and pawning was becoming a habit.[48]

If hard times on occasions prompted people to steal, they might also have prompted the poorer victim to lash out with a prosecution when, in better times, he or she might have been prepared to compound the offence or even ignore it. The working man who lost his tools, some clothing, foodstuffs, or money through theft was, like the offender, unquestionably more vulnerable to economic pressure in lean years.

Much crime during the first half of the nineteenth century was, without question, 'acquisitive'; even some of that which might, at first glance, be presumed 'protest' or 'survival'. Some sheep theft, for example, was well organised and involved large numbers of animals and long distances,[49] all of which suggests enterprise and planning rather than simply the promptings of hunger and unemployment or a desire for revenge on a particular farmer. Furthermore, one of the few seasonal studies of crime has shown that while there was a peak in both summary and indictable crime in the dead season of winter when little employment was available for agricultural workers and groups like building workers, there was also an August and autumn peak at precisely the moment when employment was at its peak: the indictable offences for the August and autumn peak were less than those for winter, but summary offences were about equal. Summary offences generally encompassed the theft of growing crops and such crops were most available in the late summer and autumn; but some indictable offences were also of this type.[50] The mobility of summertime fairs and of harvest time also provided opportunities for petty theft; and the fear of criminality among mobile workers encouraged the possessors of property to be wary of itinerant strangers.

Overall the larceny statistics for the second half of the nineteenth century also show some correlation between the peaks of offences known to the police and the years of high unemployment and need. Moreover Gatrell pinpointed a significant structural change between the two halves of the century. After the 'hungry forties' the working class rarely had to contend with the coincidence of high food prices and economic depression which so marked certain years of the late eighteenth and early nineteenth centuries. This was due, in part, to a rise in the export market for industrial goods which enabled firms to off-set short-term contractions in the home market. At the same time stable, even declining, food prices helped many sections of the working class to ride out short-term periods of unemployment. Together, Gatrell suggests, these elements help to explain the overall decline in theft and violence in the second half of the nineteenth century: put at its simplest, during this period the poor became less habituated to theft because they were less subjected to periods of severe unemployment coinciding with serious subsistence problems. In addition, the growth and the professionalisation of the new police probably had some deterrent effect; the destruction of the rookeries for urban improvements removed some of the most impenetrable criminal districts; the Vagrancy Acts meant a stricter supervision of the casual poor.[51] It might also be the case that, if indeed there is a link between people's fear of popular disorder and the fear about crime which, in turn, leads to more prosecutions, then a decrease in such fears might, in turn, lead to fewer prosecutions for petty crime. While there may have been periodic concerns about the dangerous classes during the second half of the nineteenth century, the anxieties never appear to have been as acute as in the preceding half-century.

The statistics discussed so far have generally been those relating to property offences. It was offences against the person, sometimes involving robbery and sometimes not, which provided the most spectacular and terrifying images of criminality during the eighteenth and nineteenth centuries: the Ratcliffe Highway murders, which left two families gashed and bludgeoned to death in the East End of London in December 1811 and which sent ripples of fear throughout the country; the metropolitan panics of the mid 1850s and 1862, which set a trend for describing a variety of robberies in London and the provinces as 'garottings' – on one occasion, even an attempted suicide was so described; the butchery of Jack the Ripper in East London in the autumn of 1888, which also reverberated in the provinces.[52]

Homicide is the most dramatic crime of violence. Since the disappearance of an individual is usually noticed and since a body is difficult to conceal, it has been accepted that murder is the offence probably least likely to have a large 'dark figure' and that the statistics for homicide are probably closer to the real level of the offence. Yet there remain problems, not least because until the Coroners Act of 1860 the coroners' inquests could be limited by parsimonious magistrates and even by the police.[53] Moreover, the extent to which homicide levels can be taken as a guide to the overall level of inter-personal violence is anyone's guess. While people were concerned about homicide throughout the eighteenth and nineteenth centuries, it was never a statistically significant offence. Anxiety about murder and a perceived increase in violent robbery in London led to more severe legislation in 1752, but there were only ten convictions for murder during that year and this was exceptional; the annual average for murder convictions in London and Middlesex between 1749 and 1771 was four.[54] An analysis of the Wiltshire coroners' bills between 1752 and 1796 reveals that murder as part of robbery was very rare in the county, and even when the large number of infanticides are removed from the figures, most homicides can be seen to have been committed within the family or among people known to each other (Table 2.2). In Victorian England the homicide rate reached 2 per 100,000 of the population only once, in 1865; generally it hovered around 1.5 per 100,000, falling to rarely more than 1 per 100,000 at the end of the 1880s and declining still further with the new century. In round figures this means that between 1857 and 1890 there were rarely more than 400 homicides reported to the police each year, and during the 1890s the average was below 350. Moreover a closer look at Victorian homicides reveals that, while the fear may

TABLE 2.2 *Homicides in Wiltshire, 1752–96*

Homicides committed:		
(a) by parent(s)	42 (33.3%)	(includes 31 infanticides of illegitimate offspring)
(b) by spouse	4 (3.1%)	(includes 1 wife-killing husband)
(c) by other member of family	7 (5.5%)	
(d) by person(s) clearly known to victim	11 (8.7%)	(includes 7 apprentices dying as a result of treatment received from master or mistress)
(e) as a result of fighting	14 (11.1%)	
(f) during robbery	4 (3.1%)	
(g) during riot	3 (2.3%)	
(h) by person unknown	17 (13.4%)	(12 of which appear to involve the murder of unwanted illegitimate babies)
(i) in unspecified situation	24 (19%)	(though fighting or acquaintance between the victim and the perpetrator appears probable in several instances)
Total	126	

Source: Based on the evidence in R. F. Hunnisett (ed.), Wiltshire Coroner's Bills 1752–1796, Wiltshire Record Society, xxxvi (1981)

have centred around being murdered by a burglar or a similarly ferocious member of the 'dangerous classes', in most homicides assailant and victim were known to each other, and often they were related; the very high arrest rate in cases of malicious wounding reported to the police would appear partly to have the same cause.[55] Figure 2.2 is a breakdown of all the homicides and attempted homicides reported in *The Times* for England and Wales during the years 1850 and 1860. The years have significance to the extent that they both witnessed grisly murders carried out by robbers, murders which prompted many column inches in the press. The Reverend G. E. Hollest was murdered in his house at Frimley, Surrey, by burglars in the autumn of 1850, an incident which prompted considerable concern and which was instrumental in the creation of the Surrey Constabulary. In August 1860 Mary Emsley, a seventy-year-old widow, was murdered by George Mullins, a plasterer who had done some work for the victim and who robbed her after the murder.[56] Yet murders by strangers were exceptional. Far more common were mothers accused of killing or attempting to kill their children (twenty-two in 1850 and eighteen in 1860) and husbands killing or attempting to kill their wives (twenty-two in 1850 and nineteen in 1860). Studies of homicide in nineteenth-century Britain have emphasised the high percentage of cases in which the killer and the victim were known to each other or were members of the same family.[57]

Yet few incidents of violence against the person went as far as homicide and a large number were never tried on indictment. Assault is a very broad category ranging from a threatening gesture to a savage attack which all but results in the victim's death. During the eighteenth century many cases of assault were pursued at civil law. In some instances a magistrate arbitrated between the parties, negotiating a financial settlement; he could also require the assailant to enter into a recognisance to keep the peace either towards the victim, or the monarch's subjects in general. All of this makes estimating the scale of inter-personal violence extremely problematic.

Table 2.3 gives a breakdown of the assaults taken before the Bedfordshire magistrates every five years between 1750 and 1840 noting where the assailant was indicted and where he or she was simply required to enter into a recognisance to keep the peace; it must be noted that in the latter instances the 'assault' may have been purely verbal. Most striking here is the very high number of assaults on women, only one-third of which were prosecuted on indictment; nineteen of these sixty-one assaults were by husbands on their wives. Understandably perhaps, and in contrast to the attacks on women, about eighty-five per cent of attacks on authority, in the shape of constables or overseers of the poor, were indicted. In

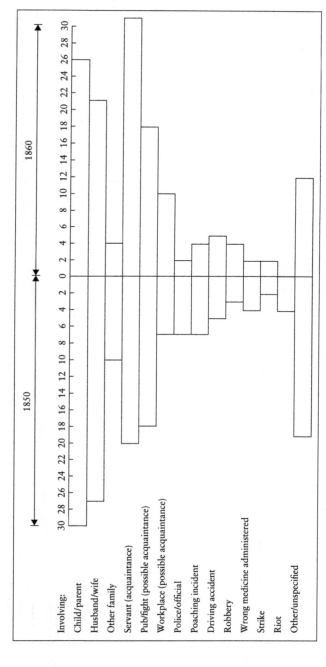

FIG 2.2 *Homicides and attempted homicides 1850 and 1860*

TABLE 2.3 *Assaults in Bedfordshire based on indictments and recognisances every five years, 1750–1840*

VICTIMS	ASSAILANTS Gentry		Professional		Farmer		Tradesman/ artisan		Husbandman/ gardener		Labourer/ servant		Women		Unknown		Total assailants
	I.	R.*	I.	R.	I.	R.	I.	R.	I.	R.	I.	R.	I.	R.	I.	R.	
Gentry	–	2	–	–	1	–	–	2	–	–	–	5	–	–	–	–	10
Professional	–	1	–	–	–	–	–	–	–	–	–	2	–	–	–	–	3
Farmer	–	–	–	–	1	1	–	1	–	–	1	8	–	–	–	–	12
Tradesman/artisan	–	–	–	–	–	–	1	6	–	1	3	6	–	2	1	2	22
Husbandman/gardener	–	–	–	–	–	–	–	–	–	1	–	2	–	–	2	–	5
Labourers/servants (including gamekeepers)	–	1	–	–	–	1	1	2	–	–	10	7	2	–	6	1	31 (19 indictments)
Constables/overseers	–	1	–	–	–	1	3	1	–	–	18	2	6	–	2	–	34 (29 indictments)
Women	–	1	1	–	–	3	3	8	1	1	10	17	2	7	3	4	61† (20 indictments)
Children	–	–	–	–	–	–	–	1	–	2	2	–	1	–	–	–	6
Unknown	–	–	–	–	–	–	3	2	1	1	15	19	–	2	22	7	72
Total indictments/recognisances	–	8	1	–	2	6	11	23	1	6	59	68	11	11	34	13	

* I. indicates indictment, R. indicates recognisance

† 19 of these 61 cases specified husbands assaulting wives; there is one incident recorded in these years of a woman brought to court for assaulting her husband

all, offences against the person constituted rather more than one-tenth of the statistics of crime available for the nineteenth century: about ten per cent of the committals made on indictments between 1834 and 1856; just over ten per cent of crimes known to the police between 1857 and the end of the century; and about 15 per cent of summary committals in the second half of the century. Assaults on authority, in the shape of policemen, formed a significant percentage of nineteenth-century assaults and declined at a slower rate than common assault; they constituted about fifteen per cent of summary prosecutions for assault in the 1860s and about twenty-one per cent in the 1890s. However the national statistics can hide important contrasts between regions.[58] Probably many of these assaults were simply men – and the typical assailant in all varieties of assault was male – resisting arrest or obstructing the police in their duty; but others were horrific in their scale of viciousness, and it was not unknown for police constables to get their retaliation in first.[59]

A degree of physical punishment meted out to dependents seems to have been accepted, or at least tolerated, across social groups during the eighteenth century and well into the nineteenth century; thus masters beat their servants, husbands their wives, parents their children. Yet there were limits. In 1786 a Bedfordshire magistrate wrote to the quarter sessions about William White of Westoning who he had committed to gaol for not finding sureties to keep the peace towards his wife, Mary:

the Man seems to have a savage stupid idea that he may beat his wife as much as he pleases provided he does not kill her: perhaps a little confinement may shew him the error and the Justices will do what is proper upon the occasion.

In 1802 William Long, a yeoman of Upper Stondon, was bound over to keep the peace towards one of his labourers, John West, after accusing West of helping himself to too much bread and cheese and then setting about him with a 'knotty stick made from a crab tree'.[60] Half a century later, in 1847, an Essex farmer noted in his diary when he horsewhipped a servant-boy who had defrauded him of money.[61] But the limits of tolerance were declining. While the statistics are problematic, a study of sentencing policies in Essex suggests that, at the end of the eighteenth and beginning of the nineteenth centuries, assailants were less likely to plead guilty, less likely to be acquitted and, if found guilty, less likely to receive a small, nominal fine and more likely to be imprisoned.[62]

Although the beating of servants was increasingly becoming unacceptable, few doubted the beneficial effects of a sound thrashing for naughty boys, but even here the evidence is contradictory. Some working-class parents, not known for gentleness towards their own children, often took strong exception to their children being beaten by teachers; yet others invited the local policeman in to chastise a difficult child.[63] Wife-beating began to cause disquiet early in the Victorian period, at least in respectable middle-class circles, and judges and magistrates began to use the law to seek to impose a more pacific concept of masculinity. Unfortunately, even on the rare occasions when such treatment resulted in death, it was possible for juries and the popular press to find mitigating circumstances. In 1850 Frederick Gilbert was acquitted of the manslaughter of his wife after it was noted in court that he was a good, sober workman and his wife had been a drunkard. Nearly forty years later Robert Knowles, a respectable Preston butcher who had killed his wife with a kick from his steel-tipped clog, had the resulting charge of murder reduced to manslaughter, and was then recommended to mercy by the jury since his wife was a drunkard and 'a scandal to her sex'.[64] Studies of violence between working-class men and women in both London and Liverpool during the third quarter of the nineteenth century suggest a decline in domestic violence, possibly because of growing respectability and rising living standards which reduced stress on the male as the principal economic provider; and possibly also because of a greater preparedness of the police to intervene. Perhaps also the cult of respectability made wives even less likely to complain since such assaults were shameful, a sign of a lack of respectability; and in the growing suburbs assaults were less public, less likely to disturb the neighbours, while the bruising was less visible than on the crowded tenement stair.[65] The question remains, of course, as to what extent the pattern of violence between working-class men and women in big cities can be taken as typical for England and Wales. In Wales the pattern appears to have been similar with a decline from the mid-century; however women in Cardiff, Swansea and Newport were not bashful about the injuries inflicted on them and their children, parading them and embarrassing police-court officials with requests for help and summonses. In Preston, however, where, in the year before the First World War, the chairman of the police court used wife-beating as a metaphor for the general level of crime, perception of a decline came only at the turn of the century.[66]

The cult of respectability may itself have contributed to one variety of homicide: of those children in Figure 2.2 allegedly killed by their mothers, at least four in 1850 and at least seven in 1860 died immediately after their birth and were illegitimate. These deaths, however, probably constituted only a tiny percentage of the incidence of infanticide during these years.

Though, in general, homicide might be one of the best-reported crimes, infanticide was notoriously under-reported and rarely came before the criminal courts. It was difficult to get coroners to hold inquests on dead infants, and even when a coroner did register a verdict of murder the assize jury was often reluctant to return a verdict indicating culpability on the mother's part.[67] Other cases, involving the deaths of older children, reveal appalling instances of neglect and ill-treatment, as in the case of Maria Hook who, aged four years, allegedly weighed only six pounds when she died following months of dreadful treatment by her stepmother.[68] The cases of family violence which reached the courts were, almost certainly, only the tip of a very nasty iceberg.

Drink was often remarked upon as a cause of violence in the family. In May 1850 Patrick Barry returned home drunk to his rooms in Jennings Buildings, Kensington, and proceeded to kick his wife to death.[69] Drink could be seen as a mitigating circumstance for the violent offender as in the case of Frederick Gilbert noted previously. However, far more common, and especially among earnest temperance reformers, drink was seen as a fundamental cause of all crime. The Reverend James Nugent, a chaplain of Liverpool Borough Prison, informed the House of Lords Select Committee on Intemperance in 1877 that nine out of ten of the convicts in that prison were there 'directly or indirectly through drink'. William Hoyle, a Lancashire cotton manufacturer and pillar of the temperance community, had published *Crime in England and Wales in the Nineteenth Century: An Historical and Critical Retrospect* the year before he appeared before the committee. He deployed statistics to demonstrate a direct correlation between the increase in crime and the increases in beer shops and public houses. Other witnesses were less zealous and suggested only a connection between crimes of violence and drink,[70] a connection explored in some detail in the sober historical analysis of Gatrell and Hadden. Placing the figures for assault and drunkenness alongside the business cycle, they have shown slight increases during years of prosperity suggesting that high wages and high employment led to a greater consumption of alcohol which, in turn, contributed to more violent crime. However, for the last quarter of the century in particular the overall trend in the statistics of both violent crime and drunkenness is downwards. This may be explained, in part, by what contemporaries perceived as the civilisation or moralisation of the population; perhaps, indeed, the Victorian virtues of morality and probity, of good works and service to others, actually succeeded in reducing the level of harm to persons and property.[71] Perhaps also there was a decrease in anxiety about small-scale, drink-related violence.[72] Such a decrease would link with the diminishing fears about the dangerous classes from the mid-nineteenth century which, it has been suggested previously, contributed to a decline in the reporting, and the prosecution, of small-scale theft. There is a further element worth considering. Recent work on gender has emphasised the notion of separate spheres and new ways of controlling women during the nineteenth century. It may be that the statistical decline in theft and, especially, violence in the second half of the nineteenth century is a reflection of a better socialisation of young, especially working-class males during this period, and that the physically aggressive behaviour regarded and accepted as traditionally masculine was being stigmatised and controlled better.

While there seems to be an interplay between criminal statistics and periodic fears of crime and disorder, it is also probable that the collection and publication of national crime statistics led to the perception of crime as a national impersonal problem. During the eighteenth century, when there were no such statistics, crime was essentially a personal problem for victims and accused. Statistics made crime national and made the criminal a national bogeyman. Crime could now be shown to be offences perpetrated on a large scale against respectable people by a group which by being measured statistically – whatever the faults of the statistics – could be defined collectively as criminals or the criminal class. This perception of criminals as a group is the subject of the next chapter.

Notes

1 Quoted in **Eric Stockdale**, *A Study of Bedford Prison 1660–1877*, Phillimore, London, 1977, p. 130. The Revd Philip Hunt who sent this warning to Peel might be considered as having been at least an accessory to what some would consider as one of the greatest thefts of the early nineteenth century; as chaplain to Lord Elgin he played a key role in the removal of the Elgin Marbles from the Acropolis.

2 **M. J. Cullen**, *The Statistical Movement in Early Victorian Britain: The Foundations of Empirical Social Research*, Harvester, Brighton, 1975, especially pp. 1–16 and 72–4. For a detailed introduction to nineteenth-century criminal statistics see **V. A. C. Gatrell** and **T. B. Hadden**, 'Criminal statistics and their interpretation', in **E. A. Wrigley** (ed.), *Nineteenth-Century Society: Essays in the Use of Quantitative Methods for the Study of Social Data*, Cambridge U.P., Cambridge, 1972.

3 **T. Barwick Lloyd Baker**, 'Abstract and inferences founded upon the official returns of England and Wales for the years 1854–59, with special reference

to the results of reformatories', *Journal of the Statistical Society*, xxiii (1860), pp. 427–54 (at pp. 436–7).

4 S. J. Stevenson, 'The "Criminal Class": Legislation, labelling and prosecution in the late nineteenth century'. Paper presented to Urban History Group, Economic History Society Conference, Cheltenham, 4 April 1986. For a more extended treatment see *idem*, 'The "Criminal Class" in the mid-Victorian city: A study of policy conducted with special reference to those made subject to the provisions of 34 & 35 Vict. c. 112 (1871) in Birmingham and East London in the early years of registration and supervision', unpublished D.Phil., Oxford University, 1983.

5 Patrick Colquhoun, *A Treatise on the Police of the Metropolis*, 3rd edn, 1796, p. vii.

6 U.C.L. Chadwick MSS 'Police Memoranda etc., undated (post 1850)', probably referring to the 1836–9 Royal Commission on Constabulary.

7 James T. Hammick, 'On the judicial statistics of England and Wales with special reference to recent returns relating to crime', *Journal of the Statistical Society*, xxx (1867), pp. 375–426 (at p. 392).

8 Clive Emsley, 'An aspect of Pitt's "terror": Prosecutions for sedition during the 1790s', *Social History*, 6 (1981), pp. 155–84; see also *idem*, 'Repression, "terror" and the rule of law in England during the decade of the French Revolution', *E.H.R.*, C (1985), pp. 801–25. Extrapolating from prosecutions in the West Country, Steve Poole estimates that there may have been as many as seven or eight times as many sedition prosecutions; S. R. Poole, 'Popular politics in Bristol, Somerset and Wiltshire, 1791–1801', unpublished Ph.D., University of Bristol, 1993, pp. 173–90.

9 Peter King, *Crime, Justice and Discretion in England 1740–1820*, Oxford U.P., Oxford, 2000, chapter 5 especially, quotation at p. 134.

10 Heather Shore, *Artful Dodgers: Youth and Crime in Early Nineteenth-Century London*, Boydell/Royal Historical Society, Woodbridge, 1999.

11 Peter King, 'Newspaper reporting, prosecution practice and perceptions of urban crime: The Colchester crime wave of 1765', *Continuity and Change*, 2 (1987), pp. 423–54.

12 Jennifer Davis, 'The London garotting panic of 1862: A moral panic and the creation of a criminal class in mid-Victorian England', in V. A. C. Gatrell, Bruce Lenman and Geoffrey Parker (eds), *Crime and the Law: The Social History of Crime in Western Europe Since 1500*, Europa, London, 1980, p. 205.

13 Cullen, *Statistical Movement*, p. 14. The committees were: the Select Committee on Criminal Commitments and Convictions and the Select Committee on the Police of the Metropolis.

14 Chris A. Williams, 'Counting crimes or counting people: Some implications of mid-nineteenth-century British police returns', *C.H.S.*, 4, 2 (2000), pp. 77–93.

15 Beds. R.O. QEV 4.

16 'Discrepant criminal statistics', *Journal of the Statistical Society*, **xxxi** (1868), pp. 349–53 (at p. 352).

17 See the discussion in **Jennifer Davis**, 'Law breaking and law enforcement: The creation of a criminal class in mid-Victorian London', unpublished Ph.D., Boston College, 1984, pp. 137–9, 152–8 and 246–51.

18 HO 45.9755. A60557.

19 **William Douglas Morrison**, *Crime and Its Causes*, London, 1891, p. 6.

20 For this legislation see below, pp. 195.

21 Perhaps the first such offender to be prosecuted was Micah Gibbs, a gentleman of Wellow who was found guilty by the Somerset quarter sessions in October 1800 of producing fraudulent certificates to the tax commissioners at Bath. He was fined £200 and sentenced to four months in Ilchester Gaol where he was to remain until the fine was paid. Somerset R.O. QS Minute Book CQ2 2/4(3).

22 **Susan S. M. Edwards**, 'Sex crimes in the nineteenth century', *New Society*, 13 September 1979, pp. 562–3. Before 1875 it was a felony to have sexual intercourse with a child aged ten or under, but only a misdemeanour with a child between ten and twelve years.

23 **E. G. Du Cane**, 'The decrease of crime', *Nineteenth Century*, **xxxiii** (1893), pp. 480–92 (at p. 485); **William Douglas Morrison**, 'The increase of crime', *Nineteenth Century*, **xxxi** (1892), pp. 950–7 (at pp. 951–2).

24 Du Cane, 'The decrease of crime', p. 485.

25 **K. K. Macnab**, 'Aspects of the history of crime in England and Wales between 1805–60', unpublished Ph.D., University of Sussex, 1965, p. 347. Macnab does remark that the decline is 'rather suspicious'.

26 **David Philips**, *Crime and Authority in Victorian England*, Croom Helm, London, 1977, pp. 132–5 and 146.

27 **Thorsten Sellin**, 'The significance of the records of crime', *Law Quarterly Review*, **lvx** (1951), pp. 489–504.

28 See, *inter alia*, **Jason Ditton**, *Contrology: Beyond the New Criminology*, Macmillan, London, 1979, especially chapter 2. For the most prolonged and sophisticated argument in favour of using statistics for the study of eighteenth-century crime see **J. M. Beattie**, *Crime and the Courts in England 1660–1800*, Oxford U.P., Oxford, 1986.

29 **V. A. C. Gatrell**, 'The decline of theft and violence in Victorian and Edwardian England', in **Gatrell**, **Lenman** and **Parker** (eds), *Crime and the Law*, p. 248.

30 **Howard Taylor**, 'Rationing crime: The political economy of criminal statistics since the 1850s', *Economic History Review*, **li** (1998), pp. 569–90; *idem*,

'The politics of the rising crime statistics of England and Wales, 1914–1960', *C.H.S.*, **2**, 1 (1998), pp. 5–28; **Robert M. Morris**, ' "Lies, damned lies, and criminal statistics": reinterpreting the criminal statistics in England and Wales', *C.H.S.*, **5**, 1 (2001), pp. 111–27.

31 **J.M. Beattie**, 'The criminality of women in eighteenth-century England', *Journal of Social History*, **viii** (1975), pp. 80–116; *idem*, *Crime and the Courts*, pp. 243–8; **David Jones**, *Crime, Protest, Community and the Police in Nineteenth-Century England*, RKP, London, 1982, pp. 132–4; King, *Crime, Justice and Discretion*, especially chapter 8; Macnab, 'Aspects of crime', especially pp. 59 and 341–8; Philips, *Crime and Authority*, pp. 147–2.

32 **Douglas Hay**, 'War, dearth and theft in the eighteenth century: The record of the English courts', *P and P*, **95** (1982), pp. 117–60: p. 146 and note 78.

33 OBP t17970426-335.

34 **Sir John Fortescue** (ed.), *The Correspondence of George III*, 6 vols, London, 1928, vip. 387; *Leicester Journal*, 24 July 1795. *The Gentleman's Magazine* commented in November 1772: 'It is worthy of observation, that during the two last years of the last war, viz. 1759, 1760, the number of criminals condemned at the Old Bailey amounted to 29 only, and the days of the Judges' attendance to 46; but that during the two last years of peace, viz. 1770, 1771, the number of criminals condemned have amounted to 151, and the days of the Judges' attendance to 99' (xlii, 541). For similar contemporary concern see Hay, 'War, dearth and theft', pp. 138 and 142.

35 Hay, 'War, dearth and theft', *passim*.

36 King, *Crime, Justice and Discretion*, pp. 156–7; **Esther Snell**, 'Discourses on criminality in the *Kentish Mercury*', *Continuity and Change*, **22**, 1 (2007), pp. 13–47.

37 King, 'Newspaper reporting, prosecution practice and urban crime'.

38 Macnab, 'Aspects of crime', especially appendices 1 and 2.

39 **T. R. Gurr**, *Rogues, Rebels and Reformers: A Political History of Crime and Conflict*, Sage, Beverley Hills, CA, 1976, p. 10; **Abdul Lodhi** and **Charles Tilly**, 'Urbanisation, crime and collective violence in nineteenth-century France', *American Journal of Sociology*, **79** (1973), pp. 296–318 (at p. 296); **J. A. Sharpe**, *Crime in Early Modern England 1550–1750*, 2nd edn, Longman, London, 1999, pp. 263–8.

40 **Norma Landau**, *The Justices of the Peace, 1679–1760*, University of California Press, Berkeley and Los Angeles, CA, 1984, p. 395.

41 See the discussion in **Gertrude Himmelfarb**, *The Idea of Poverty: England in the Early Industrial Age*, Faber and Faber, London, 1984, pp. 393–7.

42 **Clive Emsley**, *British Society and the French Wars 1793–1815*, Macmillan, London, 1979; Himmelfarb, *The Idea of Poverty*, especially pp. 100–44;

Joseph Lowe, *The Present State of England in Regard to Agriculture, Trade, and Finance*, 2nd edn, London, 1823, pp. 210–24.

43 John Rule, *The Experience of Labour in Eighteenth-Century Industry*, Croom Helm, London, 1981, pp. 95–6 and 114–19.

44 Philips, *Crime and Authority*, pp. 145–6 and 163–4.

45 OBP t18161204–20, (Dennison) and t18161204–69 (Waldon); in both instances the jury recommended mercy: in Dennison's case judgment was respited; Waldon was fined 1 shilling and discharged. OBP t18361128–64 (Field); Field, also recommended to mercy, was imprisoned for one month.

46 Beds. R.O. QSR 24/271; QSR 24/229; QSR 25/324; QSR 1830/409.

47 George Rudé, *Criminal and Victim: Crime and Society in Early Nineteenth-Century England*, Clarendon Press, Oxford, 1985, p. 78 and chapter 5, *passim*.

48 OBP t17660116-7 (Plint) and t18010114-11 (Brand); Rudé, *Criminal and Victim*, p. 93.

49 John Rule, 'The manifold causes of rural crime: sheep-stealing in England c. 1740–1840', in John Rule (ed.), *Outside the Law: Studies in Crime and Order 1650–1850*, Exeter Papers in Economic History no. 15, University of Exeter, Exeter, 1982; R. A. E. Wells, 'Sheep-rustling in Yorkshire in the age of the Industrial and Agricultural Revolutions', *Northern History*, xx (1984), pp. 127–45.

50 Janet Gyford, ' "Men of Bad Character": Property crime in Essex in the 1820s', unpublished M.A., University of Essex, 1982, pp. 63–5.

51 Gatrell, 'Decline of theft and violence', pp. 305–16; Gatrell expresses scepticism about that area upon which 'the Victorians were prone to congratulate themselves . . . most' when noting a decline in crime, namely the assault on juvenile crime from the 1850s (pp. 305–7).

52 T. A. Critchley and P. D. James, *The Maul and the Pear Tree: The Ratcliffe Highway Murders 1811*, Constable, London, 1971, pp. 79 and 96–7; Davis, 'London garotting panic', p. 205; Sindall, *Street Violence*, especially chapter 4 which emphasises the metropolitan nature of the garotting panic and the role of the press in fostering it. Sindall also notes that the statistics indicate a greater incidence of street violence in the north west than in London.
   Sir Robert Anderson publicly blamed 'the sensation-monger of the newspaper press' for the scare created by Jack the Ripper in 'Our absurd system of punishing crime', *Nineteenth Century*, xlix (1901), pp. 268–84 (at p. 269). However Anderson's own role in the Ripper affair (as head of the Criminal Investigation Branch of the Metropolitan Police) was hardly distinguished.

53 Peter King, 'The impact of urbanization on murder rates and on the geography of homicide in England and Wales, 1780–1850', *H.J.*, 53, 3 (2010), pp. 671–98 (at pp. 675–8 and 687–9).

54 John H. Langbein, 'Shaping the eighteenth-century criminal trial: A view from the Ryder sources', *University of Chicago Law Review*, 50 (1983), pp. 1–136 (at pp. 44–6). For a discussion of homicide during the eighteenth century see Beattie, *Crime and the Courts*, pp. 77–124.

55 Gatrell, 'Decline of theft and violence', pp. 286–95 and appendices A1 and A2.

56 See, *inter alia*, *The Times*, 2, 3, 5, 8, 14, 19 October 1850; 18, 20, 22, 23, 25, 27 August 1860, and 24, 26, 27 October 1860; T. A. Critchley, *A History of Police in England and Wales*, 2nd edn, Constable, London, 1978, p. 98. Although her murder was shocking, Mary Emsley was manifestly not everyone's favourite old lady. Detective Inspector Thornton, in charge of the murder investigation, reported that she 'was possessed of considerable house property situated in very low neighbourhoods of Bethnal Green, Ratcliffe, Stratford, Barking, Dagenham etc., and she was in the habit of personally collecting the greater portion of her rents on a Monday and in consequence of her frequent litigation with her tenants, her very plain way of dressing and living, she became well known at the East End of London'. According to her solicitor she had been threatened by tenants. Nor was she popular with her own family, having told them that she intended to leave all her money to build almshouses. MEPO 3/62.

57 See, for example, Philippe Chassaigne, *Ville et Violence: Tensions et conflits dans la Grande-Bretagne Victorienne (1840–1914)*, Presses de l'Université de Paris, Paris, 2005; Carolyn A. Conley, *Certain Other Countries: Homicide, Gender and National Identity in Late Nineteenth-Century England, Ireland, Scotland and Wales*, Ohio State U.P., Columbus, 2007.

58 Gatrell and Hadden, 'Criminal statistics', pp. 269–71; Gatrell, 'Decline of theft and violence', pp. 284–95 and appendix A5. For all its notoriety as a violent city the figures for Liverpool did not clearly follow the national pattern; this may, of course, have been the result of the way violence was reported. See John E. Archer, *The Monster Evil: Policing and Violence in Victorian Liverpool*, University of Liverpool Press, Liverpool, 2011, p. 52.

59 Clive Emsley, *The Great British Bobby: A History of British Policing From the 18th Century to the Present*, revised edn, Quercus, London, 2010, pp. 148–52 and 159–62.

60 Beds. R.O. QSR 15/191, and QSR 18/67.

61 Essex R.O. D/DBs F 38 Bretnall's Diary, entry for 10 November 1847 (quoted in Gyford, 'Men of Bad Character', p. 15).

62 Peter King, 'Punishing assault: The transformation of attitudes in the English Courts', *Journal of Interdisciplinary History*, xxvii (1996), pp. 43–74.

63 Stephen Humphries, *Hooligans or Rebels? An Oral History of Working-Class Childhood and Youth 1889–1939*, Basil Blackwell, Oxford, 1981, pp. 82–9; Emsley, *The English Police*, p. 80.

64 *The Times*, 7 April 1850; **A. James Hammerton**, *Cruelty and Companionship: Conflict in Nineteenth-Century Married Life*, Routledge, London, 1992, pp. 34–5. For a general and persuasive account of the developments in the courts and resistance to them, see **Martin J. Wiener**, *Men of Blood: Violence, Manliness, and Criminal Justice in Victorian England*, Cambridge U.P., Cambridge, 2004.

65 Nancy Tomes, 'A "torrent of abuse": Crimes of violence between working-class men and women in London 1840–1875', *Journal of Social History*, **xi** (1978), pp. 328–45; Archer, *The Monster Evil*, chapter 11.

66 **David J. V. Jones**, *Crime in Nineteenth-Century Wales*, University of Wales Press, Cardiff, 1992, pp. 82–3; Hammerton, *Cruelty and Companionship*, p. 42.

67 See below, pp. 104–5.

68 *The Times*, 14 August 1850.

69 *The Times*, 23 May 1850.

70 P.P. 1877 (418) xi, *Select Committee of the House of Lords on Intemperance. Third Report*, qq. 8327 and 8401–11. The Earl of Onslow, for one, was not convinced by Hoyle's use of statistics and asked him: 'Do you not think it would be no very difficult matter to prove almost anything you wished to prove by judiciously manipulating statistics from various parts of the country?' (q. 8411).

71 **Gertrude Himmelfarb**, *The Demoralization of Society: From Victorian Virtues to Modern Values*, Institute of Economic Affairs, London, 1995.

72 Gatrell and Hadden, 'Criminal statistics', pp. 370–1; Gatrell, 'Decline of theft and violence', pp. 291 and 300.

CHAPTER 3

Class perceptions

The historians who began the current interest in the history of crime tended to have a Marxist or liberal progressive perspective. Even the non-Marxists deployed the concept of class in their analyses. Theft, or 'appropriation', became a form of protest, while the criminal law became a tool for maintaining an unequal division of wealth. Gender, ethnicity and Foucauldian concepts of power and control have since eclipsed class, yet it still remains useful for thinking about the perception of crime.

When Peel proposed the consolidation and rationalisation of the criminal law to parliament in 1826 he explained that, in the previous year, 14,437 persons had been charged with various crimes; some 12,500, or six-sevenths of them, had been charged with theft.[1] Throughout the eighteenth and nineteenth centuries theft of various sorts was the principal offence which occupied the time of the criminal courts. Most thefts were petty; only a very few involved large sums of money or objects of great monetary value; only a very few involved violence. It was the quantity rather than the quality of the offences which concerned people and, arguably, this has always been the case. But once the decision had been made, albeit unconsciously, to concentrate on quantity, rather than what might be termed 'quality' crime, other things followed. Most of those prosecuted for these crimes came from the poorer sections of society and, as a consequence as the discourse of 'class' became more and more central to the analysis and perception of society, so criminality tended to be seen as, essentially, a class problem.

Counterfactual history is fraught with danger, yet, if legislators and commentators on crime had concentrated on the few big thefts or embezzlements as their benchmark for crime, rather than on the very many small thefts and incidents of disorders, then the overall perception of criminality and of the criminal class would have been very different. This is not to say that there was a middle-class conspiracy during the nineteenth century when these perceptions developed. Concern about the poor and their 'immoral' or 'disorderly' behaviour went back a long way; but fear of the poor reached a new peak in the aftermath of the French Revolution and with the experience of the fast-growing and teeming cities in the early nineteenth century. Crime was often perceived as another problem, like sanitation, within the burgeoning urban sprawls.

It was recognised that men of wealth and social standing also committed offences. Throughout the nineteenth century there were concerns about various forms of white-collar crime and corruption. Sarah Wilson has traced the foundations of twenty-first-century financial crime in Britain to the 1830s noting how even the much used Royal Commission on a Rural Constabulary suspected that crimes of fraud were increasing in contrast to a decline in violent crime.[2] Victorian novelists portrayed corrupt bankers and businessmen – Bulstrode in *Middlemarch*, Merdle in *Little Dorrit*, Melmotte in *The Way We Live Now*. Yet such offenders, however common in fiction and in newspaper and journal literature, were not perceived as members of a criminal class and were categorised as 'criminal' with some difficulty, at least until the close of the nineteenth century when biological discourse began to rival that of class in the analysis of crime and criminals. The illegal and/or immoral actions of white-collar offenders set a bad example to their social inferiors, but these offenders were 'rotten apples' within their social class.[3] It was a consoling distinction to which the middle and upper classes clung; offenders within their social milieu were exceptions and the criminal class was located elsewhere. Poor clerks caught embezzling their employer's money similarly were not regarded as part of a criminal element within society. Public debate on such offences during the 1860s and 1870s concentrated on examining employer-clerk relations. The employers were criticised for not having a proper sense of business management and ensuring that their books balanced, for not providing a better system of surveillance of clerks who could so easily be tempted by the large sums with which they often had to deal, and for paying the clerks a 'beggarly pittance' hardly commensurate with the trust and responsibility expected of them. 'We can't for a moment dispute the right of merchant princes paying what salaries they deem fit to their clerks', declared a Manchester journal, 'but we would ask, is the system of paying low salaries likely to conduce a high moral tone in the young men employed?'[4]

Yet if low wages and poverty were regarded as contributing to crime among clerks, lower social groups were commonly denied this excuse and

'the fiery ordeal of protracted idleness, and its inevitable concomitant, protracted temptation'. The longer an economic crisis continued, the greater
the temptation:

The occasional act becomes a constant habit; principle is overlaid, and
conscience drugged and stupified. . . . Nor does the return to prosperity
obliterate the evil which a long cycle of distress has produced. Work may
be resumed, and the former comforts gladden the household, but the trail
and slime of the moral evil which has dwelt in the heart and ruled there,
remains, and will evidence itself in a thousand forms.

Yet it remained the individuals within 'the operative classes' who were at
fault rather than the system.[42] For Plint's contemporaries, like the Reverend John Clay, the Chaplain of Preston Gaol, and Matthew Davenport
Hill, the Recorder of Birmingham, it was possible to argue that times of
economic prosperity also linked with the moral weakness of the working
class to tempt them into crime.[43]

The 1830s and, particularly, the 'hungry forties' witnessed apocalyptic
visions of society shared by men at opposite ends of the political spectrum.
Engels asserted that 'the incidence of crime has increased with the growth
of the working-class population and there is more crime in Britain than in
any other country in the world'. Crime was an aspect of the new social war
which worsened with every passing year. Sir Archibald Alison, the Tory
Sheriff of Lanarkshire, perceived:

destitution, profligacy, sensuality and crime [advancing] with unheard-of
rapidity in the manufacturing districts, and the dangerous classes there
massed together combine every three or four years in some general strike
or alarming insurrection, which, while it lasts, excites universal terror.[44]

It was during the 1840s that the Chartist G. W. M. Reynolds began publishing *The Mysteries of London*, which, with its sequel, were 'probably
the longest, best-selling fiction of the time'.[45] The former was inspired by
Eugene Sue's *Les Mystères de Paris*, the best-selling novel in France during
the 1840s, and with scenes of appalling savagery and violence as well as
sexual titillation, Reynolds gave his readers a frightening portrait of a brutalised, savage poor – a truly dangerous class.

In 1840 a French Police administrator, H.A. Frégier, coined the term 'the
dangerous classes.' It was readily accepted by the English middle classes
as descriptive of the creatures inhabiting the most squalid districts of the
burgeoning cities. Eleven years after Frégier's book appeared in France,
Mary Carpenter chose to publish a philanthropic treatise under the title

Reformatory Schools for the Children of the Perishing and Dangerous Classes and for Juvenile Offenders. She used 'perishing' and 'dangerous' as a way to distinguish between those who were deserving and had not yet become criminal, and those who were already tainted by prison. Gaol, she believed, harmed the child physically as well as mentally. It damaged the joints and developed 'sluggishness' and feeble-mindedness[46] – another way of explaining why the poor and the criminal looked very different in physique as well as dress.

In 1862 the Reverend H. W. Holland writing on 'professional thieves' in the *Cornhill Magazine* described how any visitor entering a thieves' district would be struck by the inhabitants' strange dress and physiognomy; the adults were 'seedy and sleepy' while the children 'lounge about, looking very suspicious and preternaturally sharp'. He went on to explain that:

Nearly all habitual thieves, male and female, die of consumption, and under or about thirty-five years of age. Drink, debauchery, irregular hours, the sudden transitions from luxuries to a low prison diet – these things soon kill them off.[47]

The question immediately posed by such descriptions is, what was the difference between the life-style and life expectancy of these 'professional thieves' and those of the poorer sections of the working class? Whatever the early statisticians may have argued about improvements in life expectancy, the tables published during the middle years of the nineteenth century revealed a significant difference between the life expectancy of the working class and that of their social superiors; and very large numbers of the working class died before the age of thirty-five. Tuberculosis, 'the Captain of the Men of Death', the 'White Plague', was a remorseless killer of the urban poor and, while it declined during the nineteenth century, it still accounted for perhaps one-third of all deaths from disease during the Victorian period.[48] Poor nutrition, in the context of long hours and hard physical labour, together with appalling and unchecked industrial diseases, ensured that even if the adjectives 'seedy' and 'sleepy' might be questioned, the physiological differences between the working class, particularly the poorer sections, and the middle class were certainly real.

In another article on thieves in the *Cornhill Magazine* Holland, who claimed to have lived among them for two years, noted that even 'the worst of them' spoke gloomily of their future, given the efforts of policemen, prisons, ragged schools and reformatories – the metaphor he used was telling and typical – 'just as a Red Indian would complain of the dwindling of his tribe before the strong march of advancing civilization'.[49] In the middle years brought to crime by poverty. Bad, uncaring parents, drink, the corrupt literature which glamorised offenders, and a general lack of moral fibre continued to be wheeled out as causes of crime. Poverty remained the hallmark of most criminals in the literature of the second half of the nineteenth century, but this was not so much because poverty was regarded as a cause of crime, but rather because crime could not be held to pay. 'Thieving is always a losing game', explained Holland. 'The money they get never does them any good; it never stays with them. It all goes in gambling, debauchery and law expenses.'[64] *The Times*, commenting on the conviction of seven thieves in 1865, believed that they had taken property valued at between £11,000 and £12,000 in six months; of course, it went on, they would not have realised anything like this sum when they fenced it, but, more importantly:

None of them were living in other than mean houses, and some tawdry jewelry about the women seems to represent the extent of their luxury. In fact, they dare not spend much, or they would attract the attention of the police, and they are thus condemned to enjoy their spoil with the same stealthy fear with which they seize it.[65]

Greenwood, in turn, emphasised:

There can be no question that that of the professional thief is a bitterly severe and laborious occupation, beset with privations that moral people have no conception of, and involving an amount of mental anxiety and torment that few human beings can withstand through a long lifetime.[66]

Even if for many the incidence of crime appeared to be decreasing, the problem was how to explain its persistence in the face of the advantages and opportunities provided by the advance of civilisation and the expansion of education. In addition to the old standbys of corrupting literature, drunkenness, uncaring and criminal parents, and the mixing of first-time offenders with recidivists in prisons, concepts of heredity and ideas drawn from developments in medical science began to be enlisted for explanation. An eighteenth-century Swiss theologian, Johann Kaspar Lavater, had launched a debate on the significance of physiognomy in the late 1780s. His ideas had, perhaps, a more profound impact on continental Europe, but Victorians confidently believed that the face portrayed the character. The fact that the skull was the shell for the brain underscored much of this way of thinking and in the early nineteenth century studies began to appear of British convicts that were rooted in the belief that detectable inordinate mental faculties led to crime. Medical men, and others, detected irredeemables from the shape of their heads, their desperate fixed expressions and their 'mental bravado'.[67] Visitors to the penal colonies in Australia often declared that the convicts had an unmistakable 'peculiarity of the visage [making them look] different from other men'.[68] A schoolmaster with experience of working in Newgate in the early 1830s noted that the features of prisoners were 'strongly marked with animal propensities'; and this seemed particularly so among some of the boys who had 'an approximation to the face of a monkey'.[69] From the middle of the century British doctors, like James Thompson who worked in Perth Prison, began collating biological analyses of convicts, thus providing an academic underpinning to the perception of 'animal propensities' by the supposedly foolproof means of empirical research. The majority of the boys in the juvenile wing of one English prison, according to Dr Forbes Winslow, had 'the cerebrum . . . badly organised, the crown of the head was nearly flat, the posterior region full. In other words, there was little or no intellect, the moral sentiments were small and the propensities large'. Forbes Winslow shared his findings with the readers of the *Morning Chronicle*,[70] thus contributing to a popular Victorian belief that facial features told character and could be deciphered.

Edwin Chadwick considered crime as a moral problem which could be resolved by effort and organisation. The investigations of medical experts, underpinned by the increasing acceptance of Darwinian ideas, began to challenge this as the nineteenth century wore on. The force of heredity implied that notions of blame and responsibility were much more problematic than Chadwick's certainties would allow. As the leading English psychologist, Henry Maudsley, lamented in *Body and Mind* in 1874:

in consequence of evil ancestral influences, individuals are born with such a flaw or warp of nature that all the care in the world will not prevent them from being vicious or criminal, or becoming insane. . . . No one can escape the tyranny of his organisation; no one can elude the destiny that is innate in him, and which unconsciously and irresistibly shapes his ends, even when he believes that he is determining them with consumate skill.[71]

Such recognition that the mastery of personal circumstances and constitution could be exceedingly difficult was given even sharper focus in the last quarter of the century by, on the one hand, the housing problem in London and the studies of the great social investigators, and, on the other, by the gradual filtering into Britain of the physiological and psychological theories of the European students of the new science of criminology or, to use the more common contemporary term, criminal anthropology.

At the bottom of the social scale in London Charles Booth found Social Class A: 'occasional labourers, loafers and semi-criminals'. This was a:

savage semi-criminal class of people [which] had its golden age in the days when whole districts of London were in their undisputed possession. They mainly desire to be left along, to be allowed to make an Alsatia of their own. Improvement in our eyes is destruction in theirs. Their discontent is their measure of our success.[72]

In meticulous detail Booth outlined the squalor and poverty in which this group lived and also the similar surroundings of his Social Class B that existed marginally above it. Such revelations fuelled the arguments of those critics of the system of outdoor relief who maintained that mistaken humanitarianism and charity were creating, rather than alleviating, the problem of the unpleasant residuum in the slum districts of cities; charity merely fostered idleness and improvidence. At the same time the work of Booth, and others, with its exposure of bad housing and inadequate diet, encouraged a perception of the residuum as the inevitable workings of social Darwinism. Arnold White, who became a central figure in warning the public about the degeneration of the British race, first expressed such concerns during the 1880s. He lamented the exodus from the bracing countryside, which produced fit and sturdy men, to the unhealthy cities, where half the poor were so mentally, morally and physically unfit that the best thing for the nation to do was to leave them alone to die out. Unfortunately the 'criminal and pauperised classes with low cerebral development renew their race more rapidly than those of higher nervous natures'.[73] Yet while criminals could still be seen as part of the residuum, lurking in their slums and, by implication, eager and ready to prey on the respectable, the increasingly popular biological explanation of crime meant that it was no longer necessary simply to define criminality largely in class terms.

The mass of petty thefts and the large number of crimes committed by juveniles continued to be a main object of concern, but it began to be acknowledged that crime was not simply a problem rooted in the poorer sections of the urban working class. Charles Booth noted that 'every social grade has its criminals, if not by conviction, at least by character'.[74] The new criminal anthropology, with its 'scientific' physiological and psychological theories, enabled the criminal to be studied more easily as an individual rather than simply as part of a class. Reduced to the simplest formula, the criminal was increasingly seen as someone who was not 'normal'; normal individuals did not assault, murder, rape, or steal from others. Criminals, therefore, became less a class of offenders by choice and rather more pathetic, and sometimes dangerous, social wreckage, produced by largely impersonal forces. L. Gordon Rylands explained:

the active causes of all kinds [of crime] are these: Defective training or total absence of any; immoral associates and bad example in prison as well as out of it; drink; idleness, and the hereditary transmission of evil tendencies. These causes, however, frequently overlap, and one is often found to be the effect of another, the only perfectly simple and absolutely final division is into two main heads, Heredity and Environment, which comprise all others.

Under the heading of Environment Rylands meant the lack of good and caring parents, the lack of a decent home (more the fault of parents than anything else), and bad company in the slums and in prison. Such problems might, he believed, be alleviated by the state taking control of children found on the streets 'without visible means of subsistence, or who seemed to be neglected by their parents'; the 'inherited tendencies' of 'embryo criminals' might thus be nipped in the bud. Theft, suicide, and 'homicidal monomania' were all hereditary failings and consequently, in Rylands' perception, it might be best to exterminate the irredeemable offender. He was not alone in drawing such conclusions.[75]

In 1890, for a series of 'Contemporary Science' books, Havelock Ellis published a critical survey of the work of the criminal anthropologists of Europe and the United States; the book went through four editions in twenty years. Ellis explained that research into the physical characteristics of criminals revealed that they were individuals incapable of living by the ordinary standards recognised by a community:

By some accident of development, by some defect of heredity or birth or training, [the criminal] belongs as it were to a lower and older social state than that in which he is actually living.

Research into the physical characteristics of the criminal, moreover, demonstrated that:

[I]n the criminal . . . there is an arrest of development. The criminal is an individual who, to some extent, remains a child his life long – a child of larger growth and with greater capacity for evil.

But this did not mean that the criminal was 'an idiot' or even 'merely weak-minded'. The criminal was far more dangerous. 'The idiot and the feeble-minded, as we know them in asylums, rarely have any criminal or dangerous instincts.'[76] Ellis's fervent advocacy of 'social hygiene', by

side effects of reducing sympathy for the poacher and making him appear more of a 'criminal'.[90]

Just as some crimes were not perceived as such by certain social groups or communities, several nineteenth-century authors, generally liberals or radicals of various hues, did urge, contrary to the overall picture given in this chapter, that poverty could lead to crime. *The Poor Man's Guardian* even went so far as to suggest that the laws of the country were made by rich men to protect the great evil – property.[91] Yet there was never any suggestion that gaoled 'criminals' were, in any sense, political prisoners. There was violent hostility to the political disfranchisement which went with admission to the workhouse or with receipt of poor relief. Admission to the workhouse or the resort to relief was a constant threat hanging over a significant percentage of the poor and one of the chief condemnations of the New Poor Law was, in Disraeli's words, that 'it announces to the world that in England poverty is a crime'.[92] However no radical group called for the political enfranchisement of men in gaol. Indeed from the corresponding societies of the 1790s to the Chartists and beyond, conviction and imprisonment for a crime meant the forfeiture of political rights. This may be explained by the notions of morality which pervaded the thought of nineteenth-century working-class activists as well as the Victorian middle class – criminals, unlike paupers, made a conscious, positive and immoral decision when they committed a crime. At the same time it may also have been a recognition by the radical activists that the working class were as much the victims of crime as the perpetrators – political reform, and parliaments chosen by universal manhood suffrage, would remove the vestiges of inequality within the law.

The literature dealing with criminals which was aimed at the working class was both moralistic and titillating as was much of that aimed at their social superiors; indeed as the nineteenth century wore on there was an increasing overlap between the reading matter of the middle class and the respectable working class. The 'last dying words', with cheap woodcuts at the top of a sheet, which were hawked at public executions throughout the eighteenth and well into the nineteenth centuries, were infused with a moralistic tone as the condemned was made to repent and to warn others against following in his, or her, footsteps. Some ballads took a similar line, like 'A Shining Night, or Dick Daring, the Poacher':

Be advised then ye young be advised too ye old,
To soberness, honesty, industry hold,
For stealing and murder may rise it is clear,
From a shining night if 'tis our delight in the season of the year.[93]

The Execution at Winchester:

Of John Smith for Horse-stealing. James Dawes, and *Wm.* Dawes, two brothers, for Burglary. Likewise Patrick Cusack, and Elenor Ryan, for the Murder of John Ryan, her husband, by Strangulation, and afterwards burning the body.

At Winchester on Friday morning the extreme sentence of the law was carried into execution on John Smith, aged 26. James Dawes, aged 30, and Wm. Dawes aged 22. Smith, whose real name was Hughes and who had been convicted of horse stealing, was a gipsey, and always led a wandering life. He professed to be a rat-catcher and basket maker, but confesed that he had subfisted chiefly on plunder. His depredations were not confined to one county, or to any single species of property but extended to house breaking, sheep stealing, and indeed to every other description of robbery. He acknowledged the offence for which he suffered, and the justice of his sentence. J. and W. Dawes brothers, were convicted of burglary, attended with personal violence to the profecutor. They were labourers, and refided at Binfted, hants. Both acknowledged their guilt, and flated the offence was planned and committed by themselves alone, and that a letter found on the premises was written by James Dawes,

and left there for the purpose of exciting fufpicion against another person whofe name was on it, but who, they declared, had not the moft diftant knowledge of the tranfaction. From the time of their condemnation, the unhappy men conducted themfelves in a manner becoming their melancholy fituation.

At the Limrick affizes Patrick Cufack Edmund Hall, and Elenor Rian, were found guilty of the murder of John Ryan, the husband of the latter culprit. Ryan was a refpectable farmer. They firft made him drunk, then put a rope round his neck and dragged him to the floor, after which, they cut off his right arm and leg, bent the other arm and leg, and then put him upon a large fire. Mrs. Ryan fainted when fentence of death was pronounced. She appeared to be about 18 years of age. Cufack and Elenor Ryan was executed on the 11th inst. at Limrick, the woman was penitent and refigned. Cufack was lefs firm. Hall has been refpited.

Lines on Viewing a Malefactor under Condemnation.

How sunk is man by coescious guilt opprest'd.
By pangs of dying virtue robb'd in reft?
No unease who has the torment of his soul,
Wild, with despair his body eye balls roll.
Black retrospection poisons every scene.
And hope which smile es all's done'd to him,
In this sad state the culp it thare i found
He started at my sight, his casual eyes flew round.
Sigh'd shook his head and fix'd them on t e ground.
Here see in mournful s loom tone he said,
As on my knee his trembling hand he laid
Here dee the state to which by my v e,
I've sad effects of company and dine.
The idea's horrid in the prime of days,

torn from my friends by my evil wars,
Perhaps e one foe malignantly may dwell,
On my sad fate, and all my vice tell.
There's madness in the thought, my brain's on fire,
Why was I born. God grant I now expire.
Vainly I strove to calm his troubled mind,
Twould brave as ease to subdue the wind,
Reluctantly I left him to his fate,
And sigh'd, to think to what a wretched state,
A man's dur'd from rectitude may fall,
What if conscience for reform may loudly call,
O may mankind from my sad fate beware
and shun these paths which lure hot to ensnare,
Fly Folly's crowd and walk in Virtue's steps,
Obsorve the laws and ev as heaven directs,
So shall your lives serenely glide away,
and Hope point, smiling, to the realms of day.

'Execution at Winchester'

This broadside of an execution in 1825 is rather more sophisticated than many in that it mixes the traditional image of bodies hanging from the gallows with a foreground based on William Hogarth's illustration (1749) of the execution of the idle apprentice at Tyburn. Many eighteenth- and early nineteenth-century execution broadsides have the simple woodcut of the executed felon at the top with, as in this case, some details of the offence, trial and execution underneath. (Courtesy of the Historical & Special Collections, Harvard Law School Library.)

Life, Trial, and SENTENCE
OF HENRY HUGHES,
For the most Horrid and Atrocious Rape committed on the body of
EMMA COOK, A CHILD ONLY EIGHT YEARS OF AGE, AT NORWOOD.

This morning (Wednesday) at the Kingston Assizes, it being generally known that the case of Rape was to come on, the town immensely crowded with persons anxious to gain an entrance to the Court to hear the proceeding against Henry Hughes who had to undergo his Trial for the inhuman crime committed on the body of Emma Cook. The usual ceremonies having been gone through, the prisoner was placed at the bar, when being called on to plead to the charge, Guilty or Not Guilty! he replied in a firm and impudent manner, "Not Guilty." Accordingly the first witness was called—

John Cook, father of the little sufferer, stated that he had a daughter named Emma, who was eight years old on the 8th of last February. This witness was called principally to prove the capability of his child to give evidence in the present case. He established this point satisfactorily.

Mary Cook sworn. Was out washing at Mrs. Attwood's, when a boy named Rayner came and told me that my daughter Emma had been taken very ill. She went home about a quarter of an hour afterwards, in consequence of a young man named Syers calling upon me and requesting me to come home. On the road he communicated to me what had befallen my child When she got into the house, found the child lying on the bed and bleeding. The little sufferer, as soon as she saw me, said, "Oh, mother, kill him, for he has made me very ill."

Emma Cook sworn. Reccollected going to Penge-wood with an infant on Monday 3rd of March ; met the Prisoner, who said to me, "There are plenty of flowers down here." Took me into the wood, but would not pick any flowers for me. He then threw me into the bushes, and lifted up my clothes.

I cried out, but the prisoner did not desist from hurting me very much. When the prisoner met me he asked me what my name was, I told him. (The little girl then proceeded to describe the conduct of the prisoner, which is wholly unfit for publication) Prisoner said while on the ground, " Lie still, or I'll eat you." Prisoner prevented me from calling out by placing his hand over my mouth. Knew the prisoner well, for he had formerly lived next door to my father. While on the ground, saw Bedser's boy running towards me but the prisoner did not leave. When the prisoner got up, he did not walk but ran away.

William Street, surgeon, sworn. Resides at Norwood, was called about three o'clock on Monday to attend Emma Cook, Found her lying on a bed in a state of great agitation. Her arms and face were much scratched. The lower parts of her person covered with blood which had flowed in considerable quantities—her dress was much stained. (The evidence of the surgeon is of course unfit for pubication, but the nature of it was to establish in the clearest manner the capital part of the charge) Had no essitation in saying that the crime had been fully completed and that great voilence must have been used.

Augustus Bedser, sworn, a boy about fifteen years of age. Reside with my father, who is a police officer at Norwood. On monday was on Penge-common in company with a boy named Christopher Rice. About two o'clock I heard the screams of a child, and ran to

the spot. On getting to the place saw the prisoner with a child on the ground. The child cried for her bonnet, when the prisoner desired her to lie still. Rice called to me, but did not answer for fear the prisoner should hear me. I becomed to Rice, but before he could get to the spot, the prisoner got up and ran away.

David Bedser, policeman sworn went in search of the prisenor as soon as I was inform of the charge against him. After searching about some time, saw a man named Syers, in Penge-wood, who told me that he saw the prisoner lying sideways among some bushes. Took the prisoner into custody to the hose where the child was lying and asked her if she new the prisoner, "Yes, that is the man who did it." The prisoner said that he was perfectly innocent of the charge.

This being the whole of the evidence the Learned Judge addressed the Jury in a very impressive manner, beseeching them zealously to consider their Verdict. "To lay asside all former feeling, and deliver their verdict according to their conscience resting solely on the evidence they had heard that day.

The Jury then retired to an adjoining room to consider their verdict, and at the expiration of about ten minutes returned with a Verdict of GUILTY !—DEATH.

Printer, and Sold, by G. HUNT, (late Quick,) 8, Little Paternoster Row, Spitalfields.

'Life, Trial, and Sentence of Henry Hughes'

This broadside, from 1834, has an even more sophisticated image at the top. By this time, however, the broadside was beginning to give way to the newspaper. (Courtesy of the Historical & Special Collections, Harvard Law School Library.)

The criminals portrayed in such ballads were commonly stereotypes that went back at least as far as the Tudors and Stuarts. In Dick Daring's case poaching led to more serious crimes, but generally speaking it was drinking and whoring which was held to have put the offender on the slippery slope to perdition. There were some ballads, however, which romanticised the 'criminal'. If 'Dick Daring' was a warning, 'Keepers and Poachers' portrayed the poacher William Taylor as a veritable Sydney Carton:

The judge and the jury unto him did say
'If you wil confess, your sweet life shall be saved.'
'Oh no,' then said William, 'that won't do at all,
For now you have got me I'll die for them all.'[94]

Ballads such as this were rooted in an oral tradition and the notion that poaching was no 'real crime'. Other 'corrupting' material was not. John Gay's *The Beggar's Opera* rapidly acquired a notorious reputation for leading young men astray, and cheap books telling of the adventures of Jack Sheppard, Dick Turpin and others were similarly looked at askance by middle-class gentlemen; though, of course, the original novels *Rookwood* (1834), which both created and immortalised Turpin's ride to York, and *Jack Sheppard* (1839) were written by the son of a respectable lawyer from the neighbourhood of Manchester, William Harrison Ainsworth. Moreover, while Ainsworth is now relegated to the rank of second-class or 'popular' novelist he was, at the time, a friendly competitor of Dickens and the two even considered collaborating. Physique, physiognomy and geography are all tokens of class in Ainsworth's novels; critics were worried by what they considered as immorality in his novels, yet the popularity of his characters was seized on by others to produce a variety of imitations in the form of ballads, 'memoirs' and plays as well as novels.[95] Increasingly, with the developments in printing and publishing, and with the growth of literacy in the second half of the nineteenth century, the availability and the amount of this literature became greater. Printers and publishers found an appreciative audience for both adventure stories and lurid tales of ''orrible murder'; all the better if they had a basis in fact. In 1868 a man could defend his sons' behaviour before a court on the grounds that literature romanticising criminals had corrupted them, while in 1884 it was said of Ernest Castles, a nineteen-year-old who shot a police constable in Oldham, that his 'mind has been corrupted by the reading of trashy literature'.[96] In addition to 'trashy literature' there was a growth in the representation of exhibitions, marketable souvenirs and popular theatrical representations particularly of violent crimes and criminals. These may, it has been convincingly argued, have contributed to the statistical decline in violent crime during the nineteenth century, though the power of such literature either to improve or corrupt is not really ascertainable.[97] The question also remains: how much did the written representation of crime and criminals shape people's understanding of the issues?

Police officers, prison officers, some magistrates and some judges experienced crime and criminals relatively frequently because of their jobs and functions. But most people were victims or witnesses of crime only rarely. Most people in the eighteenth and nineteenth centuries learned about crime from media representations – the written word, the play, the drawing. The problem here was that media entrepreneurs, be they editors or theatrical producers, commonly went for the sensational, often violent story and chose to portray the characters in their stories in stereotypical ways. These representations, in turn, helped to foster and reinforce criminal stereotypes, interacting all the time with popular understanding of, and popular sympathies for right and wrong. Petty pilferage at work was scarcely a crime, unlike theft from a friend or neighbour; a public house argument which led to blows, or striking a policeman interfering in such an argument outside a pub, might not be perceived as a crime, but extreme violence and murder, whatever the circumstances, generally was.

The argument here is not to deny the existence of a criminal class, or at least groups of professional criminals. There were individuals and groups who made a significant part of their living from activities which lay outside the law; yet the word 'class' implies a large number, and a more homogeneous group than actually existed. But while these individuals may have affected most of the very spectacular and large-scale thefts during the eighteenth and nineteenth centuries, the overwhelming majority of offences were not of this variety. Nineteenth-century experts and commentators looked at who were being processed by the police, the courts and the prisons, never seriously questioned the idea that the multitude of petty thefts (sometimes with the addition of assaults and disorderly conduct) should be the benchmark of criminality, and they then set out to find the causes of this criminality. Since the great majority of offenders came from one social class it was logical to locate the causes of crime within what were generally perceived as the vices of this class. There would be many today who would accept some of the Victorian notions of links between vice and crime: strong drink appears to have contributed to some instances of disorder and inter-personal violence; a poor man may have yielded to temptation because of his poverty, yet not every poor man stole, and it might be argued that such nebulous concepts as strength of character and morality do come into play here. The problem was that most nineteenth-century analysts of crime ignored the seasonal and uncertain nature of much employment, and the gruelling aspects of the working-class existence; these certainly contributed to physiological differences between the classes and they probably encouraged the 'vices' (drink, cheap crime literature, rowdiness, consorting with prostitutes) when times were good and when the poor had money in their pockets.

Notes

1 *Hansard*, new series, xiv (1826), cols 1218–19.

2 **Sarah Wilson**, *The Origins of Modern Financial Crime: Historical Problems and Current Problems in Britain*, Routledge, London, 2014, p. 83.

3 It has been argued that the enforcement of the 1833 Factory Act was guided by the 'rotten apple' thesis and that factory inspectors made the consoling distinction between a majority of respectable employers who would never break the law (though they did) and 'rotten apples'. **W. G. Carson**, 'The institutionalization of ambiguity: Early British Factory Acts', in **Gilbert Geis** and **Ezra Stotland** (eds), *White-Collar Crime: Theory and Research*, Sage, Beverley Hills, 1980, pp. 166–7. For a useful historical survey of white-collar crime see **George Robb**, *White-Collar Crime in Modern England: Financial Fraud and Business Morality 1845–1929*, Cambridge U.P., Cambridge, 1992.

4 **Gregory Anderson**, *Victorian Clerks*, Manchester U.P., Manchester, 1976, pp. 37–40.

5 **Henry Fielding**, *An Enquiry Into the Causes of the Late Increase of Robbers*, 2nd edn, London, 1751, p. xxiii.

6 *Ibid.*, p. 7.

7 *Ibid.*, p. 69.

8 **Henry Fielding**, *The History of the Life of the Late Mr Jonathan Wild the Great*, Everyman edition, London, 1973, p. 18.

9 *Punch*, for example, commented: 'It is true that the criminal may have been led by the example of aristocratic sinners to disregard the injunctions of revealed religion against the adulterer, the gamester, and the drunkard; and having imitated the "pleasant follies" of the great without possessing the requisite means for such enjoyments, the man of pleasure has degenerated into the man of crime. It is true that the poor and ignorant may have claims upon the wealth and intelligence of the rich and learned; but are we to pause to inquire whether want may have driven the destitute to theft, or the absence of early instruction have left physical desires of the offender's native superior

to its moral restraints. Certainly not, whilst we have the gallows.' *Punch*, vol. 1, 20 November 1841.

10 *PP.* 1812 (127), ii, *Select Committee on the Nightly Watch of the Metropolis*, appendix 8, pp. 34–9.

11 **Jonas Hanway**, *The Defects of Police, the Cause of Immorality and the Continual Robberies Committed, Particularly in and about the Metropolis*, London, 1775, p. 273.

12 **Jonas Hanway**, *Observations on the Causes of the Dissoluteness Which Reigns Among the Lower Classes of the People; the Propensity of Some to Petty Larceny: And the Danger of Gaming, Concubinage, and an Excessive Fondness for Amusement in High Life*, London, 1772, p. 38.

13 *Ibid.*, p. 15.

14 Hanway, *The Defects of Police*, p. 241.

15 **Patrick Colquhoun**, *A Treatise on the Commerce and Police of the River Thames*, London, 1800, pp. 37–8 and 40.

16 **Patrick Colquhoun**, *A Treatise on the Police of the Metropolis*, 3rd edn, London, 1796, p. 88. Colquhoun's argument here was highly questionable. It was generally accepted that the most 'correct' and 'energetic' police of the eighteenth century were to be found in France, yet the pre-Revolution rural police, the *maréchaussée*, had problems with brigands, the like of which simply did not exist in Britain. Furthermore the revolutionary wars, during which Colquhoun was writing, witnessed an increase in brigandage in France, the Low Countries and the Rhineland.

17 For the popularity of the *Treatise on the Police* see **Sir Leon Radzinowicz**, *A History of English Criminal Law*, 5 vols, Stevens, London, 1948–86, iii, pp. 221 note 2, and 227–8.

18 'Reflections occasioned by the perusal of a recent treatise on Indigence, etc.', *Monthly Magazine*, **xxvi** (1808), pp. 108–12 (at p. 111).

19 Colquhoun, *Treatise on the Police*, p. 88.

20 *P.P.* 1816 (510) v, *Report on the State of the Police of the Metropolis*, pp. 29, 143–4 and 212.

21 *Ibid.*, pp. 29–30 (for comments on shopkeepers) and pp. 42, 56 and 63 (for comments on parents); *P.P.* 1828 (533) vi, *Select Committee on the Police of the Metropolis*, p. 57 (shopkeepers) and pp. 48, 59, 85 and 145 (parents).

22 *P.P.* 1816 (510) v, *Report on the State of the Police of the Metropolis*, pp. 18–21, 38–41 and 48–9.

23 *Hansard*, new series, xiii (1825), col. 300; *Hansard* new series, xiv (1826), col. 1243. Though it probably needs to be emphasised that in each of these instances the discussion was centred on rural, rather than urban, crime.

24 *P.P.* 1828 (533) vi, *Select Committee on the Police of the Metropolis*, p. 38; for suggestions that unemployment and poverty may have contributed to crime see pp. 56, 84, 134 and 226.

25 *P.P.* 1816 (510) v, *Report on the State of the Police of the Metropolis*, p. 215.

26 *P.P.* 1828 (533) vi, *Select Committee on the Police of the Metropolis*, pp. 40 and 63.

27 Fielding, *An Enquiry*, p. 4.

28 Colquhoun, *A Treatise on the Police*, p. vii.

29 U.C.L. Chadwick MSS 11 f. 2.

30 *P.P.* 1839 (169) xix, *Royal Commission on Constabulary*, pp. 7, 10.

31 *Ibid.*, p. 68.

32 **Raphael Samuel**, 'Comers and goers', in **H. J. Dyos** and **M. Wolff** (eds), *The Victorian City*, 2 vols, RKP, London, 1973, chapter 5. For similar statements about vagrancy being a cause of crime see *P.P.* 1852–3 (71) xxxvi, *Select Committee on Police*, qq. 844–5, 1416, 1423–4, 1775, 3004–7 and 3722.

33 *P.P.* 1839 (169) xix, *Royal Commission on Constabulary*, pp. 34 and 67.

34 **David Philips**, 'Three "moral entrepreneurs" and the creation of a "criminal class" in England, c. 1790s–1840s', *Crime, histoire et sociétés/Crime, history and societies*, **7** (2003), pp. 79–107. **A. W. Ager**, *Crime and Poverty in 19th-Century England: An Economy of Makeshifts*, Bloomsbury, London, 2014 stresses the significance of the New Poor Law as a possible spur to criminal activity for the poor.

35 *P.P.* 1834 (599) viii, *Select Committee on Inquiry Into Drunkenness*, p. vi.

36 **Heather Shore**, *Artful Dodgers: Youth and Crime in Early Nineteenth-Century London*, Boydell/Royal Historical Society, Woodbridge, 1999. **Susan Magarey** has written of the 'invention' of juvenile delinquency between 1820 and 1850 ('The invention of juvenile delinquency in early nineteenth-century England', *Labour History*, **34** (1978), pp. 11–27). There may have been a growth in the concern about juvenile offenders during this period but eighteenth-century commentators like Henry Fielding and Jonas Hanway also expressed anxiety about criminal activities committed by boys and young men, while Peter King and Joan Noel have pointed out an increase in prosecutions of juveniles in the generation before Magarey's study. **Peter King** and **Joan Noel**, 'The origins of "The Problem of Juvenile Delinquency": The growth of juvenile prosecutions in the late eighteenth and early nineteenth centuries', *C.J.H.*, **14** (1993), pp. 17–41.

37 **Jelinger C. Symons**, *Special Report on Reformatories in Gloucestershire, Shropshire, Worcestershire, Herefordshire and Monmouthshire, and in Wales* (Printed in the Minutes of the Parliamentary Committee on Education, *P.P.* 1857–8), p. 236.

38 John Glyde, jun., *The Moral, Social and Religious Condition of Ipswich in the Middle of the Nineteenth Century*, Ipswich, 1850, reprinted S. R. Publishers, Wakefield, 1971, p. 66. The same point was made by Lord Brougham: 'Those who had the mere power to read perused only the narratives of banditti, of swindlers, of thieves; they filled their minds with that species of information which only polluted', *Hansard*, 3rd series, xc (1847), col. 200.

39 Glyde, *Moral Condition of Ipswich*, p. 111.

40 Symons, *Special Report on Reformatories*, p. 223.

41 David Vincent, *Bread, Knowledge and Freedom: A Study of Nineteenth-Century Working Class Autobiography*, Europa, London, 1981, p. 49.

42 Thomas Plint, *Crime in England: Its Relation, Character, and Extent as Developed From 1901 to 1848*, London, 1851, pp. 84–5. For similar explanations about crime in Suffolk see John Glyde, jun., *Suffolk in the Nineteenth Century: Physical, Social, Moral, Religious and Industrial*, London, 1856, pp. 132–3 and 156–8.

43 John Clay, 'On the effect of good or bad times on committals to prison', *Journal of the Statistical Society*, xviii (1855), pp. 74–9; M. D. Hill, *Suggestions for the Repression of Crime, Contained in Charges Delivered to Grand Juries of Birmingham*, London, 1857, p. 109.

44 Both quotations are in David Philips, *Crime and Authority in Victorian England*, Croom Helm, London, 1977, pp. 13–4.

45 Gertrude Himmelfarb, *The Idea of Poverty: England in the Early Industrial Age*, Faber and Faber, London, 1984, p. 435.

46 Aurélie Baudry-Palmer, 'Addressing Juvenile anti-social behaviour in Victorian England: Mary Carpenter and the reformatory schools', in Sarah Pickford (ed.), *Anti-Social Behaviour in Britain: Victorian and Contemporary Perspectives*, Palgrave Macmillan, London, 2014.

47 H. W. Holland, 'Professional thieves', *Cornhill Magazine*, vi (1862), pp. 640–53 (at p. 653).

48 Anthony S. Wohl, *Endangered Lives: Public Health in Victorian Britain*, Methuen, London, 1984, pp. 130–1.

49 H. W. Holland, 'Thieves and thieving', *Cornhill Magazine*, ii (1860), pp. 32–44 (at p. 339).

50 J. Ginswick (ed.), *Labour and the Poor in England and Wales*, 8 vols, Frank Cass, London, 1983, i, p. 79.

51 Charles Dickens, 'On duty with inspector field', *Household Words*, iii (1851), pp. 265–70.

52 J. Ormsby, 'A day's pleasure with the criminal classes', *Cornhill Magazine*, ix (1864), pp. 627–40.

53 Henry Mayhew, *The Morning Chronicle Surveyor of Labour and the Poor: The Metropolitan Districts*, Caliban Books, Firle, 1980, i, p. 40. The letters were published in the *Morning Chronicle* between 19 October 1849 and 12 December 1850.

54 *Ibid.*, i, pp. 90, 94, 102 and 107.

55 *Ibid.*, ii, pp. 239–40.

56 Henry Mayhew *et al.*, *London Labour and the London Poor*, 4 vols, London, 1861–2, i, pp. 2–3, 43 and 148.

57 *Ibid.*, iv, pp. 29, 30.

58 *Ibid.*, iv, p. 25.

59 For a good critical assessment of Mayhew see David Englander, 'Henry Mayhew and the criminal classes of Victorian England: The case reopened', in Louis A. Knafla (ed.), *Crime Gender and Sexuality in Criminal Prosecutions: Criminal Justice History*, 17, Greenwood Press, Westport, CT, 2002; for an uncritical use, see Donald Thomas, *The Victorian Underworld*, John Murray, London, 1998, chapters 1 and 2.

60 Mayhew *et al.*, *London Labour and the London Poor*, iv, p. xii.

61 James Greenwood, *The Seven Curses of London*, London, 1869 (reprinted, Basil Blackwell, Oxford, 1981), p. 57.

62 *The Times*, 29 March 1870.

63 Greenwood, *Seven Curses*, pp. 42 and 83.

64 Holland, 'Professional thieves', p. 653.

65 *The Times*, 14 April 1865.

66 Greenwood, *Seven Curses*, p. 59.

67 David de Guistino, *Conquest of Mind: Phrenology and Victorian Social Thought*, Croom Helm, London, 1975, pp. 145–53.

68 Quoted in Richard White, *Inventing Australia: Images and Identity 1788–1980*, Allen and Unwin, Sydney, 1981, p. 66.

69 Quoted in Philip Priestley, *Victorian Prison Lives: English Prison Biography*, Methuen, London, 1985, p. 78.

70 *Morning Chronicle*, 11 March 1850.

71 Quoted in Martin J. Wiener, *Reconstructing the Criminal: Culture, Law, and Policy in England, 1830–1914*, Cambridge U.P., Cambridge, 1990, p. 169.

72 Charles Booth, *Life and Labour of the People in London. 1st series, Poverty*, 4 vols, London, 1902, i, p. 174.

73 Arnold White, *Problems of a Great City*, London, 1886, p. 47.

74 Booth, *Life and Labour, Poverty*, i, p. 175.

75 L. Gordon Rylands, *Crime: Its Causes and Its Remedy*, London, 1889, pp. 46, 71, 92 and 251–2. For similar conclusions about the need to exterminate irredeemable offenders see **Leon Radzinowicz** and **Roger Hood**, *The Emergence of Penal Policy in Victorian and Edwardian England*, Clarendon Press, Oxford, 1990, pp. 239–40.

76 **Havelock Ellis**, *The Criminal*, London, 1890, pp. 206, 214 and 229.

77 *Idem, The Task of Social Hygiene*, London, 1912, p. 2.

78 **W. D. Morrison**, *Crime and Its Causes*, London, 1891, pp. 85, 140 and 199.

79 *Idem*, 'The increase of crime', *Nineteenth Century*, **xxxi** (1892), pp. 950–7 (at p. 957); *idem, Crime and Its Causes*, pp. 141–2.

80 Radzinowicz and Hood, *The Emergence of Penal Policy*, especially pp. 15–17. There is an illuminating comparative study in **Daniel Pick**, *Faces of Degeneration: A European Disorder, c.1848–c.1918*, Cambridge U.P., Cambridge, 1989, see especially chapter 7.

81 Wiener, *Reconstructing the Criminal*, p. 235.

82 Holland, 'Thieves and thieving', p. 340.

83 **Michael Sturma**, 'Eye of the beholder: The stereotype of women convicts, 1788–1852', *Labour History*, 34 (1978), pp. 3–10.

84 Quoted in **Frances Finnegan**, *Poverty and Prostitution: A Study of Victorian Prostitutes in York*, Cambridge U.P., Cambridge, 1979, p. 7. See also **Judith R. Walkowitz**, *Prostitution and Victorian Society: Women, Class and the State*, Cambridge U.P., Cambridge, 1980, pp. 25, 38–9 and 41–5.

85 Ellis, *The Criminal*, p. 221.

86 **Bernard Waites**, 'The effects of the First World War on aspects of the class structure of English society', unpublished Ph.D., The Open University, 1983, pp. 56–7.

87 **Douglas Hay**, 'Poaching and the game laws on Cannock Chase', in **Douglas Hay, Peter Linebaugh, E. P. Thompson** *et al.* (eds), *Albion's Fatal Tree: Crime and Society in Eighteenth-Century England*, Allen Lane, London, 1975.

88 *Sussex Express*, 1 March 1879.

89 Sharpe, *Crime in Early Modern England*, chapter 4, especially pp. 110–11; **R. A. E. Wells**, 'Sheep-rustling in Yorkshire in the age of the Industrial and Agricultural Revolutions', *Northern History*, **xx** (1984), pp. 127–45 (at p. 139).

90 **David Jones**, *Crime, Protest, Community and Police in Nineteenth-Century Britain*, RKP, London, 1982, pp. 78–9 and 83–4.

91 Himmelfarb, *The Idea of Poverty*, p. 234.

92 Quoted in *ibid.*, p. 182.

93 V. de Sola Pinto and A.E. Rodway, *The Common Muse: Popular British Ballad Poetry From the Fifteenth to the Twentieth Century*, Chatto and Windus, London, 1957, p. 236.

94 Recorded on *Waterloo-Peterloo: English Folksongs and Broadsides 1780– 1830*, by the Critics Group, Argo Record Company, 1968.

95 Himmelfarb, *The Idea of Poverty*, chapter xvii. It is interesting to note how time gave respectability. The *Athenaeum*'s reviewer of Ainsworth's *Jack Sheppard* condemned it as a 'bad book' because it contained all the 'inherent coarseness and vulgarity of the subject'. He drew a contrast with Fielding's *Jonathan Wild* and Gay's *The Beggar's Opera* whose effect was to 'raise the public in the moral and intellectual scale' (quoted in *ibid.*, p. 428.) The reviewer was clearly ignorant of the obloquy heaped on *The Beggar's Opera* at least until the end of the eighteenth century and the accusations that the character of Macheath was so glamorous that many young men were seeking to emulate him as highwaymen.

96 *Illustrated London News*, 30 May 1868; *The Times*, 23 May 1884. Summing up the case of a soldier in the Rifle Brigade who had attempted to kill his girlfriend as part of a suicide pact, the judge commented: 'He supposed these people had been reading novels.' *The Times*, 18 July 1860.

97 Rosalind Crone, *Violent Victorians: Popular Entertainment in Nineteenth-Century London*, Manchester University Press, Manchester, 2012.

identity, though Blackstone's main concern was with the law of property. The principle of *feme covert* held that any woman charged with a felony in company with her husband could argue that she acted under his direction and thus gain an acquittal. Serious felonies such as murder could not be so excused, yet many others were. Blackstone stressed that the principle applied only to married women. Most of the women appearing before the courts in this period were single. It seems possible, however, that *feme covert* worked with traditional ideas of patriarchy to give considerable benefit to women, especially in magistrates' courts, well into the nineteenth century. The principle appears, for example, to have discouraged employers in the Yorkshire worsted factories from prosecuting women for appropriating materials in all but the strongest cases. It is possible also that the principle was interpreted sufficiently broadly to put young women under the age of majority under the 'coverage' of their fathers.[11]

Feme covert offers one reason why some women escaped the courts in the eighteenth and early nineteenth centuries. Yet, as the principle fell out of use and ceased to appear in the instruction books written for magistrates, the number of female offenders before the courts continued to fall. Moreover it is particularly striking that, towards the end of the nineteenth century, there was a preponderance of female recidivists. There were more women than men among those 'habitual offenders' convicted twenty times or more which suggests that the stigma attached to a female offender, and the consequent difficulties of surviving in honest employment after a period of imprisonment, was even greater than that attached to a male. There is another implication here: if some women committed more crimes than men (or at least were arrested and convicted more often), and thus were appearing more often in the criminal statistics, then the overall decline in women offenders in the second half of the nineteenth century was even greater than the statistics imply. Lucia Zedner has suggested that the decline in the statistics may be explained by a changing diagnosis of serious female offenders as the nineteenth century wore on. Rather than morally corrupt and depraved, such offenders began to be seen as feeble-minded or prisoners of their 'special bodily functions' (to use Maudsley's term) and were thus moved out of the criminal justice sphere.[12] The use of the terms 'kleptomaniac' for women thieves from the middle class or 'nymphomaniac' for women demonstrating any form of sexual desire was symptomatic of this, linking, as it did, the offence/disease with female sexuality and using this to re-emphasise woman's secondary position in nature.

While notions of patriarchy reinforced by the principle of *feme covert* may have kept women from the courts, it is unlikely that there was any significant 'dark figure' that would put the number of female offenders on a par with male offenders. Criminal activity, however, was often gendered. Poaching in the sense of shooting, snaring or trapping game was almost always conducted by men. But women were involved in the black market carrying and selling of poached game and also, more commonly, in collecting eggs. Field girls were ideally situated for informing poachers, and even gamekeepers, of the whereabouts of game birds' nests.[13] Country women stole milk by unlawfully milking cows, but countrymen and women alike were guilty of stealing poultry, growing crops and wood.[14] Breaking and entering and robbery at night tended to be male offences, and overall men appear to have taken a much wider range of goods than women. The evidence from late-eighteenth and early-nineteenth-century London suggests that in cases of shoplifting women tended to take gloves, stockings and textiles; but then these were goods sold by mercers and linen drapers where women tended to be the main customers. Women's clothing was useful for theft since petticoats and cloaks offered places for concealment. Shopkeepers and their assistants were often wary of women with cloaks, and in court lawyers and judges might ask if a cloak was worn by the accused as a way of implying intent. Men were more inclined to take goods that were smaller and that could be concealed in a hand, but some male thieves were prepared to walk out of a shop brazenly with their booty. Men also commonly took goods of greater value than women, such as hardware, jewellery, clocks and watches. Both sexes took food and clothing. More women than men were prosecuted for picking pockets, though the archetypal pickpocket in early-nineteenth-century London was commonly described as an assertive, precocious young male. The offence itself appears to have been gendered in time and place. Men tended to be accused of committing the offence in crowds and in daylight; women were more often accused of picking pockets after dark and in less public places. Such female offenders were also commonly accused of being prostitutes.[15]

Contemporary opinion often considered that women brought before the courts were connected in some way with prostitution. As was suggested earlier, for the Victorians 'prostitutes' were the female equivalent, or female half, of the criminal class. The prostitute was the total negation of the ideal of womanhood in the Victorian period but also in the rather less repressive Hanoverian century. Significantly, eighteenth-century criminal biographies often described the offender-hero as being brought to crime by involvement with a prostitute or continuing in his life of crime so as to support his lust for them. Commentators on juvenile delinquency in the early nineteenth century were concerned about young males falling under the influence of corrupting women and girls. This kind of portrayal re-emphasised the social mores of the day by offering an awful warning of what happened when the natural order of things was broken and when men became subordinate to independent or masterful, and therefore unnatural, women.[16]

Prostitutes, it has been suggested, started trouble in pubs 'to draw the police away from the scene of an intended burglary'; they were also 'in league with pickpockets'.[17] Some prostitutes did rob their clients, and the dark figure here is probably considerable since victims were often reluctant to come forward.[18] Any man who brought a prosecution or made a report to the police could find himself vilified by the courts, particularly with the increasing presence of lawyers in criminal trials from the late eighteenth century; defence lawyers could have a field day with the morals and sullied respectability of such victims. Tangentially, at least one pimp in Victorian London sought to discipline his women by means of prosecutions for theft.[19] Equally difficult to assess in numerical terms were the brutal physical assaults inflicted on prostitutes by their clients, often the worse for drink, or by their pimps; very few of these were reported. The isolation and danger of the 'profession' is reflected in the fact that all of Jack the Ripper's victims were prostitutes at some time in their lives, and so too, a few years later, were the London victims of Thomas Neill Cream.[20] Contemporary comments about the prostitute, as with the professional criminal, invariably tell us rather more about Victorian perceptions than about the women themselves. In the mid-nineteenth century, prostitutes were to be catalogued with the detritus of society; they were 'dissolute', 'fallen', 'wretched', the 'Great Social Evil' of a society that was eager to stress its morality and progress. Dickens described the life of Sikes's Nancy as 'squandered in the streets and among the most noisome stews and dens of London'. She was '[t]he miserable companion of thieves and ruffians, the fallen outcast of low haunts, the associate of the scourings of the jails and hulks'.[21] 'Abandoned prostitute' and 'hardened offender' were almost synonymous for women transported for theft; and policemen arresting drunken women commonly catalogued them as 'prostitutes'. Towards the end of the century, however, with the developments of psychiatry and the increasing reluctance to perceive of crime and criminals less as simply immoral and more as not 'normal', prostitutes began to be catalogued as coming from the feeble-minded.[22]

Prostitution was not, in itself, a criminal offence; the prostitution offences were specifically soliciting, living off immoral earnings, and running 'houses of ill fame', but these were enforced selectively. In elegant, nineteenth-century York, for example, the influential groups of Catholics, Evangelicals and Quakers took a much stricter line than the worthies of the fast-growing seaport of Hull where prostitution, around the docks, was a much greater problem. But then the respectable worthies of Hull rarely had occasion to walk in the dockland streets after dark.[23] In Cambridge, since the early modern period, the university authorities had extensive powers over those that its proctors defined as 'streetwalkers'. During the nineteenth century, in spite of the condemnation raised far beyond Cambridge by scandals that resulted from these powers, the university steadfastly hung on to them.[24] The elegant London brothels like the Argyll Rooms, Kate Hamilton's and Mott's were largely ignored by the police. Manifestly neither the proprietors, nor the women who catered for gentlemen in these establishments, were perceived as members of a criminal class or as professional criminals; and at this end of the market the profits were handsome. The less salubrious 'houses of ill fame' were more vulnerable, though even in some of the poorest districts the police did not interfere with them. Indeed, there appear to have been considerable differences in the ways that the police of different towns responded to prostitution, and this seems largely to have been the result of local directives from either the watch committee or the chief constable.[25] But even where police action was vigorous, this might merely solve one problem by creating another. In London towards the end of the century, moves against brothels and their keepers resulted in the entrepreneurs of sex opening massage parlours, or using flats which escaped the legal definition of a brothel.[26]

In general the larcenies committed by women appear to have been very petty. Significantly, the only summary offence during the Victorian period for which the number of women convicted was consistently higher than the number of men, was that of 'unlawfully pledging or disposing' under the Pawnbroker's Act.[27] But small thefts, with the goods being pledged at pawnbrokers, also brought women before the higher courts. 'I took these [three spoons and a fork, valued at four shillings] with the intention to pawn them, and when I got my wages to take them out,' declared Elizabeth McLaren, a twenty-four-year-old cook, to the Central Criminal Court in February 1838. 'I took them to the pawnbrokers, they would not lend me much, and I took them back. The washerwoman, who wanted my place, told my master of it.' Nineteen years later Mary Shellito, a laundress, was before the same court for pawning washing entrusted to her; the woman searcher at Barking Police Station found eight pawn tickets in Shellito's possession.[28]

Theft, of course, was not just committed by poor cooks and washerwomen. Respectable, middle-class women also found themselves charged, most notably, with shoplifting. By the end of the Regency period London had growing numbers of charity bazaars and emporiums selling all kinds of clothing and encouraging shoppers to buy with ready cash rather than credit. There were some who feared that their ostentatious window displays, the tactile experiences offered inside and the pressure of none too respectable proprietors encouraged some women to steal. The emergence of the department store later in the century perpetuated the anxiety. Middle-class women who stole from the changing consumer outlets had individual motives, but nineteenth-century commentators sought explanations within contemporary discourses. Thus, initially, middle-class women were seen as tempted by cheap shops that undermined traditional shopkeepers. By the mid-1850s their thefts were beginning to be seen as having biological origins and, a generation later, doctors and criminologists were defining 'kleptomania' as a mental illness related to irregular menstrual cycles, difficult pregnancies, the menopause and a range of other problems that were believed particularly to play upon the frailties of women.[29]

It is tempting to take the incidence of homicide as a measure of the pattern of inter-personal violence in a society, but this can only ever be an assumption that it would be difficult, if not impossible, to verify. Violence was most commonly associated with men. Historians have charted new models of masculinity emerging from the late seventeenth century that increasingly rejected any ready recourse to violence by men to preserve their honour or reputation. There was a new politeness, a greater concern with the skills of conversation, with new, restrained standards of behaviour, and with ways of acquiring reputation through public activity, church and work. The shift is detectable in eighteenth-century London among the elite and the middling sort.[30] It did not mean a quick end to violence between men, and by men against women; and the working-class 'hard man' remained a figure attracting respect well into the twentieth century.[31] The courts of Victorian England, however, appear increasingly to have taken it upon themselves to discipline men for violent behaviour and to impose the levels of acceptable behaviour. The extent to which provocation was accepted by judges as a defence in cases of homicide – both manslaughter and murder – was increasingly restricted and men who assaulted or killed were treated with much more severity at the end of Victoria's reign than at the beginning.[32]

While they made up the overwhelming majority of violent offenders, men were not alone in being violent. Some women beat, or otherwise ill-treated, servants and apprentices; on occasions such violence caused death or injury and landed the assailants in court.[33] Women fought each other;

less commonly they fought with men and a few fought with the police. Jane Smith, for example, fiercely assaulted two police officers in Hull when they tried to arrest her for being drunk and disorderly. A local newspaper turned to classical allusions for its description:

The prisoner was of amazonian build, and had conducted herself more like a fury than anything else. She was obliged to be hand cuffed and have her legs strapped together to keep her from kicking any one she came near, and it took five men to convey her in a cart to the station house.[34]

Like their menfolk Irish women had a particular reputation for violence.[35] Among the criminal anthropologists of nineteenth-century Europe the violent female offender was regarded as even more vicious and dangerous than her male counterpart; and it was common, in different theories, for violent female behaviour to be linked to the menstrual cycle.[36]

Although 'unnatural' women used their fists, feet and weapons to commit assaults and murder, it was the female poisoner who, almost by definition, acted secretly and without overt physical aggression, who became a *bête noire* of the nineteenth century.[37] The horror of the female poisoner was probably sharpened by the idea of domesticity and the preparation of food being central elements within the woman's separate sphere of behaviour. Wilkie Collins created the passionate, unscrupulous poisoner, Miss Gwilt, for his labyrinthine *Armadale* (1866), but there was also the occasional 'real' story for the press to latch on to. Eliza Fenning, a servant girl, was executed in 1815 for allegedly attempting to kill the family that employed her with poisoned dumplings.[38] Later in the century came the *causes célèbres* of Florence Bravo, Adelaide Bartlett and Florence Maybrick whose husbands died in suspicious circumstances; the cases were further spiced by adultery.[39] The wife who was accused of murdering her husband generated enormous popular interest. The offence was the ultimate negation of the behaviour expected of the dutiful wife, and it also reached into the ranks of the respectable middle classes. Yet, for all its notoriety, it was a rare occurrence with perhaps one conviction every three or four years.[40] In the early Victorian period women made up forty per cent of all those tried for murder; but when, towards the end of the century, the statistics for the murder of infants under a year old were separated out, the number of women accused of murder fell to fewer than a quarter of the total tried for the offence.[41]

New-born child murder, often described as infanticide, was overwhelmingly a female crime. Like the prostitute and the female poisoner, the murdering mother was a negation of the ideal of womanhood, but throughout the period 1750–1900 the all-male juries and judges were often more moderate in their treatment of an accused than a strict implementation of the law would have allowed. Until 1803 the crime of infanticide was supposed to be tried under an act of 1624. This act had been prompted by concerns about bastardy and immorality; it made the offence capital and presumed that a woman who had concealed the death of an illegitimate child had murdered it. Proof of concealment was required, but the accused had the task of proving, with at least one witness, that a dead infant had been born dead. By the middle of the eighteenth century the act was increasingly perceived as cruel and harsh. In addition, there were changing attitudes towards the nature of evidence and new requirements in the standard of proof. More and more juries required the prosecution to prove the killing for a guilty verdict and thus, to all intents and purposes, they turned trials under the 1624 act into murder trials. Juries also increasingly accepted that evidence of a woman having made some suitable preparations for her child's birth was sufficient grounds for acquittal. There was an attempt to reform the law in the 1770s, but legislative change did not come until 1803.[42]

The act of 1803 was not the work of penal reformers. It was introduced by the conservative Lord Chief Justice, Lord Ellenborough, who was keen to limit the latitude that was increasingly to be found in the courts in such cases. He also drew on concerns about rising levels of illegitimacy; rising poor rates were already aggravated by the French wars and were thought to be worsening as a result of immoral women turning to the parish for assistance. The bill introduced by Ellenborough was the subject of considerable debate and amendment within parliament – another example of the fact that capital statutes were not simply nodded through, even when emanating from a conservative figure in a period of relative conservative ascendency. The 1803 act made new-born child murder like any other murder, in that the prosecution was required to prove the offence. But where the murder charge failed the jury could return a verdict of 'concealment of birth' which carried a penalty of up to two years in prison. Again however, as the nineteenth century progressed, jury attitudes continued to act as a check on convictions. In 1857, for example, Eliza Higgins, a twenty-one-year-old domestic servant lodged in a London workhouse, was tried for the wilful murder of her baby daughter; an Old Bailey jury found her guilty of manslaughter, recommended mercy, and commented that 'the bastardy laws had a strong tendency to increase this class of crim'.[43] Witnesses before the 1866 Royal Commission on Capital Punishment testified that juries were reluctant to convict as long as the death sentence remained. 'Practically the law of infanticide hardly prevails,' declared J. H. Parry, a barrister with long experience in the criminal courts. 'Almost always now juries find concealment of birth; and . . . I also find that there is a great reluctance to hang women.'[44] Perhaps part of this 'general reluctance' was the result of juries recognising the plight of the accused. Most of the women charged with infanticide during the eighteenth and nineteenth centuries were young, commonly servants, desperate to maintain their positions and their respectability.[45]

Desperate attempts to preserve respectability, and also a determination on the part of married working-class women to limit the size of their families, could also lead to abortions, or to the use of baby farmers, the least scrupulous of whom might be better described as baby disposers. The law regarding abortion was progressively tightened during the nineteenth century. Before 1803 abortion was punished by a fine or a short term of imprisonment, and there was no penalty at all for abortion before 'quickening' – that is, when the woman could feel the movement of the foetus at about thirteen weeks. In 1837 the concept of quickening was removed; but until the 1861 Offences against the Person Act it was only the abortionist, and not the pregnant woman, who was guilty of an offence. Legislating against abortifacients was virtually impossible since so many of them were sold as purgatives and remedies for other ailments. Throughout the Victorian period much of the press carried advertisements for a great variety of pills to remove 'obstructions' – a euphemism for an unwanted foetus; and those marketing the products sought ways round the law by, for example, requiring purchasers to make a declaration that they were not pregnant, or by insisting that the pills should not be taken during pregnancy. If the pills failed (and invariably they were quite useless), there was always recourse to an abortionist. Middle-class women might be able to call on the services of a practising doctor; in working-class communities unqualified women who acted as midwives and nurses, and who laid out the dead, appear also to have been generally accepted and employed as abortionists. Baby farmers were individuals, generally women, who, for a fee, would keep children in their own homes.[46] In some instances 'keeping' appears to have been tacitly recognised as a synonym for allowing to die through lack of food and care, or even murdering. The revelations of baby farming in South London, which culminated in the execution of Mary Waters in 1870, led to the Infant Life Protection Act of 1872. This required all persons keeping more than one infant in their homes for more than twenty-four hours to register with local authorities; the local authorities themselves had to draw up regulations regarding facilities and numbers. The new act did not solve the problem; but then parliament recognised that there was a need for cheap baby care. So too, it would seem, did the all-male courts which continued to be lenient with baby farmers accused of negligence as well as mothers accused of infanticide. Overall however, there is little evidence to suggest that the criminal justice system was ever greatly concerned with abortion.[47]

During the seventeenth and eighteenth centuries there was an acceptance that a man might physically chastise his wife. The new ideas of masculinity, however, whittled away at the tolerance of such behaviour and, as noted earlier, at least from the late eighteenth century the courts were beginning to take a more critical view of wife-beating. Initially Georgian artisans appear to have been largely immune to these trends and they seem also to have been among the most violent towards their women folk. They feared competition from low-paid female labour, but they depended upon their wives to help support the family. They bonded with each other in their workplaces, pubs and clubs, and heavy drinking was central to the artisan culture. Their attitudes and their drinking arguably fostered domestic violence. In the early nineteenth century, however, a change is detectable as radical working-class spokesmen who urged political and economic reform also began to speak out loudly and publicly against wife-beating.[48] Moreover, they urged, a properly respectful and submissive wife deserved protection. Such views became increasingly common across all social classes in Victorian Britain, though within the working-class family particularly, economic pressures and tensions contributed to the continuation of domestic violence. Nevertheless, even in the poorer urban working-class districts where such violence continued to have vestiges of acceptance, neighbours might intervene when a husband exceeded the boundaries that a community recognised; and rural communities might still charivari such a husband.

In general the Victorian courts continued to take an increasingly hostile attitude towards the husband who assaulted a dutiful, virtuous wife, and in 1853 an Act for the Better Prevention of Aggravated Assault Upon Women and Children set out to specify and limit the amount of chastisement which a husband or father could administer. Nevertheless, 'aggravation' on the part of the wife continued to be considered by some as a just cause, or at least a mitigating circumstance for chastisement, even when such chastisement resulted in death.[49] In 1886 a Birmingham surgeon, Furneaux Jordan, explained to his, and probably to others' satisfaction, that on the basis of his observations most battered and murdered wives were of distinct physical types. Their skin:

was often clear, delicate, perhaps rosy. Their hair-growth was never heavy nor long, and the eyebrows were spare and refined. Their upper spinal curves were so formed to give a somewhat convex appearance to the back and shoulders and a more or less forward pose to the head.

But most importantly, they 'had sharp tongues in their heads and an unfailing – unfailing by repetition – supply of irritating topics on which to exercise them'.[50] In addition to such suggestions that the wife who was beaten was asking for it, the wife who responded with counter-violence was likely to receive a sentence from a court in excess of that meted out to violent husbands.

The scale of wife-beating is impossible to assess. The police were dissuaded from becoming involved in domestic disputes, while many women were reluctant to take their family's principal breadwinner to court or simply failed to give evidence in court, recognising the impact that even a short spell of imprisonment or a small fine could have on the family budget. A study of spousal abuse in late-nineteenth-century Northampton deploys evidence suggesting a slight increase in the offence in the last quarter of the century, and argues that this could have been the result of a crisis of self-esteem among the town's shoemakers deprived of traditional sports and leisure under increased supervision by factory foremen and police officers.[51] Others, however, have suggested that there was a decrease in the scale of such violence towards the end of the century as rising living standards reduced stress on the male as economic provider and as new legislation and rulings were enforced. An amendment to the Matrimonial Clauses Act of 1878 enabled magistrates to order separations in cases where husbands had been convicted of aggravated assaults on their wives, and the husband could also be required to pay a set weekly sum for the maintenance of his wife and children if it was deemed necessary for their future well-being. In 1891 the ruling in the case *R. v. Jackson* finally settled the law that it was illegal for a husband to beat or imprison his wife; the Summary Jurisdiction (Married Women) Act of 1895 allowed women to decide for themselves on separation without the need for a magistrate's order. But it is equally possible that growing respectability inhibited wives even more from complaining, while the noise and results of 'domestic disputes' were less apparent behind the net curtains and garden walls of the increasing working-class streets of suburbia. As James Hammerton has concluded, it is not possible to sustain any conclusions about a decline in domestic violence before 1914 on the evidence available.[52]

The wife-beater, increasingly demonised as the nineteenth century wore on, was perceived essentially as a working-class problem. However, from the middle of the century feminist critics and conservative moralists began to put more and more stress on the standards to be expected from husbands in marriage. In consequence, there appears to have been a growing intolerance of overbearing male behaviour whatever an individual's class.[53] The shift was a gradual one, reflected in legislation such as the Matrimonial Clauses Act and court decisions. In the courts the judiciary often led the way, sometimes inflicting heavy sentences on violent husbands when the jury was inclined to recommend mercy because of a wife-victim's drunkenness, scolding, or failure to provide the appropriate domestic arrangements for her husband and children. Such situations generated friction between judge and jury; the same kind of mind set prompted a massive petitioning and press campaign for clemency in the case of George Hall, a Birmingham jeweller's stamper who shot his new but 'adulterous' young wife.[54] Yet for many, the problem of family violence was so abhorrent that it could scarcely be discussed and it was submerged under pieties about the ideal harmony of the family in which the father was dominant and masterful while the mother and children were dutiful and submissive.

Violence by men against women was not confined to marriage. The workplace, as well as the home, provided the spatial context for such violence, as well as for male on male and female on female violence. Similarly the social context of courtship might result in incidents of male assault.[55] While the dominant, masterful male was presumed to have a rational, enlightened mind, it was also recognised that within his body there was located an unruly sexual urge. Again this was contrasted with the ideal female who was regarded as irrational and prey to her emotions yet, at the same time, sexually passive. The double standard was made explicit in 1871 in the report of the Royal Commission on the Contagious Diseases Acts. The Commission rejected the idea of regular examinations of soldiers and sailors for venereal diseases, as was required of prostitutes under these acts, on the grounds that:

there is no comparison to be made between prostitutes and the men who consort with them. With the one sex the offence is committed as a matter of gain; with the other it is an irregular indulgence of a natural impulse.[56]

At the beginning of the twentieth century the Royal Commission on the Metropolitan Police underlined this double standard further when it rejected the idea of sexual equality in the offence of soliciting. It insisted that legislation to criminalise a man for propositioning a woman, at least if she did not 'resent it, or, at any rate, [showed] no resentment or annoyance', would simply not be acceptable 'to the community at large'.[57] Notions of this sort contributed to problems in cases of that most appalling of offences committed by members of one sex on the other – rape.

Embarrassment, fear, and even ignorance ensured that many victims of rape and sexual assault sought no legal redress. In June 1824 parliament discussed the use of summary punishments for men 'lewdly and obscenely exposing the person'. T. G. B. Estcourt reported the opinion of magistrates:

that the offence was so frequent, and it was so difficult to prevail upon females to overcome their natural delicacy, and prosecute the offender in a court of justice, that some summary punishment was almost indispensible.[58]

Ann Spowage, a maidservant in Nottinghamshire, was rescued from rape by a passer-by in September 1857, but it was eleven days before she gave a deposition to the police. 'I complained about it to my mistress on the Thursday after. I was so shy I hardly dare mention it.'[59] The number of prosecutions for rape and attempted rape remained small throughout the period. In some instances, perhaps the majority, the matter appears to have been settled out of court. Magistrates and grand juries commonly dismissed accusations of rape or attempted rape. It seems probable that more offenders were pursued on charges of indecent assault which were heard at quarter sessions rather than assizes. These were less expensive for the prosecutor, less embarrassing for the victim, in as much as she escaped lengthy cross-examination by a defence counsel, and more likely to end with a conviction since, with rape being a capital offence until 1841, juries again appear to have been reluctant to convict.[60] Eighteenth-century evidence suggests that such prosecutions were more common in rural than urban areas, probably because of the support which the victim received from family and friends.[61] Most offences in the Black Country between 1835 and 1860 concerned girls under sixteen years, and often under ten;[62] this also suggests the family acting as the prime movers in a prosecution. However, not all women in rural districts were as fortunate. Female servants in the countryside were as unprotected from, and as vulnerable to, sexual harassment as any of their urban counterparts; and few in the communities, to which these women were usually strangers, appear to have cared.[63]

Rape trials were invariably as much an examination of the character and purity of the accused as they were of the events of the alleged offence.

There was concern that the accused could be the victim of a malicious prosecution, or that, with his natural and powerful sexual urges, the man had been unwarrantably encouraged. The victim needed to show evidence of a vigorous resistance to the attack, and of untarnished honour up until the moment it occurred. As Carolyn Conley has concluded, rape victims were suspect on three counts: they were women, they were admitting to have been outside the supervision of their male protectors, and they were declaring their loss of sexual innocence in public. 'Judges and jurors frequently concluded that no man should lose his respectability, let alone his freedom, for the mere seduction of such unworthy creatures.'[64] The point was put most forcibly in a paper by Charles Routh to the British Gynaecological Society in 1886. Routh took as his subject 'Nymphomania'. He considered incest unthinkable, and insisted that in rape cases signs of assault were insufficient in themselves; the doctor should consider whether the complainant 'is . . . addicted to masturbation? Has her mind been deteriorated by prurient ideas?' and he concluded of all women complaining of sexual assault: 'Except upon the strongest corroborating evidence, the presumption is that they are liars, plausible liars, cunning liars.'[65]

While on several occasions the courts insisted that prostitutes had as much right to protection from rape and sexual assault as any other woman, the reality of court proceedings and jury decisions often suggested otherwise. The case of Mary Duggan, though not specifically involving sexual assault, is illustrative of this. One night in February 1850 Duggan, 'a woman of abandoned character', had left a Yorkshire pub in company of three men; all four had gone into a neighbouring field. The following morning Duggan was found dead 'with her person exposed and much bruised'. The judge directed the jury to acquit the three defendants charged with causing her death since:

these facts did not amount to the crime of manslaughter. The woman, being intoxicated, had voluntarily accompanied the prisoners; and she was not like an infant who, unable to take care of itself, had been left exposed to the cold and died in consequence.[66]

Rape was overwhelmingly a male offence committed against women. Child sexual abuse was also almost always an offence committed by men. Notions of masculinity were deployed alongside those of class when such cases came to court. The abusers were labelled as 'monsters'; their offences were a negation of the ideal of the Victorian gentleman and the father as moral protector. Almost always the assumption was that this was also a crime committed by the most vicious lurking within the residuum, and these ideas were played out in court as defendants sought to stress that they were respectable fathers, or that they were being traduced by evil women motivated by malice or thwarted in blackmail attempts. The character of the accused and the accuser in such cases was always important, and the evidence suggests that members of the working class were more likely to be convicted of such offences than members of the middle class.[67]

The contemporary interest in the history of crime began as part of a wider attempt to find the voice of those who had been largely ignored in studies of the past. The initial focus on the working class has shifted to exploring gender relations and, to a lesser extent, race. The latter issue remains little explored, in part perhaps because between 1750 and 1900 England was not a particularly heterogeneous society; its people were largely white and native born. The Irish were seen as different, and the districts that were home to poor Irish were commonly stigmatised as criminal and dangerous. The thousands of Jews that fled East and Central Europe at the end of the Victorian period created a panic in the country and, particularly, in towns and cities into which they moved; they spoke an unknown language, dressed differently and the men wore large beards and strange haircuts. Outsiders and strangers commonly prompted suspicion, but numbers also appear to have had significance. The evidence and the research are limited but the experience of London and Liverpool suggests that the increasing inclination to see people of a different skin colour as inferior had repercussions in the general population, and also in the courts.

Gender was different but here too ideas evolved and stereotypes appear to have become more tightly defined. The patriarchal society that developed expected that men and women limit their activities to their respective spheres. Certain male offenders might be glamourised since their offending reflected the male virtues of courage, daring and initiative. In rough working-class districts the 'hard man' might achieve an appeal precisely because he showed the toughness and independence to which others might aspire. But perhaps the clearest example is the romantic highwaymen whose appeal spanned the spectrum of social class, though the tendency to invest some literary highwaymen with gentility was obviously directed at the more respectable reader. A romantic highwayman like Ainsworth's Dick Turpin was quite different from Dickens's brutal Bill Sikes; but even Sikes had the attributes of daring and shrewdness. In contrast, by her criminal actions the female offender, in the Victorian period particularly, was seen as challenging, even denying the social position designated for women. Furthermore, while the patriarchal society boasted of protecting the weaker sex, and while the legal process increasingly sought to uphold

48 Anna Clark, *The Struggle for the Breeches: Gender and the Making of the British Working Class*, University of California Press, Berkeley, CA, 1995, chapter 5.

49 Chadwick, *Bureaucratic Mercy*, pp. 313–19.

50 Furneaux Jordan, *Character as Seen in Body and Parentage*, London, 1886, p. 3.

51 Mary Beth Emmerichs, 'Five shillings and costs: Petty offenders in late-Victorian Northampton', Ph.D., University of Pennsylvania, 1991, chapter 7, *passim*.

52 Conley, *The Unwritten Law*, pp. 71–81; Maeve Doggett, *Marriage, Wife-Beating and the Law in Victorian England*, Weidenfeld and Nicholson, London, 1992; Nancy Tomes, 'A "Torrent of Abuse": Crimes of violence between working-class men and women in London, 1840–1875', *Journal of Social History*, 11 (1977–78), pp. 328–45; A. James Hammerton, *Cruelty and Companionship: Conflict in Nineteenth-Century married Life*, Routledge, London, 1992, p. 42.

53 Hammerton, *Cruelty and Companionship, passim*.

54 Wiener, *Men of Blood*, pp. 224–7.

55 Shani D'Cruze, *Crimes of Outrage: Sex, Violence and Victorian Working Women*, U.C.L. Press, London, 1998, *passim*.

56 P.P. 1871 (C.408–1) xix, *Report From the Royal Commission on the Administration and Operation of the Contagious Diseases Acts 1866–9*, p. 17. In contrast to the Commission's conclusion, however, there were witnesses who recognised the double standard. R. B. Williams, for example, a committee member of the Rescue Society, protested: 'One of the root causes of prostitution is the widely prevalent immoral sentiment that the quality which is so strongly demanded in women is not to be required in our sex – that incontinency on the part of men is comparatively venial, and that men may have access to women who are not wives. These Acts are based on the same vicious principle, and operate to protect and encourage men in their illicit indulgences. As they thus provide for vice, so will their educational effect be to teach men, and especially young men, that they must have a continual supply of fallen women for their sensual gratification.' *Ibid., Minutes of Evidence*, q. 20, 292.

57 P.P. 1908 (C.4156) *Report of the Royal Commission upon the Duties of the Metropolitan Police*, p. 127.

58 *Hansard*, new series, xi (1824) col. 1082.

59 Notts. R.O. Q.S.D. Deposition of Ann Spowage, 15 September 1857.

60 Anna Clark, *Women's Silence, Men's Violence: Sexual Assault in England 1770–1845*, Pandora, London, 1987; Antony Simpson, 'The "Blackmail

Myth" and the prosecution of rape and its attempt in 18th century London: The creation of a legal tradition', *Journal of Criminal Law and Criminology*, 77 (1986), pp. 101–50; and Gatrell, *The Hanging Tree*, chapter 17.

61 Beattie, *Crime and the Courts*, p. 130.

62 Philips, *Crime and Authority*, p. 269.

63 Jill Barber, ' "Stolen Goods": The sexual harrassment of female servants in West Wales during the nineteenth century', *Rural History*, 4 (1993), pp. 123–36.

64 Conley, *The Unwritten Law*, pp. 81–95; quotation at p. 95.

65 Quoted in McLaren, *A Prescription for Murder*, pp. 84–5. McLaren also quotes Lawson Tait, the eminent Birmingham gynaecologist and surgeon who was infuriated by the 1885 legislation which raised the age of consent to sixteen and which he believed could lead to the ruin of respectable gentlemen. Tait persuaded the authorities to let him investigate the subsequent complaints made in the Birmingham area, and out of one hundred he considered that only six should result in prosecution.

66 *The Times*, 16 March 1850.

67 Louise A. Jackson, *Child Sexual Abuse in Victorian England*, Routledge, London, 2000, especially chapter 6.

68 David Taylor, 'Cass, coverdale and consent: The metropolitan police and working-class women in late Victorian London', *Cultural and Social History*, 12 (2015), pp. 113–36.

CHAPTER 5

Perceptions of place

Contemporaries who thought and wrote about crime in England between 1750 and 1900 perceived it largely as an urban problem. London, the largest city in Western Europe, was the focus for the concerns of both Henry Fielding and Patrick Colquhoun. The former lamented that:

Whoever . . . considers the Cities of London and Westminster, with the late vast Addition of their Suburbs; the great Irregularity of their Buildings, the immense Number of Lanes, Alleys, Courts and Byeplaces; must think that, had they been intended for the very Purpose of Concealment, they could scarce have been better contrived.

Colquhoun described London as:

not only the grand magazine of the British Empire, but also the general receptacle for the idle and depraved of almost every Country, and certainly from every quarter of the dominions of the Crown; – where the temptations and resources for criminal pleasures – gambling – fraud and depredation, as well as for pursuits of honest industry almost exceed imagination.[1]

Most of the more alarming and best publicised of nineteenth-century crimes were committed in London.[2] Yet some contemporaries looked beyond the metropolis and found crime in the burgeoning urban environments with their teeming, anonymous populations and their uneducated, nomadic poor living in insanitary slums. Thomas Plint fused the assessments of Fielding and Colquhoun when he declared that:

The pickpocket and the thief can find no nesting-place amongst the statesmen of Cumberland and Westmoreland, or the miners of Durham

and Cornwall. They fly to Birmingham, London, Manchester, Liverpool,
Leeds. They congregate where there is plenty of plunder, and verge
enough to hide in.

In 1867 James T. Hammick emphasised 'that the criminal classes are, for the
most part, congregated in the towns'. For the Reverend William Douglas
Morrison it could 'easily be ascertained without the aid of any figures' that
cities were 'the nurseries of modern crime'. Implicit in Hammick and Morrison, and explicit in Plint, was the idea that crime in rural society was not
as serious. This was articulated by some opponents of the new police in the
1830s and 1840s. 'In cities', according to the Reverend Charles Brereton:

the majority of thieves exist in gangs, practise fraud by profession, and
live by a constant series of depredations . . . criminals in the country only
occasionally once or twice a year steal a sheep, pig, corn, hay, wood,
turnips, poultry as the case may be.

This was just one of the many reasons why, according to Brereton, the
Metropolitan Police model was inapplicable to rural England. Towards the
end of the century such ideas had been developed by enthusiasts for the Settlement Movement who urged young gentlemen to spend time doing 'good
works' in slum areas like London's East End. What was lacking in these
districts, according to Canon Barnett, the founder of Toynbee Hall, was 'a
leisured class . . . who will see that the laws are carried out and generally
keep the social life going'. Canon Henry Scott Holland, an early enthusiast
for Oxford House, summed this up with his call to young gentlemen to
'Come and be the squires of East London'.[3] This can best be understood in
terms of the vision of a contented rustic England which developed during
the nineteenth century and in which the stability and tranquillity of rural
society were emphasised to compensate for the terrors of urbanisation and
recurrent concern about the effects of the industrial economy.

The attempts of various sociologists and social anthropologists to
explain the differences between rural and urban life-styles has given a theoretical underpinning to the belief that rural crime and urban crime are
markedly different. According to the *Gemeinschaft-Gesellschaft* dichotomy proposed by the German sociologist Ferdinand Tönnies in traditional
society, generally equated with rural society, people live in a face to face
community where social mobility is low, and behaviours and actions are
legitimated in terms of custom and precedent; modern society, in contrast,
is impersonal and a variety of voluntarily formed associations regulate
different aspects of social life.[4] *Anomie*, or social instability particularly

resulting from the disruption or disappearance of value systems in the teeming new cities of the nineteenth century, has also been popular in explaining a growth of crime during the great period of industrialisation and urbanisation. At the close of the nineteenth century some European criminologists and social investigators, notably Emile Durkheim, were concerned that the city, together with the spread of 'modern civilisation', was destabilising the 'equilibrium' of some individuals, prompting degeneracy and deviance. In the words of Havelock Ellis: 'Like insanity, criminality flourishes among migrants, and our civilisation is bringing us all, more or less into the position of migrants'.[5] These concepts implicitly, though perhaps not always consciously, informed the understanding of many older historians. J. J. Tobias, for example, concluded that:

The large towns during much of the nineteenth century failed to provide the support which former country dwellers had known in the smaller communities from which they came. Entry into the criminal class was a means of finding support; it was entry into an association, informal but none the less, members of which could be found almost everywhere.[6]

To some extent the setting can dictate the form and style of crime. It appears that, from the early modern period there has been a long-term decline in violence and murder across Western Europe. Yet the evidence from the British Isles suggests that for much of the nineteenth century rapid urbanisation led to a temporary increase in violent crime in the big, expanding towns compared to rural districts.[7] White-collar crime depends on particular forms of economic and social structure generally rooted in a bureaucratic and urbanised society. Street robbery, by definition, could not happen in a corn field or forest; similarly poaching and sheep-stealing could really only be rural offences, though not necessarily committed by rural dwellers. Nineteenth-century urban and industrial areas in the Midlands, East Anglia and Lancashire contained poachers who made regular forays into the neighbouring countryside.[8] Some London gangs were suspected of secretly killing other animals, notably horses, and then offering to buy the carcasses from the owners for dog meat.[9] Sheep-stealers and rustlers were drawn similarly from both town and country, as well as from a variety of social groups; and motives were varied. Rural and urban poverty could be a spur, though it seems possible that in some districts there was almost a tradition of periodically improving the family diet with stolen mutton. Sometimes resentment or revenge appears to have motivated the rural sheep-stealer; and, on occasions, as in the case of poaching, sheep were taken to provide butchers with illicit meat for the urban market.[10]

Arson, while it was occasionally employed as a weapon during trade disputes,[11] was primarily a rural offence, and environment was a contributory element. The farmer's house was known and probably isolated; his barns and ricks, like his sheep and other livestock, were vulnerable on dark nights in ways that factories, or workshops in tolerably lighted streets, sometimes with night watchmen and subject to increasing police patrols, were not. A casual agricultural labourer, angered or victimised by a farmer acting as employer or Poor Law official, could exact prompt revenge and the chances of getting away with it seemed reasonable. At the very end of 1841 the Reverend Henry Owen, a magistrate living at Haveringham in Suffolk, saw £80-worth of his corn go up in flames. The Chief Constable believed that the outrage was committed 'in consequence of the Revd Mr Owen having punished some persons of bad character in the neighbourhood'.[12] In 1845 William Grange set fire to the hay and corn stacks of John Handysides, a farmer of Ackham in the North Riding, when Handysides dismissed him without payment. Grange declared at his trial that he intended to show Handysides 'an example that farmers should treat their labourers with respect and not clandestinely as he had done'. He was found guilty and transported. The Chief Constable of the East Riding reported to the quarter sessions in January 1864 that the 'illiterate rustic' was easily offended and that:

the majority of these evil-doers, of course, are those who have been discharged from their employments, or punished for offences, or refused favours, or warned to be on their good behaviour, or deluded into an idea of wrong or an insult to their families.[13]

Insurance companies rightly recognised that the problem was not one-sided and warned their agents to enquire whether farmers were deemed 'obnoxious' in their locality before undertaking to offer their services; in addition they surcharged unpopular farmers who were already policyholders.[14]

About half of those arrested for arson in the East Riding during the 1860s were agricultural labourers and several of these were itinerants, locally known as Wolds Rangers – defined by a prosecuting counsel as 'a man who travels the Wolds getting work from day to day and consequently being fully conversant with the district'.[15] Vagrants were allegedly involved with a wave of arson in North Wales, the border countries and the Midlands during the 1860s. According to one contemporary, from then until the end of the century arson remained 'a favourite method of [vagrants] venting spite'.[16]

Rural arson was not always the work of isolated individuals; sometimes villagers assisted the arsonist by impeding, or at best offering no assistance to fire-fighters.[17] The epidemic of incendiarism in East Anglia in the 1830s and 1840s appears to have been the work of a few, generally young men, single and unemployed, who were growing aware that there was no future for them on the land. Their protests struck a chord with others in the labouring community and may have contributed to the gentry's re-examination of its role in the community and to the provision of allotments and better housing.[18] However it would be wrong to understand every instance of rural arson in terms of class war. Henry Clapham set fire to his brother's stack at Burton Pidsea in the East Riding as part of a family feud.[19] George Serle, alias Edwin Serle, alias Walter Tomlinson, alias Cockayne, alias Thompson, born in Belper, Derbyshire, and a horse-trimmer by trade, had a long career of starting fires. In 1854 he was sentenced to one year's hard labour for arson in Derbyshire; five years later he was sentenced to five years' penal servitude for setting fire to stacks of wheat and hay at Biggleswade, Bedfordshire. Shortly after the end of this sentence the Nottinghamshire Lent Assizes of 1866 gave him fifteen years' penal servitude for a similar offence.[20] Serle appears to have delighted in lighting fires. But, of course, a few fires were started by property owners seeking to defraud their insurance companies, while others were simply the result of children playing with matches.[21]

Animal maiming was also overwhelmingly a rural crime, for obvious reasons; and it had other similarities with arson. Personal feuds between members of the same social class, revenge, and elements of social protest can be detected among the motives. The brutal, grisly, often very bloody and messy injuries inflicted on the sexual organs of a few of the animal victims suggest that some of the perpetrators might also have been seeking other forms of gratification. There were also some instances of horses being killed as a result of attempted 'horse magic', as teamsmen eager to make their masters' horses the best groomed, with the shiniest coats, employed secret remedies which turned out to be lethal.[22]

The availability of shot-guns in rural areas, combining with the greater problems of surveillance, meant that pot-shots were sometimes taken at informants and policemen. This was especially the case in Suffolk during the rural disorders of the 1840s. In March 1844 Charles Grimmer, a farmer of Pakefield near Lowestoft, heard two shots outside his house and on going to a window he received a shot-gun blast in the shoulder. 'Mr Grimmer', noted the Chief Constable:

has on several occasions taken an active part with Police to detect a gang of thieves that reside near him which is the cause assigned for the attempt upon his life.[23]

Rural communities, however, were not the only ones in which informers and certain types of offender could find themselves set upon or ostracised.

The level of sophistication might also contribute both to types of crime and to responses to crime. The rural poor often did not see Christianity and Paganism as mutually exclusive. They combined the two within their distinctive world view, though Paganism became less significant as the nineteenth century wore on.[24] Girls in rural districts, anxious to discover future husbands or to attract particular young men, sometimes butchered and mistreated animals in ways which sickened rational and sensitive Victorians. In February 1848 Mary Brice, Jane Matthews and Sarah Page were brought before Bletsoe Petty Sessions for torturing a cat. They were fined and sentenced to short periods of hard labour in the house of correction. The prison chaplain was appalled by their offence:

The three females . . . had the barbarous cruelty – a cruelty that sickens the very heart, to open up with a pair of scissors the body of a living cat, and take out her heart . . . the motive was most ignorant and superstitious. It was the belief that, by sticking pins in the poor animal's heart, and then burying it in the earth, they would bring back their lovers. This happened in a village in Bedfordshire in the year 1848![25]

When crimes were committed against them, at least up until the middle of the nineteenth century, the rural poor seem to have been as inclined to go to 'cunning' or 'wise' men as to constables or policemen. It was even alleged that an escaped thief in Norfolk consulted a 'cunning' woman for a 'safe conduct'. These 'cunning' men and women were professionals who charged fees and whose expertise could be purchased to thwart witches and tell fortunes in addition to identifying thieves and finding stolen, or lost, property.[26] There were other ways of dealing with witches, but in the eyes of the law these could constitute assault. The Reverend R. M. Healey was asked by a wheelwright to say a few words over a sow which, the wheelwright believed, was being 'overlooked' by a witch. The traditional way of dealing with a witch who 'overlooked' a victim or an animal was to stick pins in her chair, or otherwise draw her blood and thus render her powerless. The wheelwright confessed that he had not done this as the witch would take him before the Spilsby magistrates, and Victorian magistrates were 'that iggnerant' that they would have fined him. At Cromer in 1847 a group of boys was brought before the magistrates for stoning the poor woman who carried the local letter bag; they wanted to draw the blood 'of the old witch'.[27]

Some historians, though not specifically with reference to Britain, have detected more significant differences between rural and urban crime. Rural society, it was once assumed, was more primitive, and therefore had a higher incidence of inter-personal crime than urban areas. In the latter the disorganisation created by urban growth, or simply the greater opportunity for theft provided by the urban environment, led to a greater incidence of property crime.[28] Such conclusions fit comfortably with both Marxist and Modernization theories of social and economic development, though they are not helped by Peter King's analysis of prosecutions for violence which reveal an increase in the expanding towns and cities but not in rural areas. Furthermore it has been emphasised by J. A. Sharpe that property crime, as measured by indictments and executions for property offences, fell markedly between the early seventeenth and early eighteenth centuries, namely during the period generally portrayed as so significant for the rise of English capitalism.[29]

Towns and cities appeared to both eighteenth- and nineteenth-century social commentators as anonymous, dangerous and dirty, particularly those areas where the poorer sections of the community lived. When the poor had only one room for the family then the courtyard, the street and the pub became centres for leisure and recreation, for meeting and arguing; the courtyard and the street became sites for displaying wares, selling hot food and dumping rubbish. Many streets, in consequence, appeared to be owned by the poor; and the elite could never know these teeming, jostling masses in the way that they knew retainers on their estates or supposed that their predecessors had known whole communities. The poor became exotic 'wandering tribes' to be described by a Mayhew; they also became objects of social policy to enable the respectable among them to prosper and, through the notorious 'less eligibility' aspects of the New Poor Law, to make those work who were assumed to be idle and indolent. At the same time there emerged a romantic view of a former Golden Age: for Fielding this was before the corruption of society, and especially of the poor, by the luxury and wealth created by trade; for William Cobbett it was before the development of 'the thing' and 'the infernal wen' of London. The Golden Age was to be found in a romantic Merrie England, and even before Joseph Strutt had published his *Glig Gamena Angel-Deod, or the Sports and Pastimes of the People of England* (1801) or William Thomas had coined the word 'folklore',[30] gentlemen were in pursuit of the popular recreations of rural England so as to preserve them in 'Calendars' or 'Everyday Books'. Historians critical of the shape of the Industrial Revolution and what it meant for the working class, once implied that it saw the destruction of a reasonably contented rural society. More recently, historians of the customs and rituals of the old rural community have followed a similar tack; the new economic order of industrialising Britain, in its attempt to establish a rational and compliant workforce, battered away remorselessly at the old popular culture with its undeniable brutality, horseplay and lack of deference. The reconstruction of custom and ritual in rural, or 'preindustrial' communities, has been invaluable; yet some of the conclusions drawn about the criminalisation of aspects of traditional behaviour might tend to mislead.

Largesse was a customary rural practice at harvest time and was a way of supplementing harvest wages. In some areas the chosen chief of a gang of labourers would request money from any person passing a field wherein harvesting was in progress. Elsewhere labourers solicited largesse by going from door to door in a neighbourhood. The behaviour had an implicit element of threat, but it was also a levy 'made on the whole community, as a recognition of and reward for the labourer's work during harvest'.[31] Yet this leads to key questions: Where, if at all, can a line be drawn between largesse and extortion? And what was the difference between largesse, which folklorists could find acceptable in a rural community, and extortion which was repugnant? The notion of largesse manifestly did not enter into Lord Fortescue's condemnation of 'sturdy beggars' infesting parts of Devonshire in the 1850s:

Numbers of sturdy beggars, particularly in summer, invade our farmhouses and cottages and in the absence of the men extort money or provisions from the women who they find at home. Indeed in this house I have for some years kept at my own expense an assistant constable in the shape of a trusty labourer to repel the above class of visitors, some of whom when they have been saucy I have committed to Bridewell where they have almost invariably been recognised as old offenders.

Fielder King, a substantial landholder in Hampshire and Sussex spoke similarly of 'vagrants . . . alarming the females in the house and obtaining alms from fear rather than charity'.[32]

The problem of Liverpudlian 'cornermen' further demonstrates the problems relating to largess and extortion, but in the urban environment. In the 1870s a murder by 'cornermen', young men who congregated in the streets and sometimes requested/demanded 'a treat' from passers-by, led to a panic in the national press. The cornermen, according to one local paper, were 'well-known dock loafers; beings who will do anything and everything but be honest and work for a living'. In August 1874 a young warehouse porter, on his way home from a day out with his wife and brother, was accosted on the corner of Tithebarn Street and Lower Milk Street. He

refused to give the sixpence treat to a group of men who beat him sense-
less. He later died of his injuries. The national press reporting the incident
claimed that the local population backed his assailants, though in reality
the situation was much more complex. Some individuals may have presumed it was a typical pub brawl and others had no wish to risk life and
limb by getting involved or suggesting that they supported the police. Yet
some people called for help; the principal assailant was identified and he,
together with accomplices, was tried, sentenced to death and executed.[33]

Mumming was another way of extracting money or goods in the rural
community. The mummers performed their plays for all ranks of people
which, in some ways, emphasised the social cohesion of the old society.
Mumming became increasingly obsolete as the nineteenth century progressed.[34] At New Year in Bradford during the 1860s, however, mummers –
men and boys with blackened faces – crossed into middle-class districts
and even forced their way into middle-class homes demanding money and
drink.[35] In 1887 a correspondent of *The Times* expressed alarm about 'the
increasingly aggressive character of the roughs' who were to be found in
London's suburbs:

*At Essex Villas, Kensington, yesterday, upon my wife reaching home
with a box outside her brougham, a rough who had followed, waiting
until the coachman drove off, forced his way into the hall, and refused to
leave until he was given something. While the police were being sent for
he, during 10 minutes, indulged in the most loathsome abuse, evidently
hoping to terrify the lady into acceding to his demands. He only left
when the policeman appeared in the street, and then he only strolled
away, for, as he stated, he did not care for all the police in London. The
policeman would take no action, merely seeing him down the street in a
leisurely fashion. At the police station I am informed my only remedy is
by summons.*[36]

The Kensington rough described previously appears to have made no
attempt to offer any service, other than his departure, for his payment. But
several questions are posed by each variety of urban extortion described
here, especially, when money was demanded in the form of largesse or to
reward mumming. Liverpool Cornermen, Bradford Mummers and London 'roughs' were hardly reinforcing community cohesion; they wanted
something, and were prepared to use intimidation and even at times
physical violence to get it. But what did the rural practitioners of largesse
and mumming think that they were doing? Their behaviour may, at one
time, have reinforced community solidarity. Yet recent historical research

has pushed unified village communities further and further back in time; there are doubts about their existence in the mid-sixteenth century;[37] and whether the average, typical mummer or harvest gang leader (whatever such a being was) ever consciously thought in such terms is highly debatable. Furthermore, even in the second half of the eighteenth century, much harvesting was being done by itinerant labouring gangs, and any demands for largesse on their part cannot realistically be construed as reinforcing a local community. During the eighteenth and nineteenth centuries there was an assault on forms of popular culture such as largesse and mumming; the question remains as to when such institutions were ever accepted by all participants in the ritual in the ideal form which was allegedly destroyed by the assault on popular culture. It is important never to glamourize nasty, intimidating and violent behaviour with the cloak of popular tradition; and it is not just cynicism or class prejudice to suggest that some of the men who sought alms and/or largesse in the late eighteenth and early nineteenth centuries were just as nasty and unscrupulous as Lord Fortescue and Fielder King implied.

Urbanisation did not destroy the ability of groups bound by work, ethnic, religious or other ties from existing as communities; nor did it leave the new urban dweller as an isolated individual among a society of strangers. Irish immigrants, and their descendants, remained in readily identifiable enclaves. New migrants sometimes came with recommendations to those from their villages who had gone before. These immigrants brought practices from their rural backgrounds with them, which, like keeping pigs and faction fights were often ill-suited to their cramped urban dwellings. Such behaviour, while it concerned and alienated the native population, may have served to reinforce the communities' Irishness. Moreover Irish 'criminality' was regarded as rooted in violence and public disorder rather than theft. The immigration by Jews from Holland and Germany in the eighteenth century and from Eastern Europe at the end of the nineteenth century reveals similar communal solidarity, but the forms of criminality were different. But a comparison of Irish and Jewish immigrants in nineteenth-century British cities also provided an object lesson against the simple equating of immigrant ghetto areas with criminal areas. The Irish were notorious for alleged criminality, though their offences were primarily of the public order variety as is evidenced by a cursory glance at the headlines of any nineteenth-century urban newspaper produced in a town with a significant Irish population, as well as by court records.[38] Jews committed the same kinds of crime as the English and serious alarm about crime and the Jewish 'race' scarcely materialised before the widespread immigration at the

close of the nineteenth century. The concern prompted a reforming campaign by respectable, well-to-do Anglo-Jewry, and partly because of this,
together with the strict regulations imposed on tenants in the tenements
built for immigrants by Jewish philanthropists, the Jewish immigrants from
East Europe acquired a reputation (generally, and not always deserved) for
keeping out of trouble. This was even the case when the tenements were
sited in what were formerly notorious districts.[39] But the historian must be
careful of making a special case of immigrants; Robert Roberts who was
brought up in 'the classic slum' in Salford at the beginning of the twentieth
century, recalled how his community was a village with his parents' corner
shop one of the focal points. The 'village' had man-made boundaries: railway tracks to the north and south, a different slum village to the east and,
to the west, 'lay the middle classes, bay-windowed and begardened'.[40]

The principal problem with the urban-rural division in seeking to
understand crime is that it is simply too crude. Urban and rural are opposite ends of a spectrum and however the extremes are defined, there is a
vast area between them. Indeed for much of the eighteenth and nineteenth
centuries most of the English lived in neither big industrial cities nor on the
land, but in small towns, some of which, like Exeter and York, boasted the
title of city. These small towns were centres for rural society, and had been
for centuries: they had markets and fairs; some were the meeting places for
quarter sessions and assizes; and some, as boroughs, had their own courts.
The focus of these towns remained essentially rural. At the same time,
there were areas which, while rural in setting, were focused on burgeoning
economic and industrial development. The industrial villages of the West
Riding provide one example; the pit villages in the coalfields of Durham
and Northumberland provide another.

Urban and rural also break down significantly at the extremes. No
two cities are entirely similar and different economic structures and different functions provide opportunities for different types of crime. Seaports
and garrison towns offered wider opportunities for the 'victimless crime'
of prostitution. Ipswich was a garrison town and, with a population of
nearly 33,000 in the mid-nineteenth century, it was alleged to have fifty-
two brothels.[41] Seaports also generated other forms of crime. In 1811 the
magistrates of the Thames Police Office reported:

*In our District and Experience . . . we find Riots and dangerous affrays
among foreign seamen (many of whom continue on shore until they are
destitute and then seek a support by plunder) the most prevalent offences
and most difficult to be prevented.*[42]

Discharged merchant seamen, their pockets bulging with pay, encouraged other forms of offences. 'Street robberies and particularly larceny from the person (chiefly committed on seafaring people)' appeared the most prevalent forms of crime in the Whitechapel district of Regency London; the perpetrators, according to the magistrates, were 'pickpockets and prostitutes'.[43] The docks and warehouses of major ports provided greater opportunities, if not greater rewards than the much smaller canal wharfs of, for example, Manchester and Birmingham. The prevalence of small metal trades, together with the employment of boys to take unfinished goods from one small workshop to another, was considered a key element contributing to the scale of juvenile offences in mid-nineteenth-century Birmingham.[44]

Almost a century ago the Chicago 'School' of Human Ecology demonstrated that it is possible to generalise about urban social structure particularly with reference to the zonal arrangements of land-use, physical conditions and demographic structure. Drawing on such conclusions R. N. Davidson suggested an 'eclectic typology of the urban environment' for portraying urban neighbourhoods in terms of their crime characteristics; 'eclectic because of the stubborn refusal of the ecological dimensions to provide a neat framework to the classification'.[45] While it is not possible for the historian to amass the data of the modern criminologist and thus parallel all of Davidson's nuances, a rough division of the city into centre, commercial and industrial zones, inner-city residential districts and suburbs is useful in helping to comprehend the criminal characteristics of urban neighbourhoods in the past.

The city centre attracts crowds to its shops and its entertainments. These crowds provide opportunities for the pickpocket and the prostitute. Shops provide opportunities for shoplifting and, together with offices, for burglary. Entertainments provide the possibilities for affrays and minor assaults. The commercial and industrial zones, often near the centre, provide opportunities for theft and embezzlement though, because the number of people permitted legitimate access is fewer, the level of personal victimisation is also less. However much they structured their perceptions of criminality within contemporary ideology both Fielding and Colquhoun saw the wealth of the metropolis as fostering crime. Colquhoun was particularly concerned about thefts from warehouses and ships on the Thames. Court records, and Arthur Harding's recollections of East End dockers bringing home tea and selling it to corner shopkeepers, reveal such depredations continuing throughout the nineteenth century.[46] In mid-nineteenth-century Manchester the Chief Constable denied that the factory system had encouraged theft, but 'the warehousing system, from the value and the portable nature of the property left lying about in great ranges of rooms, was to a certain degree prolific of theft'.[47] John Rawlinson, a London Police Magistrate, told the Select Committee on the Police of the Metropolis in 1828 that the increasing exposure of goods in shop doors encouraged theft. A decade later the Superintendent of D Division of the Metropolitan Police bemoaned:

the too frequent practice of shopkeepers exposing their goods for sale outside of their shops [which] affords an easy facility to plunder, together with the ready mode of disposing of such plunder at Marine store shops, old clothes shops etc.

In 1865, echoing the comments of Colonel James Fraser, the Commissioner of the City of London Police, *The Times* expressed amazement at 'the unsuspecting confidence of the commercial, or, at least, the shop-keeping world'. As for pilfering from industrial areas, the Superintendent of K Division of the Metropolitan Police informed the Constabulary Force Commissioners that:

Robberies to an immense extent are daily occurring by workmen at large Factories, but I am informed by the Principals, that the men would not submit to be searched indiscriminately and continually, and that the combination amongst them is so strong that a strike would be the result.[48]

It is apparent that there was a vast amount of theft from the workplace in mid-nineteenth-century London, but it is impossible to put a figure on how much was taken, where from, or by whom.

In contemporary society there is a high concentration of crime and of offenders in certain inner-city residential areas. Davidson divides these areas into two basic sub-types: residual areas, in which there is an element of social cohesion and a degree of balance in the demographic structure; and transitional areas, with high turnovers of population and few family units. There was considerable mobility in the nineteenth-century city, even among the respectable working class; indeed moving could be a mark of respectability with a move being the only way that a family could get new lodgings which did not require immediate repairs.[49] Yet movement was often not very far within the city and it remains possible to detect both residual and transitional districts.

Not every residual district appeared prone to crime, but some were notorious. Irish districts were singled out as particularly criminal: the Bedern in York, Caribee Island and Stafford Street in Wolverhampton offer good examples during the thirty or forty years following the potato famine. But criminality here was, primarily, a problem of public order. Some, and not simply Irish districts, became virtual 'no-go areas' for the police and, more particularly, for the rent collector and landlord.[50] It may be that there was a high level of theft within such districts which, because of the inhabitants' antipathy to the police, was never reported. Victims might also be intimidated into not bringing charges and this, David Jones has suggested, could be one reason why the statistics might belie the undoubted criminality of the 'China' district of mid-nineteenth-century Merthyr Tydfil, a 'frontier town of the industrial revolution'. While respectable society rejected the population of 'China', that population itself reveals bonds of family, self-respect, independence and a unity of self-interest.[51] The bonds uniting the community of 'China' could be found in other poor areas such as the Jago, or Nicol, in Arthur Harding's childhood London. The police, and others, stigmatised such areas as the aphorism 'guarding St James by watching St Giles' testifies of itself. Until its destruction in the mid-nineteenth century, notably by the cutting of New Oxford Street, the St Giles 'rookery' was regarded with horror by respectable Londoners and the Reverend Thomas Beames explicitly compared it with the Faubourg St Antoine of Paris, notorious for its plebeian revolutionaries. Moreover, as one area was cleared, so the mantle of most criminal district or street was passed to another.[52]

Some residual areas, especially those where the landlords and rent collectors were reluctant to go and where repairs were never made, may have been worse in respect of poverty and squalor than transitional districts with their lodging houses – at least after the creation of the system of lodging house supervision in the mid-nineteenth century. Transitional areas were probably the worst centres of anomie, though there are problems in employing this concept to explain crime: what is the justification for seeing crime as the result of an ill-defined 'social disorganisation' when crime might just as well be considered as a fundamental component of such disorganisation?

Lodging houses with their rootless, generally single, populations were suspect at least from the 1750s. Henry Fielding quoted his friend and colleague, Saunders Welch, High Constable of Holborn, on the subject. Welch considered that some of the worst of such houses were to be found in St Giles and in St George, Bloomsbury:

with miserable Beds from the Cellar to the Garret, for . . . Twopenny Lodgers . . . in these Beds, several of which are in the same Room, Men

and Women, often Strangers to each other, lie promiscuously, the Price of
a double Bed being no more than Threepence, as an Encouragement to
them to lie together . . . as these Places are thus adapted to Whoredom,
so are they no less provided for Drunkenness, Gin being sold in them
all at a Penny a Quartern . . . in the Execution of Search Warrants.
Mr Welch rarely finds less than Twenty of these Houses open for the
Receipt of all Comers at the latest Hours . . . in one of these Houses, and
that not a large one, he hath numbered 68 Persons of both Sexes, the
Stench of whom was so intolerable, that it compelled him in a very short
time to quit the Place.[53]

Similar images recur throughout the nineteenth century and further illus-
trate the concerns about itinerants and those with no permanent employment, as well as the determination to equate criminality with physical
ugliness. Angus Reach, whose description of a 'low lodging house' in
Angel Meadow, Manchester, was quoted earlier, reported the city's chief
constable as speaking warily of 'a considerable floating population, and a
smaller number of persons who are known both to work and steal'.[54]

The police stigmatised certain lodging house districts as criminal and,
while these were generally the cheapest and poorest, the labelling may
have become self-fulfilling with those who could avoid lodgings in a stigmatised area making every effort so to do. At the same time, given that the
'crime' problem was understood as centring on the mass of petty thefts, a
majority of the offenders responsible for these activities probably were to
be found in these districts.

Low lodging houses in St Giles and other poor districts of London, in
Angel Meadow and Deansgate, Manchester, in Thomas Street, Birmingham, and in other cities had notorious reputations. The inhabitants of
all such districts were doubly vulnerable: on the one hand, having been
defined as what modern sociologists call 'police property',[55] they suffered
regular police searches; on the other, unlike the Irish or the people of Merthyr's 'China', their lack of community cohesion militated against any
resistance or unity of self-interest. The property of anyone staying in such
a lodging house, which obviously would not have been much, was also at
risk, for most things could be pawned; any property too meagre for the
pawnbroker could be taken to the dolly shop, and there was always the
second-hand clothes dealer and the rag and bone man. Again estimates of
crime within the transitional neighbourhood, and especially one stigmatised as criminal, are impossible given the relationship between the inhabitants and the police.

Many of the poorer inner-city residential areas became even less salubrious as cities expanded and new transport systems fostered the spread of
suburban residential districts. The better districts have much lower offender
and offence rates in contemporary society; during the nineteenth century, in
comparison with residual and transitory areas of the inner city, public order
offences in the suburbs appear to have been tiny. Thefts from gardens and
burglaries seem to have been the typical offences. The spread of suburbs
may have contributed to the fact that the statistics of burglary and housebreaking resisted the general decline in crime from the middle of the nineteenth century. Indicative that suburban districts were the more likely target
of the professional, calculating house burglar is the fact that it was in these
districts of metropolitan London where, from the mid-1880s, policemen on
night beats were authorised to carry revolvers. This authorisation came in
the wake of two particular burglaries by armed men in Islington and Wim-
bledon in the summer of 1883 and because of concern over the availability
of cheap revolvers manufactured in Germany. It was, however, also the case
that from early on police patrolling some fringe districts of London had
been issued with edged weapons: cutlasses for the men on foot and sabres
for those who were mounted. These weapons were countenanced because
of the large size and lonely nature of the beats in these districts, often in the
countryside, and the consequent inability of a man to get speedy assistance
from the constable on a neighbouring beat should he be attacked.[56]

Suburban residential districts, like the elegant and fashionable areas
which were still to be found in the centre of some cities, had their own
kinds of offenders. The different kinds of white-collar offenders were often
to be found living here, and these districts contained a high proportion of
domestic servants, among whose numbers lurked some who filched from
their employers and, occasionally, even illicitly pawned pieces of their
employer's property.

The smaller towns and cities also had their mixture of respectable housing and narrow squalid courts harbouring different kinds of offender and
providing the opportunities for different kinds of offence. The respectable
inhabitants of mid-nineteenth-century Horncastle, Lincolnshire, for example, with a population just reaching 4,500 in 1841, were concerned about
their 'lawless and immoral' inhabitants. Dog Kennel Yard in particular was
notorious for its brothels and prostitution. During the 1840s the town was
plagued by two gangs: Frank Kent led a group of adolescents who special-
ised in aggressively harassing country people and vagrants; Jack Sharpe, a
labourer, and Maskell Spencer, a blacksmith, led a different group known
as 'The Gang', whose offences included poaching and robbery.[57]

Similar gangs, or at least groups of young men in persistent and varied trouble with the authorities, were to be found in rural villages. In the summer of 1825 two young men, James Redman, aged twenty and James Grummet, aged twenty-three, were charged with stealing pistols from troopers of the Bedfordshire Yeomanry Cavalry. The troopers had stopped at the Royal Oak public house in the village of Houghton Conquest on their way home from a training exercise and, foolishly, they had left their pistols in the holsters on their saddles. The local constable had considerable difficulty in hanging on to his prisoners; villagers assaulted him and there were attempts to break the prisoners out of the village cage. At the Midsummer Quarter Sessions Grummet alone was convicted. He was positively identified as taking a pistol; Redman was not. Grummet was sentenced to three months' hard labour. He was no stranger to Bedford Gaol having received similar sentences for game offences in May 1818 and December 1819. On each occasion the gaoler described his behaviour as 'indifferent'. Redman had also been in trouble before. At the Epiphany Sessions in 1822 the Grand Jury had thrown out a bill of indictment brought against him for theft; eighteen months later he was sentenced to one month's hard labour for stealing a duck. In 1824, with two others, he was bound over to keep the peace towards Thomas Sharp of Wilstead. While visiting Houghton Conquest, Sharp had gone into the Royal Oak. Showing rather more valour than discretion Sharp suggested that Redman moderate his language whereupon, aided by the two others Redman ferociously assaulted him. When William and James Page were arrested in 1823 for stealing stockings from a draper's stall at Silsoe Fair, William Page bemoaned that there were seven or eight in Houghton Conquest far worse than him and that 'it was the first time that he had ever got into the Gang'. James Page protested: 'I am not the worst', and named seven who, he believed, were worse, including James Redman and James Grummet. A few weeks after his acquittal for the theft of the yeomanry pistol, Redman was committed for trial on a charge of housebreaking, together with John Hosler, aged nineteen, and Joseph Redman, aged twenty-six. Hosler was also on James Page's list and had received a sentence of two months' hard labour for wood theft in 1825. At the Bedfordshire Lent Assizes in 1826 all three were found guilty and sentenced to death. All were reprieved: Joseph Redman's apparent previous good behaviour told in his favour since he was given only one year's hard labour; James Redman and John Hosler were transported for life.[58]

Houghton Conquest, where the Redmans, Grummet and Hosler resided, was notorious. During the late sixteenth and early seventeenth centuries it had been a thriving and important country village; over the following century it had declined but in the second and third decades of the nineteenth century its population soared from 507 and 505 recorded respectively in the censuses of 1801 and 1811, to 651 in 1821 and 796 in 1831. The sudden growth of the parish, far above that for Bedfordshire as a whole, possibly led contemporary gentlemen to view it with suspicion; though it should be emphasised that the Parish Register of Houghton Conquest records Grummets and Redmans from the end of the sixteenth and beginning of the seventeenth centuries respectively.[59] According to the Reverend J. W. Burgon, vicar of St Mary's Oxford and subsequently Dean of Chichester, who wrote a brief history of the village during the 1870s, there was a popular saying that 'Bedford gaol would fall when it did not contain a Houghton man'. The streets were said to be unsafe after dark; the roads were impassable in winter. Burgon maintained that the reason for the village's unsavoury nature was the lack of any stable and responsible gentry. The gentry families in the village during its heyday had died out in the seventeenth and early eighteenth centuries. Houghton Park had repeatedly changed hands. The church living became increasingly undesirable; Dr William Pearce, the Master of Jesus College, Cambridge, who held the living between 1786 and 1820, was non-resident. Burgon dated the beginning of a slow improvement from the appointment of the Reverend Thomas Barber as rector in 1821. Barber enforced order in church 'by the power of his lungs' and on the streets 'by the weight of his arm'. He carried a stick, and sometimes used it; and, according to Burgon, as a magistrate he succeeded in getting some of the worst offenders transported.[60] Barber could not have sentenced men to transportation, but he was the magistrate who committed the Redmans, Grummet and Hosler for trial.

Burgon's analysis of why Houghton Conquest became so notorious says as much about his, and his contemporaries', perception of rural life, as it does about the village itself. After analysing the residences of criminals in mid-nineteenth-century Suffolk John Glyde was astonished by the result: about one-third of the county population were urban dwellers, yet they committed only about one-fifth of the crime. 'The simplicity and innocence of peasant life exists only in imagination.' The poor criminal villagers, he feared, had been left 'morally and physically a prey to their passions' by landowners, clergy and employers.[61]

Burgon's and Glyde's conclusions fit with the nineteenth-century image of two kinds of village – 'open' and 'closed'; a perception which emerged with the Poor Law investigations conducted at the first half of the century. In the closed village, control was firmly in the hands of a single landowner, or a small group of like-minded gentlemen. Their aims were to keep poor rates to a minimum and to preserve their personal amenities such as the views over their country houses or parks. To these ends they bought up land and enclosed commons to make larger agricultural units, game reserves and parks; they also limited settlement and building. Their control meant that they exercised a powerful influence over the local population; only hard-working, deferential, moral labourers were allowed settlement and the consequent relief in hard times. Open villages had no such controls. They were sprawling and usually very much larger; shopkeepers and independent artisans built cottages for rent which often turned into rural slums. The occupants of these slums provided labour for local farmers in both open and closed villages.[62] Some open villages might be squatter settlements providing labour for a nearby town. Headington Quarry, formerly a waste area on the edge of Shotover Common on the outskirts of Oxford, provides a good example. Many of the men here worked as quarrymen or brickmakers. Physical toughness was regarded as a virtue in the village. Disputes were settled without recourse to the police who patrolled Headington in pairs. Outsiders gave the village a wide birth.[63] Other open villages were viewed with similar horror and were accused of being centres of rural immorality and vice and, in consequence, the havens of burglars and other dangerous criminals. Francis Howells was one of the investigators appointed by the Poor Law Commissioners in 1848 to study the effectiveness of the law of settlement and removal. Among his findings Howells reported how, around 1840, Lord Manvers had pulled down several cottages at Laxton in Nottinghamshire so as to be rid of the occupants. The evicted families found temporary shelter in the workhouse:

I think it is right to say . . . that these people had become troublesome as poachers and as idle dissolute characters; and I believe that Lord Manvers was considered to have done a good thing when he broke up this gang of bad characters. They did not remain long in the [work] house, but went out and took up their abode in the neighbouring village of Egmanton, where Mr Barrow told me he thought they were the foundation of a gang of burglars. Mr Barrow adds 'We have broken up two different gangs of burglars in Egmanton', an open parish. And this perhaps, is one of the worst evils that the open parishes suffer from the close parishes, that they receive into them the bad characters to whom the owners of close parishes are naturally unwilling to give shelter, and whom they wish to get rid of if they can.[64]

The open-closed village dichotomy was not as clear-cut as implied by the poor law literature and those commentators who fretted about idle, disorderly and criminal rural labourers.[65] Detailed analysis of closed villages with resident gentry reveals that these could also contain frequent offenders. Westfirle is a case in point: the Gage family owned ninety-eight per cent of the available acreage in the village and were the largest single employer, yet over one-third of those prosecuted for criminal offences between 1820 and 1850 were prosecuted on more than one occasion and some of the offenders had criminal careers not unlike the Grummets and Redmans of Houghton Conquest.[66] At the same time research into rural protest suggests, not surprisingly perhaps, that it was the larger villages – the 'open' villages – with their greater proportion of agricultural labourers to employing farmers, and their distinctly higher percentage of independent artisans, which were more likely to participate in such behaviour.[67] Though, occasionally, a few magistrates and gentlemen might sympathise, the machine-smashing, the incendiarism, the destruction of game and of property, and the riotous assemblies which popular protest involved, were all crimes. Moralising contemporaries had little difficulty in making an intellectual leap at this point: if the idle and immoral poor participated in these crimes, then they would also participate in others; poaching thus became the first step on the road to a life of crime. To the extent that they probably contained proportionally more poachers, open villages were more criminal; few permanent labourers seem to have been convicted for poaching on the land of their employer.[68] Also poaching gangs could work together with some independent villagers; butchers, for example, were useful to a variety of poachers and sheep-stealers; innkeepers might purchase game themselves, or be able to pass it on to, or via, their clientele.

Some industrial villages were 'closed' inasmuch as they were built and run by the employer and his immediate subordinates. While the employer might look to his workforce's moral and intellectual improvement by restricting strong drink, providing schools for children and a mechanics' institute for his men, he could also enforce discipline through evictions and dependence by establishing his own store. Given that the village could be remote such stores could be a boon; it was the requirements and restrictions that went with it which made the truck system so hated by workers. When the employer was also the local magistrate, his power was complete. 'If the men took any measures against the masters they would not be employed' commented Thomas Jones Phillips, clerk of the peace at Bedwellty, while explaining to a parliamentary committee in 1842 that there had been no prosecutions in Monmouth under the Truck Act since the iron masters were also the magistrates.[69] But not all industrial villages functioned in this way. In some instances building development was left to independent tradesmen within the village. Furthermore mining, which was probably the most common reason for the creation of new industrial villages during the late eighteenth and nineteenth centuries, was an industry which was far less susceptible to rigorous regulations and supervision of the labour force than factory work. Miners were feared as violent and unruly during the eighteenth century; the image persisted well into the nineteenth century. In 1847 Jelinger Symons told a parliamentary committee that the mining district of Monmouthshire contained 'a larger proportion of escaped criminals and dissolute people of both sexes than almost any other populace'.[70] Thousands poured into County Durham in the second quarter of the nineteenth century to meet the requirements of industry, especially the demand for miners. The pit strike of 1831–32 was noted for its ferocity. After the creation of the county constabulary, policemen were commonly assaulted in pit villages; in 1842 it was argued that the relatively crime-free agricultural districts of the county were financing the police presence in the colliery districts. Yet for all that contemporaries branded the Durham miners as dangerous and criminal, theft does not appear to have been much of a problem in pit villages. In his reports to the *Morning Chronicle* Angus Reach found that the mining districts of Northumberland and Durham contradicted 'the theories generally entertained upon the connection of ignorance with crime by presenting the least criminal section of the population of England'. Statistically Reach found that there was a smaller proportion of offenders in the mining districts of Cornwall, Cumberland and Staffordshire. He concluded that the small amount of theft in the north east was probably due to the power of Methodism:

aided by the comparatively isolated condition in which the mining population lives – seldom or never coming in contact with the members of any industrial class except their own, and little exposed to the influences and excitements of great towns.[71]

It is equally likely that, in the event of a theft, a mining community was reluctant to involve the authorities, especially the police who guarded blacklegs and assisted at evictions during strikes. Justice for theft in a pit village, at least during the first half of the nineteenth century, may have been rougher and speedier than that sanctioned by the state, but responses probably varied with the nature of the incident.[72]

Environment had an inter-relationship with crime, but not simply along the lines that the urban-rural division might suggest. During the eighteenth and nineteenth centuries industrialisation and urbanisation changed communities, but the experience was not so shattering that people, especially poor immigrants spreading to cities or sprawling open villages, ceased to live in, and to perceive themselves as part of, communities. Some communities tended to be more law abiding than others, but theorists of crime, policemen and the respectable classes in general tended to think that any areas where the poor teemed and where there was no visible form of elite control and surveillance, were havens for the dangerous classes. Popular disorder, even when it had recognisable and even modest aims – food at a fair price, the traditional right to use common land – was increasingly perceived as dangerous and criminal. Popular exuberance at fairs and wakes, the noise and 'disorder' which spilled over from pubs, crowded courts, tenements and streets, was viewed similarly, even though it was condoned by the immediate community in which it occurred and, occasionally, might have involved the meting out of popular justice. Some of this disorder and exuberance was criminal in a narrow sense of the word, even if in some degree tolerated by the rural or urban community in which it occurred. But it seems to have been difficult for those contemporaries fired by 'respectability' and ideas of progress, fortified by Malthusian theory, and recognising that they lived in a society which was changing at a frighteningly rapid rate under the twin impact of urbanisation and industrialisation, to perceive continuities in community behaviour and the difference between different forms of offence.

Notes

1 **Henry Fielding**, *An Enquiry Into the Causes of the Late Increase of Robbers*, 2nd edn, London, 1751, p. 116; **Patrick Colquhoun**, *A Treatise on the Police of the Metropolis*, 3rd edn, revised and enlarged, London, 1796, pp. xi–xii.

2 Among the exceptions to the predominance of London crimes in creating fear was the grisly murder of four-year-old Francis Saville Kent at Road, Wilts, in January 1860. The fascination with the case was partly due, however, to the difficulties experienced by the authorities in identifying the murderer – Francis's sister, Constance. The case is the subject of **Kate Summerscale**, *The Suspicions of Mr Whicher, or the Murder at Rose Hill House*, Bloomsbury, London, 2008.

3 **Thomas Plint**, *Crime in England: Its Relation, Character, and Extent as Developed From 1801 to 1848*, London, 1851, p. 19; **James T. Hammick**, 'On the judicial statistics of England and Wales with special reference to recent returns relating to crime', *Journal of the Statistical Society*, **xxx** (1867),

pp. 375–426 (at p. 391); **William Douglas Morrison**, 'The increase of crime', *Nineteenth Century*, **xxxi** (1892), pp. 950–7 (at p. 956); **C. D. Brereton**, *A Refutation of the First Report of the Constabulary Force Commissioners*, 3 parts, London, n.d., Part 1, p. 73; Barnett and Scott Holland are quoted in **Mandy Ashworth**, *The Oxford House in Bethnal Green*, Oxford House, London, 1984, p. 7. Angus Reach was something of an exception. In his mid-century reports for the *Morning Chronicle* he noted that 'where great bodies of people, the vast proportion of them labouring poor, are crammed together, crime must abound'. But he also emphasised that there was far more rural crime than many people imagined, indeed the amount was 'of startling magnitude to the many who naturally connect rustic beauties with rural innocence, and take but little account of the fact that the agricultural labourer endures more habitual and more pinched hunger and cold amid his fair fields and woods, than the factory operative amid the dust and smoke of his alley and his mill'. **J. Ginswick** (ed.), *Labour and the Poor in England and Wales*, 8 vols, Frank Cass, London, 1983 i, p. 6.

4 Ferdinand Tönnies, *Community and Society*, trans. and supplemented by Charles P. Loomis, RKP, London, 1955. *Gemeinschaft* is generally translated as 'community'; *Gesellschaft* as 'association', 'organisation' or even 'society'.

5 Havelock Ellis, *The Criminal*, London, 1890, p. 297. For a useful introductory critique see **Howard Zehr**, *Crime and the Development of Modern Society*, Croom Helm, London, 1976, pp. 20–9; see also **Robert A. Nye**, *Crime, Madness and Politics in Modern France: The Medical Concept of National Decline*, Princeton U.P., Princeton, NJ, 1984, especially pp. 149 and 171.

6 J. J. Tobias, *Crime and Industrial Society in the Nineteenth Century*, Penguin, Harmondsworth, 1972, p. 108.

7 Peter King, 'The impact of urbanization on murder rates and on the geography of homicide in England and Wales, 1780–1850', *H.J.*, **53**, 3 (2010), pp. 671–98.

8 David Jones, *Crime, Protest, Community and Police in Nineteenth-Century Britain*, RKP, London, 1982, p. 66; **John E. Archer**, 'Poaching gangs and violence: The urban-rural divide in nineteenth-century Lancashire', *British Journal of Criminology*, **39** (1999), pp. 25–38; **Harvey Osborne** and **Michael Winstanley**, 'Rural and urban poaching in Victorian England', *Rural History*, **17**, 2 (2006), pp. 187–212.

9 John E. Archer, *'By a Flash and a Scare.' Arson, Animal Maiming and Poaching in East Anglia 1815–1870*, Clarendon Press, Oxford, 1990, p. 211, n. 43.

10 John G. Rule, 'The manifold causes of rural crime: Sheep-stealing in England c. 1740–1840', in **John Rule** (ed.), *Outside the Law: Studies in Crime and Order 1650–1850*, Exeter Papers in Economic History, no. 15, University

of Exeter, Exeter, 1982; **R. A. E. Wells**, 'Sheep-rustling in Yorkshire in the age of the industrial and agricultural revolutions', *Northern History*, **xx** (1984), pp. 127–45. See also **K. P. Baun**, 'Social protest, popular disturbances and public order in Dorset, 1790–1838', unpublished Ph.D., University of Reading, 1984, pp. 136–8.

11 **E. J. Hobsbawm**, 'The machine breakers', *P and P*, 1 (1952), pp. 57–70; for an example of arson apparently linked with a trade dispute in early nineteenth-century Liverpool see HO 40.18.53–56, Messrs Gregson and Bury to Peel, and Charles Lawrence to Peel, both 22 March 1824. In July 1842 the board of the Norwich Union resolved to discontinue cotton mill insurance as renewals fell due because of incendiarism in the north west, though it must be remembered that the Norwich Union's strength lay in the insurance of farm stock. Norwich Union Fire Insurance Society Board Minutes, 18 July 1842. My thanks to Dr Roger Ryan for this reference and for general information on this point.

12 Suffolk R.O. (Ipswich Branch) 2577/1, Chief Constable to Home Secretary, 2 January 1842; See also **R. P. Hastings**, *Essays in North Riding History 1780–1850*, North Yorkshire County Record Office Publications no. 28 (1981), p. 101; **Janet Gyford**, *Men of Bad Character: The Witham Fires of 1820*, Studies in Essex History No. 1, Essex Record Office, Essex, 1991.

13 Humberside R.O. Chief Constable to quarter sessions, 5 January 1864. I am grateful to David Foster for his quotation and for permission to use and cite his unpublished material on arson in East Yorkshire.

14 Norwich Union Fire Insurance Society, Board Minutes, 31 August 1835, July 1841, 4 December 1843, 4 January 1847. Once again I am indebted to Dr Ryan for this.

15 *York Herald*, 26 March 1864. Dr Foster has information on the occupation of eighteen of the forty-two persons arrested for arson between 1863 and 1870; the largest group – eight – were agricultural labourers and/or Wolds Rangers.

16 **C. J. Ribton-Turner**, *A History of Vagrants and Vagrancy*, London, 1887, p. 313. For this, and the arson outbreak in North Wales, the border counties and the Midlands see Jones, *Crime, Protest, Community*, pp. 202–3.

17 Jones, *Crime, Protest, Community*, p. 48; **Michael J. Carter**, *Peasants and Poachers: A Study in Rural Disorder in Norfolk*, Boydell Press, Woodbridge, 1980, pp. 28–9; **Timothy Shakeseff**, *Rural Conflict, Crime and Protest: Herefordshire 1800–1860*, Boydell Press, Woodbridge, 2003, p. 191.

18 Archer, *'By a flash and a scare'*, p. 256; Shakesheff, *Rural Conflict*, pp. 195–200.

19 *Beverley Guardian*, 22 October 1864.

20 Beds. R.O. QGV 10/4/13.

21 A. J. Peacock, 'Village radicalism in East Anglia 1800–50', in **J. P. D. Dunbabin** (ed.), *Rural Discontent in Nineteenth-Century Britain*, Faber and Faber, London, 1974, pp. 32–3. Beds. R.O. QEV 4, Chief Constable's letter 15 October 1844 reports eight accidental fires 'two of which occurred by children playing with Lucifer matches'. Four of the eighteen arrested in East Yorks. for whom occupations are given, were children.

22 Archer, *'By a flash and a scare'*, chapter 8.

23 Suffolk R.O. (Ipswich Branch) 2577/1, Chief Constable to Home Secretary, 16 March 1844.

24 **James Obelkevich**, *Religion and Rural Society: South Lindsey 1825–75*, Clarendon Press, Oxford, 1976, chapter 6, *passim*; **J. F. C. Harrison**, *The Second Coming: Popular Millenarianism 1780–1850*, RKP, London, 1978, chapter 3, *passim*, esp. pp. 41–2.

25 Beds. R.O. QGR 1/23 Prison Chaplain's report 4 April 1848; *Bedford Times*, 11 March 1848; for similar behaviour in South Lincolnshire see Obelkevich, *Religion and Rural Society*, p. 292.

26 **John Glyde**, *The Norfolk Garland*, London, 1872, pp. 58–9; Beds. R.O. QSR 1824/384 and 1827/368; Obelkevich, *Religion and Rural Society*, pp. 287–91; **John Rule**, 'Methodism, popular beliefs and village culture in Cornwall 1800–50', in **Robert D. Storch** (ed.), *Popular Culture and Custom in Nineteenth-Century England*, Croom Helm, London, 1982, p. 63.

27 Obelkevich, *Religion and Rural Society*, pp. 275 and 286; Glyde, *Norfolk Garland*, pp. 50–1.

28 **Clive Emsley**, *Crime, Police and Penal Policy: European Experiences 1750–1940*, Oxford U.P., Oxford, 2007, pp. 4, 6 and 127–8.

29 King, 'The impact of urbanisation on murder rates'; **J. A. Sharpe**, *Crime in Early Modern England 1550–1750*, 2nd edn, Longman, London, 1984, chapter 3, *passim* and pp. 252–3.

30 In a letter printed in *Athenaeum*, 22 August 1846.

31 **Bob Bushaway**, *By Rite: Custom, Ceremony and Community in England 1700–1880*, Junction Books, London, 1982, pp. 131–2.

32 HO 45.4609 Fortescue to Palmerston, 17 January 1853; *P.P.* 1852–53 (71) xxxvi *Report of the Select Committee on Police*, q. 415.

33 **John E. Archer**, *The Monster Evil: Policing and Violence in Victorian Liverpool*, University of Liverpool Press, Liverpool, 2011, pp. 93–6.

34 Bushaway, *By Rite*, p. 158.

35 Storch, *Popular Culture*, pp. 1–2.

36 *The Times*, 21 October 1887.

37 Sharpe, *Crime in Early Modern England*, pp. 103–4.

38 Frances Finnegan, *Poverty and Prejudice: A Study of Irish Immigrants in York 1840–75*, Cork U.P., Cork, 1982, chapter 9, *passim*; R. E. Swift, ' "Another Stafford Street row": Law, order and the Irish presence in mid-Victorian Wolverhampton', *Immigrants and Minorities*, 3 (1984), pp. 5–29.

39 Jerry White, *Rothschild Buildings: Life in an East End Tenement Block 1887–1920*, RKP, London, 1980; V. D. Lipman, 'Jewish settlement in the East end of London 1840–1940: The topographical and statistical background', in Aubrey Newman (ed.), *The Jewish East End 1840–1939*, The Jewish Historical Society of England, London, 1981, pp. 25–6 and 32.

40 Robert Roberts, *The Classic Slum: Salford Life in the First Quarter of the Century*, Penguin, Harmondsworth, 1973, p. 16.

41 John Glyde, jun., *The Moral, Social and Religious Condition of Ipswich in the Middle of the Nineteenth Century*, Ipswich, 1850, reprinted S.R. Publishers, Wakefield, 1971, p. 57.

42 HO 42.114.147–8.

43 HO 42.114.178–80.

44 Tobias, *Crime and Industrial Society*, p. 173; *P.P. 1847*, vii, *Select Committee on Juvenile Offenders*, q. 227; Barbara Weinberger, 'Law breakers and law enforcers in the late Victorian city: Birmingham 1867–77', unpublished Ph.D., University of Warwick, 1981, pp. 136–40, notes an apparent decline in theft from employers by the 1870s.

45 R. N. Davidson, *Crime and Environment*, Croom Helm, London, 1981, p. 89; for the whole 'typology' see pp. 89–93.

46 Raphael Samuel (ed.), *East End Underworld: Chapters in the Life of Arthur Harding*, RKP, London, 1981, pp. 16–17.

47 Ginswick (ed.), *Labour and the Poor*, i, p. 39.

48 *P.P. 1828*, (533) vi, *Select Committee on the Police of the Metropolis*, p. 57; U.C.L. Chadwick MSS 11 f. 2; see also ff. 4–5, response of the Superintendent of K Division; *The Times*, 25 March and 14 April 1865; U.C.L. Chadwick MSS 11 f. 27.

49 David Englander, *Landlord and Tenant in Urban Britain 1838–1918*, Oxford U.P., Oxford, 1983, pp. 7–9.

50 Englander, *Landlord and Tenant*, pp. 34–6; Timothy Cavanagh, *Scotland Yard Past and Present: Experiences of Thirty-Seven Years*, London, 1893, pp. 24–7. See also Charles Dickens's fulminations in 'On an Amateur Beat' in *The Uncommercial Traveller*.

51 Jones, *Crime, Protest, Community*, pp. 108–9.

52 Thomas Beames, *The Rookeries of London, Past, Present and Prospective*, 2nd edn, London, 1852, pp. 65–8 and see also pp. 25, 26. White, *Rothschild*

Buildings, pp. 131–2; Lipman, 'Jewish settlement', pp. 25–6; Weinberger, 'Law breakers and law enforcers', pp. 243–4.

53 Fielding, *An Enquiry*, pp. 141–2. Thirty years later William Blizard described similar dwellings constituting 'a sort of distinct town, or district [of London], calculated for the reception of the darkest and most dangerous enemies to society . . . the owners of these houses make no secret of their being for the entertainment of THIEVES!': **William Blizard, *Desultory Reflections on Police*,** London, 1785, pp. 30–1.

54 Ginswick (ed.), *Labour and the Poor*, i, p. 39.

55 'A category becomes police property, when the dominant powers of society (in the economy, polity, etc.) leave the problems of social control of that category to the police.' **J. A. Lee,** 'Some structural aspects of police deviance in relations with minority groups', in **C. Shearing** (ed.), *Organisational Police Deviance*, Butterworth, Toronto, 1981, pp. 53–4.

56 **Clive Emsley,** ' "The thump of wood on a swede turnip": Police violence in nineteenth-century England', *C.J.H.*, **6** (1985), pp. 125–49 (at pp. 136–8).

57 **B. J. Davey,** *Lawless and Immoral: Policing a County Town 1838–57*, Leicester U.P., Leicester, 1983.

58 *Cambridge and Hertford Independent Press*, 16 July 1825; Beds. R.O. QGC 10/1; QSR 25/1823/330; QSR 25/1824/248; QSR 26/1825/309–16 and 367–72.

59 The population of Bedfordshire increased as follows: 1801–63, 393; 1811–70, 213; 1821–83, 716; 1831–95, 400. Thus between 1811 and 1831 the county population increased by some 36 per cent; the increase in the population of Houghton Conquest for the same period was 57.6 per cent.

60 Beds. R.O. P11/28/2/139–65. The parish register of Houghton Conquest suggests a marked decline of gentry families after 1700. **F. G. Emmison,** *Bedfordshire Parish Registers*, xliv MS vols (1931–53), xli (1950).

61 **John Glyde,** jun., *Suffolk in the Nineteenth Century: Physical, Social, Moral, Religious and Industrial*, London, 1856, pp. 146–7; **John Glyde,** 'Localities of crime in Suffolk', *Journal of the Statistical Society*, **xix** (1856), pp. 102–6.

62 **Dennis R. Mills,** *Lord and Peasant in Nineteenth-Century Britain*, Croom Helm, London, 1980, p. 24. But note that not all agricultural proletarians lived in open villages; some lived in towns and might have a twenty-mile round trip walking to and from work. Finnegan, *Poverty and Prejudice*, p. 64.

63 **Raphael Samuel,** ' "Quarry Roughs": Life and labour in Headington Quarry, 1860–1920', in **Raphael Samuel** (ed.), *Village Life and Labour*, RKP, London, 1975.

64 **Dennis R. Mills,** 'Francis Howell's report on the operation of the Laws of Settlement in Nottinghamshire 1848', *Transactions of the Thoroton Society of Nottinghamshire*, 76 (1972), pp. 46–52 (at p. 51).

65 Mills, *Lord and Peasant, passim.*

66 **Shirley Chase,** 'Crime and policing in a nineteenth-century "closed" village: Westfirle, East Sussex 1820–50', unpublished research paper. My thanks to Ms Chase for permission to read and make reference to this paper. Similar patterns of frequent offenders can be found in other Sussex villages both 'closed' and 'open'.

67 **E. J. Hobsbawm** and **George Rudé,** *Captain Swing,* Lawrence and Wishart, London, 1969, pp. 172–89; **B. Reney,** *The Class Struggle in Nineteenth-Century Oxfordshire: The Social and Communal Background to the Otmoor Disturbances of 1830 to 1935,* Ruskin College, Oxford, History Workshop Pamphlet, 3, 1970.

68 Jones, *Crime, Protest, Community,* p. 74.

69 *P.P.* 1842, ix, *Select Committee on the Payment of Wages,* q. 1584; there were similar comments passed with reference to Batley [qq. 280–84], Bradford [qq. 181–83], Chorley [qq. 1771 and 1774] and Pentwyn Works, Pontypool [qq. 2352–58].

70 *P.P.* 1847, xxvii, part 11 *Select Committee on Education in Wales,* p. 290.

71 Ginswick (ed.), *Labour and the Poor,* ii, pp. 60–1.

72 **James C. Burke,** 'Crime and criminality in County Durham 1840–55', unpublished M.A., University of Durham, 1980, pp. 123–33. **David Philips,** *Crime and Authority in Victorian England,* Croom Helm, London, 1977, p. 213, shows that Staffordshire miners were prepared to prosecute if workmates stole from each other.

CHAPTER 6

Fiddles, perks and pilferage

The focus on crime as something committed by 'criminals' belonging to a particular social group, together with the notion that burgeoning nineteenth-century cities were the refuge of this group, helped to lead contemporaries away from a serious consideration and appreciation of one major centre of criminal activity – the workplace. The reorganisation of manufacturing processes during the eighteenth and nineteenth centuries led some historians to conclude that there was a criminalisation of traditional work practices and of some 'rights' claimed by workers during the period. At the same time the development of sophisticated financial institutions and the growth of, for example, bureaucratised systems of welfare provided opportunities for appropriation by employees drawn from respectable, and often high-status, social groups.

A study of late-twentieth-century workplace crime concluded that the phenomenon was widespread and that 'in many jobs . . . it [is] often abnormal *not* to fiddle'. The word 'fiddle' is preferred since:

morally it is relatively neutral. It is . . . a 'weasel word'. It allows us to look at part-time crime not so much with complaisance as with empathy. Using the word 'fiddle', we can more readily appreciate the world-view or cosmology of the fiddler.[1]

Contemporary workplace crime in this analysis is determined not by class or social group, but by occupational structure. Every transaction involving commodities has the potential for dishonesty, but the expropriation of a commodity is not always perceived of as 'theft' either by the offender or by the victim. There is an assumption that 'theft', in the form of burglary from a warehouse, is different from 'theft', in the form of pilferage by a warehouseman. At the same time, should the owner of the warehouse send underweight goods from that warehouse to another businessman, then his appropriation can be termed 'breach of contract' and not a criminal offence. Perhaps fiddling between businessmen is currently the most common form of fraud, and was the most common form of fraud during the eighteenth and nineteenth centuries. Unfortunately embezzlement and fraud are noted for their under-reporting and many such offences never become public. Moreover research into these topics requires accessing the archives of private business concerns rather than the public record of the courts and the press.

Workplace crime or 'fiddles' come under a variety of alternative headings, most of which are not neutral words but are those used by employers or by agents of the law. Perquisites or 'perks' can be tolerated by an employer; they can also be the objects of periodic clampdowns. Generally a 'perk' is regarded by the workforce as an entitlement, though it can sometimes be abused to an extent that few employees could, or would seek to justify. It is a hazy line that separates perks from pilferage or small-scale theft at the workplace. Pilferage can be practised by virtually an entire workforce at a particular workplace or in a particular job; in a few instances it might shade into more organised and more large-scale theft. A third kind of workplace crime comes under the heading of fraud: this can involve deception on the part of both an employer and his employees to profit at the expense of a third party; it can involve deception on the part of an individual selling goods to, or performing a service for, another. Examples of all of these crimes, or 'fiddles', abound throughout the eighteenth and nineteenth centuries.

The largest single employment sector in Britain during the eighteenth, and for much of the nineteenth century, was agriculture. Various labourers and agricultural communities claimed a whole series of allowances or perks which were gradually whittled down or subjected to greater control and supervision. Gleaning was the best-known allowance whereby, after the harvest had been gathered, women and children entered the fields and collected scattered grain which the harvesters had missed.[2] Corn or beans collected in this way could form a significant part of the poor rural family's diet or wage. The custom had biblical authority, though it was clearly practised differently from place to place. During the eighteenth century it was known for individuals to object violently to anyone from outside the community seeking to glean in local fields; and farmers who tried to prevent gleaning, or who turned hogs and cattle out to graze on stubble and thus denied access to the poor, were the objects of popular odium and even assault. In *The Farmer's Kalendar* (1771) Arthur Young criticised farmers who denied gleaning to the poor; but Young was also concerned about abuses by the gleaners and, when they sold the straw, they did not give Prior all the money that they received. Five years later farmer Thomas Wiles employed James Smith to thresh his barley; he observed Smith put some of the barley into his own sack. John Palmer, a miller of Luton, was indicted in 1817 for defrauding William Williams. Palmer had received four bushels of wheat for grinding, but had only returned three and a half bushels of wheat and flour mixed. Agricultural instruments were pilfered from the workplace; occasionally perhaps because they could be used at home:

I Never Intended Keeping the Spade . . . I took the Spade to dig Potatoes again . . . I Placed the Spade where any one might See It and It Remained there three hours as the Moon Shone Bright If I Intended Keeping the Spade I should of hid It.[15]

But some of the implements taken were most likely acquired for what they would fetch when sold.

'Chips' claimed by the workers in the Royal Dockyards constitute the best-known example of an eighteenth-century industrial workplace fiddle. The government was involved directly; its attempts to save money in the yards prompted a succession of investigations which, among other things, drew attention to the workforce's perquisites and, subsequently, provided historians with a wealth of detail. Other evidence has been left by the steady trickle of offenders dealt with by the disciplinary procedures of the yards themselves or prosecuted in the courts.[16] Originally chips constituted scrap wood which men were permitted to take home from the yards to use as firewood. By the early seventeenth century the authorities considered that perquisite was being abused, not the least when in 1634 a boat-load of 3,500 one-foot-long wooden tree-nails was seized at Deptford; the tree-nails had been made by two men out of the chips which they had collected in six years' work in the royal yards. A succession of attempts was made to end or at least to limit the size of chips; a regulation of 1753 stated that they should consist of no more than could be carried, untied, under one arm. But the ambiguity continued until, in 1801, the government succeeded in commuting them to a cash payment. Ambiguity existed also over what constituted chips and who was permitted to take them from the yards. It was alleged that men spent the last half hour of the working day sawing up new and useful wood to take out as chips. Technically only men working in the yards were allowed them, yet many others left the yards carrying chips such as wives and children who brought in lunch for their menfolk, and even individuals who, for example, visited to celebrate the launching of a ship. Chips were also stretched in some minds to include nails, paint, ropes, sail-cloth and, indeed, anything which could not be nailed down. During the American War of Independence it was alleged that receivers in Portsmouth were paying 1s.3d. for five pounds of used copper nails; this was more than the average daily wage for the unskilled yard labourer. When, in 1801, the skilled men were asked to state how much they would be prepared to accept to forgo their daily bundle, they estimated the value at 8d.; the basic daily rate for a skilled shipwright or caulker then stood at 2s.1d., though, because of the exigencies of war, they were probably earning three times that amount. But pay in the royal yards was always in arrears: at the close of the Seven Years War wages were fifteen months late and throughout the war against Revolutionary France they were at least three months late. For this reason, if for no other, chips were essential to the workman's existence and the right was preserved with tenacity. Yard officials, themselves taking unofficial earnings in the form of fees and indulging in a variety of fiddles, were aware of the financial problems of their workforce and this may have fostered a degree of laxity and toleration. Juries in dockyard areas were reluctant to convict the smaller offenders, partly it seems because they accepted chips as a man's right and partly also, perhaps, because they were aware of the essential nature of the chips to the family economy of the workman. Informers were unpopular and sometimes were subjected to counter charges. The commutation of chips was accompanied by a more regular system of wage payment, though it was not until July 1813 that the men began to be paid on a regular weekly basis. This, together with stricter supervision and policing, probably succeeded in reducing the amount of material taken from the yards, but pilferage was never completely eradicated.[17]

In the same way that it sought to reduce dockyard costs by controlling the perks of manual labourers, the Admiralty also sought to rationalise the salary system for its clerical establishment and to abolish their unofficial emoluments. Clerks took fees for making out bills, certificates, contracts, warrants and so forth, tasks which produced between two- and three-fifths of their annual income. In the Navy Office clerks also performed 'agency business' by which they settled the accounts of contractors, officers and seamen, and used Navy Office stationery and postage in so doing. The commutation of these perks and the new salary scales were ill-considered and prompted much unrest; in 1800 the clerks in the Navy Office embarked on a go-slow so as to obtain overtime payments.[18]

The Royal Dockyards were exceptional during the eighteenth century for the large number of workers employed on a single site. Elsewhere *adjudged under the Bum-boat Act, to be paid by every person convicted of conveying goods pilfered from vessels, is regularly discharged; by which means the delinquents, instead of going to gaol, are enabled to return to their former criminal pursuits. Some of the members of this club, although apparently common labourers, are said to have their houses furnished in a very superior style and to be possessed of property in the funds to the extent of from £1,500 to £3,000.*[32]

It seems unlikely that these extremely wealthy dockers existed outside Colquhoun's fertile imagination, yet clubbing together to pay the fine of a workmate caught, prosecuted and convicted, continued to be practised well into the nineteenth century.[33]

Canal boatmen were said to remove cloth, ironmongery, liquor, sugar, tea, indeed anything which could be turned to their own use or sold off to a receiver. Some receivers were grocers like Harding's Aunt Liza; others were master manufacturers who took the goods from the boatmen and subsequently sold them as if their own. A variety of dodges were employed to ensure that the loss of goods was not discovered until the boatmen were well clear.[34] The replacement of canal transport by the railway did not end such pilferage, it simply changed its location, changed the problems for the fiddlers and for those whose task it was to prevent them. The Constabulary Commissioners noted that carrying firms were 'immediately interested only in the prevention of those depredations in which the losses admit of distinct specification, and for which they can be made accountable'.[35] The firms whose goods were carried were, as their evidence to the Commissioners testifies, well aware of the potential for loss through pilferage and probably made allowance. During the eighteenth century coalmine owners often loaded more coal into canal boats than was listed on manifests; this was partly because of the difficulties involved in gauging a boat's weight but also because they were well aware that the boatmen sold coal on route and paid off lock-keepers and other officials for an easy, unimpeded journey.[36] Other employers tolerated fiddles which did not hit them personally, but which could be passed on to the purchaser. At the end of the nineteenth century dairy owners admitted that they took the dishonesty of their milkmen into account when calculating wages. The most common fiddle was 'bobbing', or watering the milk and selling the surplus at a profit; such adulteration of milk by milkmen, however, was probably the least of the causes for the atrocious quality of cheap milk in the cities.[37] James Greenwood maintained that the London General Omnibus Company was able to keep their conductors' pay at 4s. for a seventeen-hour day because of an understanding by the employers and their employees that the latter were pocketing a percentage of the daily takings. It was, according to Charles Booth, 'almost as though the omnibus had been hired from the company, and was run by the men on their own account'.[38] An increase in wages and the introduction, not without opposition, of the bell punch finally put an end to this or at least limited the conductor's opportunities for personal profit.

Railway companies had similar problems as a result of the large number of their staff that were entrusted with receiving and handling money. Honest, accidental errors were made; some men could not cope with the tasks required of them. But some ticket clerks deliberately short-changed customers; and some senior clerks over-recorded the contents of men's pay-packets to pocket the excess themselves. In such instances proving deliberate embezzlement could be difficult and, where proof was insufficient for a court case, the employers resorted to their own private justice. Dismissal for such 'financial irregularities' was not necessarily more lenient than prosecution; a man who left trusted employment without a reference could find difficulty in finding other employment, let alone respectable, regular employment.[39]

In general the workplace offences discussed so far were those committed by employees, and some historians have sought to categorise these as responses to change in the economic structure. It has, for example, been suggested that the shift to centralised, factory-based manufacture was less the result of this system's proven technical superiority and more the result of concerns about embezzlement and labour discipline under the outwork system.[40] Similarly the criminalisation of workplace perks has been taken as another aspect of the destruction of artisan culture and of the alienation of the worker from the product of his labour. This broad perception suggests further that in rural areas farmers increasingly distanced themselves socially from their labourers and adopted stricter notions of private property that contributed to enclosure. This, in turn, reduced the poor rural dweller to a wage labourer denied the right to graze animals, to pick up fallen wood, to glean from the fields which he had sown and reaped with his labour. The land was property; using it, or taking things from it when not sanctioned by the owner, was an offence against that property:

Since property was a thing, it became possible to define offences as crimes against things, rather than as injuries to men. This enabled the law to assume, with its robes, the postures of impartiality: it was neutral as between every degree of man, and defended only the inviolability of

*the ownership of things. In the seventeenth century labour had been
only partly free, but the labourer still asserted large claims (sometimes as
perquisites) to his own labour's product. As, in the eighteenth century,
labour became more and more free, so labour's product came to be seen
as something totally distinct, the property of landowner or employer, and
to be defended by the threat of the gallows.*[41]

Such analyses are attractive; they draw together and relate changes in society and the economy with changes in the law, its interpretation and enforcement. There is evidence of a close link between industrial development and
prosecution for industrial theft in some areas. In early nineteenth-century
Wigan, for example, the law appears to have been administered humanely
and impartially by the local magistracy, except when it was involved
with industry. Employers were rarely prosecuted, and if convicted were
only moderately fined for operating the truck system; on the other hand
heavy sentences were imposed even for first offences of industrial theft.
Workers, including children, were commonly prosecuted for breach of
contract in leaving work without proper notice, and the sentence in this
case involved a heavy fine.[42] The Master and Servant Act 1823 worked
explicitly in the employer's favour in that he could only be prosecuted in
civil law for breach of contract; the employee was liable to criminal prosecution for the same offence. Prosecutions for industrial theft rose markedly in the Black Country between 1835 and 1860: from about fifteen per
cent of all larcenies prosecuted to about forty per cent or from about ten
per cent of all prosecutions in one year to about one-third. The increase
coincided with a change in the composition of the local magistracy from
a majority of landed aristocracy and gentry to one of coal owners and
industrialists – the principal local employers. Furthermore the Criminal
Justice Act 1855 authorised summary trial for these petty offences; prosecution thus became cheaper and quicker, and there was a qualitative leap
in the number of prosecutions during the years immediately following the
act.[43] An analysis of prosecutions under this act at eight police courts in
mid-nineteenth-century London reveals employee theft to have been the
most common offence, but equally it reveals that most of these prosecutions were undertaken by small tradesmen and masters, not by the larger
firms and the bigger employers.[44] Yet it is also clear that employers did
not always resort to the law to control their workforce; even in the late
nineteenth century employers tolerated some fiddles, especially when their
profits were untouched. They might choose to make an example of a single individual as a warning to others, and only then if his offences were in

excess of the generally accepted and tolerated level. The London Omnibus Company acted in this fashion, and generally preferred dismissal to prosecution. Alternatively, as the Superintendent of K Division of the Metropolitan Police informed the Constabulary Commissioners, some employers did not take action because of the solidarity among their workforce, fearing a strike if they did so.[45]

Peter Linebaugh's study of those executed on London's Tyburn tree during the eighteenth century stresses the significance of the growth of the monetary wage and the volume of legislation passed with the aim of controlling the outworker. 'Just as the "rights of man" presupposed doctrines of legal "wrongs", so the monetary abstraction of human labour as wages presupposed criminalizing customary appropriation.'[46] Yet it is difficult to sustain the argument that this legislation criminalised what had been legal or at most tolerated before, and passionate as Linebaugh's book is, there are times when it refuses to engage with some of the parallel studies which challenge his assertions. J. A. Sharpe has emphasised that, in the half-century before 1640, it was probably easier to regulate industrial production by patent of monopoly rather than by parliamentary statute.[47] During this period parliamentary government was in decline; the events of the 1640s reversed this process and if there appears something of a flood of legislation relating to outwork during the eighteenth century, it must be remembered that, partly owing to the availability of parliament after 1688 (it now had to meet annually), there was simply very much more legislation of all kinds passed in the eighteenth century. From Tudor times, even before, outworkers could be prosecuted for detaining waste; what legislation of 1749 and 1777 did was to put a time limit on this return – twenty-one days in the first instance, and eight in the second. The Act of 1749 gave magistrates acting summarily the power to punish embezzling outworkers with sentences of prison or corporal punishment from the outset, rather than with the financial penalties for first offences and prison or corporal punishment if the offenders could not pay, as established under earlier legislation. Evidence is fragmentary, yet it appears that a very high proportion of offenders convicted before 1749 could not, or would not pay fines and consequently received corporal punishment. The 1749 Act appears thus to have codified the practice of the courts rather than changed the law both in this respect, and also in as much as the receivers of embezzled goods, who were generally from a more well-to-do social background than the outworkers, continued to be subjected to financial penalties. The receivers had generally paid their fines before 1749, and besides it was against legislative practice to subject men who could be of some substance to immediate corporal punishment. Yet not all legislation relating to embezzlement during the eighteenth century made offenders liable to immediate custodial or corporal punishment. The most common outwork offence was short-reeling and this was the subject of separate legislation in 1774 which led to a small fine; five shillings for a first offence, rather than prison or whipping, was the most common punishment. There had been modifications in the doctrine that larceny could not be committed by persons to whom goods were temporarily transferred by the owner.[48] Yet, during the eighteenth century, no-one appears to have contemplated plugging the loophole in the security of property provided by outwork; there was no attempt to change the legal situation which rendered outworkers only liable to summary prosecution for embezzlement rather than to indictments for larceny before quarter sessions or assizes.

The view that the period of massive industrialisation and capitalisation witnessed a deliberate and corresponding criminalisation of certain work practices and that workplace theft is best understood as a defence of customary rights against attempts to impose a new system of wage discipline is open to two further objections. First, it tends to limit workplace crime to one social group and to put a blanket legitimation on their activities. Second, there is precious little evidence that the bulk of workplace crime was ever conceived as a protest against a new wage discipline. Similarly there is little evidence that customary rights were preferred to the new wages. Thrums, chips and cabbage may have been defended as a legitimate right for the workman, yet not necessarily in preference to a regular wage. Workplace offences were not always directed against the employer, and the taking of a man's half-finished work, subsequently finished and sold by another as his own – a common offence in the late eighteenth-century metal trades – can hardly be construed as a legitimate perk.[49] When dockers or boatmen or railwaymen 'knocked off' cargo, their actions may have been sanctioned by a form of tradition and protected by communal solidarity, yet they could never have been defended in court as was attempted, not without success or a sympathetic hearing, by weavers who had taken thrums, colliers who had taken coals and rural labourers who had taken wood or gleanings without authority. Furthermore there were other offences committed by employees at their place of work for which the word perk is in no sense applicable: the shopman who took money from the till, or who took anything else that caught his eye; the domestic servant who appropriated his or, more commonly, her employer's property. The number of such cases which came before the courts almost certainly constitute only a tiny fraction of the number of offences which occurred and which were discovered. On occasions an employer might mark his money or his goods to check up on such petty pilfering:

John Fewkes of Basford in the County of Nottingham, cordwainer, maketh oaths and saith the prisoner William Parnell has worked for me for about 6 months last and during that period I have missed different articles belonging to me. I also keep a Beer Shop which the prisoner frequented and I have lately missed tobacco therefrom . . . on the morning of Thursday the 9 August I marked 16 papers of tobacco by putting my name in the inside of them and I put them in the draw where they were usually kept in the Bar.[50]

Domestic servants and occasionally other employees, might also be 'tested' for honesty with coinage or paper money left where they were likely to see it.[51] The dismissal of a dishonest servant was far easier, far cheaper and, perhaps, less demeaning or embarrassing than a prosecution. Lastly, the question might be posed: if fiddling is to be condoned by one social group, why not by another which also took advantage of a lack of work-place supervision? White-collar offences, almost by definition workplace offences, and fiddles by different kinds of tradesmen, were also subjects of controlling legislation, though admittedly this was often less well struc-tured and, for a variety of reasons less well enforced.

James Greenwood reserved some of his most savage denunciations for the shopkeeper who used false weights and measures or who adulterated food and drink. Such an offender was:

by far a greater villain than the half-starved wretch who snatches a leg of mutton from a butcher's hook, or some article of drapery temptingly flaunting outside the shop of the clothier, because in the one case the crime is perpetrated that a soul and a woefully lean body may be saved from severance, and in the other case the iniquity is made to pander to the wrongdoer's covertous desire to grow fat, to wear magnificent jewellery, and to air his unwieldly carcase annually at Margate.[52]

But such frauds long-predated the tradition of an annual seaside holiday. In the mid-eighteenth century they were compounded by regional varia-tions in weights and measures; localities cherished their variations and this impeded the proposals of a parliamentary committee in 1758 that national standards be adopted and that all weights below one pound should be made of gold, silver, brass, copper or bell metal, and all those above a pound should be made of brass, copper, bell metal or cast iron.[53] There was also the problem of laxity among local authorities and/or their officials.

A miller who returned short weight of flour could be indicted for fraud, but most traders guilty of market-place offences were dealt with under the common law. Market juries, local magistrates and part-time inspectors of weights and measures were responsible for acting against corrupt practices. This area has been little studied, but it is conceivable that external events, such as a bad harvest leading to a food shortage and high prices, on the one hand, tempted unscrupulous market traders and bakers to maximise their profits by defrauding their customers and, on the other, encouraged men to be on the look-out for such frauds and to prosecute. In April 1795, for example, as food shortages threatened, three men were brought before petty sessions in Wiltshire accused of selling underweight bread.[54] In 1802, following hard on the heels of another subsistence crisis, Bedfordshire magistrates meeting in petty sessions at Biggleswade reported that the local inspector of weights and measures had conducted an inspection for the first time in living memory and as a result eighty-seven persons were summonsed. The magistrates 'presuming ignorance in all Persons against whom such Informations were exhibited fined each in the lowest Penalties allowable by Law and took away the defective Balances, Weights and Measures'. The role of inspector, like that of constable, did not suit many. The widow of John Kilpin, one of the inspectors in Bedfordshire, explained that her husband had 'dreaded and disliked' his tasks and kept putting them off, hating to leave his family 'to be exposed to the Abusive Insulting language and rough treatment of the People to whom he was sent'.[55] Significantly when the new police were established, many senior officers were given the tasks of inspectors of weights and measures.

The adulteration of food and drink was an even more difficult offence to police. John Bright, while President of the Board of Trade, maintained that 'adulteration . . . arises from the very great and, perhaps, inevitable competition in business; and that to a large extent it is prompted by the ignorance of customers'. He went on to say that it would be quite impossible, as well as intolerable, to have inspectors continually checking goods in shops. These comments infuriated James Greenwood who pointed out that France and Germany had both a better system of inspection and much stiffer penalties.[56] To the extent that an investigation of adulteration required the taking of samples and analysis of samples, however, Bright had a point. Qualified and competent chemists were not plentiful, while the cost of sufficient inspectors would have been looked at askance by the Treasury, by parliament and by taxpayers. Change came gradually, beginning with the Food and Drugs Act of 1860; but the number of inspectors remained small and the fines imposed on offenders were trifling – in 1899

4,319 prosecutions were brought for adulterating food and the average fine was £1.16s.8d.[57] The offenders in such instances were labelled not so much as 'criminals' but as 'rotten apples'; among some of their fellows they might simply have been perceived as 'unlucky'.

Some shopkeepers did well out of systems of truck, even after early nineteenth-century legislation sought to put an end to the practice. The problem with truck legislation was that the magistrates who were to enforce it were often the employers who practised it, especially as industrialists became more prominent on magisterial benches. Employer magistrates would not have heard cases brought against themselves for infringing the Truck Acts: the Victorian elite was not so hypocritical as to have tolerated such behaviour; after all they considered that the law was just and impartial and therefore it had to be seen as such.[58] Yet it is difficult to expect that employer magistrates would not have had sympathy for their fellows as victims, or acting as prosecutors, in cases of industrial theft, or as defendants in cases brought under the Truck or Factory Acts.

The expansion of capitalism provided opportunities for more extensive and more profitable workplace fiddles by a variety of company directors, bankers, managers and clerks. The self-regulating money market of the City of London run by financial 'experts', coupled with a general public largely ignorant of the jargon of business documents and legal contracts, provided tempting opportunities for the fraudster. The excesses of the railway mania of the 1840s demonstrated the possibilities in a particularly stark fashion, but it has been estimated that as many as one in six of all company promotions during the nineteenth century were fraudulent.[59] Some of the banking frauds and cases of embezzlement involved enormous sums of money. In 1857 it was revealed that Colonel W. Petri Waugh was indebted to the London and Eastern Banking Company for £244,000 which was just £6,000 less than the entire subscribed capital of the bank. The Colonel was a director of the bank and he had acted with the connivance of J. E. Stephens, the manager. Petri Waugh fled to Spain, where he started a mining company; but his only criminal offence was holding funds while he was a bankrupt. Stephens had committed no criminal offence.[60] In 1882 Charles Magniac, Liberal M.P. for Bedford, received an urgent summons to London by telegraph. He met one of his partners in Matheson and Jardine on the railway station platform:

we both agreed that some fraud must have been committed implicating the firm. This I found on my arrival proved to be the case, but the amount is so gigantic and incredible. . . . Over a million in sterling.

offenders was less likely to provoke a crisis of confidence in the institution for which they worked than the prosecution of directors, managers or clerks. But, more importantly when it came to prosecution, the workplace crimes of working-class offenders, generally, were easier to detect and, in legal terms, their offences were easier to comprehend and to prove. Even so it would seem that only a tiny percentage of such offences were prosecuted, and only then when other sanctions, such as dismissal, seemed inappropriate, when it was felt that an example must be made to limit such offences, or when a particular offender had chanced his arm just a little too far.[72] Eighteenth- and nineteenth-century workplace crime was manifestly not simply the product of industrialisation, the desire of workers to strike back at an employer or at the developing capitalist system, or to preserve their traditional rights and a vibrant popular culture. An understanding of such crime is severely restricted when explained solely as an element of the developing struggle between capital and labour. It was not the new workplace alone which provided opportunities for fiddles; it was not new attempts to control the workforce which alone criminalised practices of long standing. The milkman 'bobbing' the milk, the petty official of the New Poor Law embezzling from the sums in his care, the government official demanding, or the contractor offering, a secret commission, all fall outside the simple class analysis. Most work, from casual labour to professional, provided opportunities for crime or, if legislation had not yet caught up with it, for what might be termed immoral profiteering.

Notes

1 **Gerald Mars**, Cheats at Work: An anthropology of workplace crime, Unwin Paperbacks, London, 1983, pp. 18 and 164. The concept of a 'weasel word' is drawn from **Jason Ditton**, 'Perks, pilferage and the fiddle: The historical structure of an invisible wage', Theory and Society, 4 (1977), pp. 39–71.

2 **Bob Bushaway**, *By Rite: Custom, ceremony and community in England 1700–1880*, Junction Books, London, 1982, pp. 138–48; **David H. Morgan**, 'The place of harvesters in nineteenth-century village life', in **Raphael Samuel** (ed.), *Village Life and Labour*, RKP, London, 1975, pp. 53–61.

3 Beds. R.O. QSR 15/1785/81.

4 Quoted in Bushaway, *By Rite*, p. 141.

5 **Peter King**, 'Gleaners, farmers and the failure of legal sanctions in England 1750–1850', *P and P*, **125** (1989) pp. 116–50 (at p. 124).

6 Beds. R.O. QSR 16/1790/46.

7 King, 'Gleaners, farmers and the failure of legal sanctions'; Morgan, 'The place of harvesters', p. 57.

8 Quoted in **Alasdair Clayre** (ed.), *Nature and Industrialization*, Oxford U.P., 1977, p. 23.

9 **James Obelkevich**, *Religion and Rural Society: South Lindsey 1825–75*, Clarendon Press, Oxford, 1976, p. 60.

10 **Peter King**, *Crime, Justice and Discretion in England 1740–1820*, Oxford U.P., 2000, p. 100.

11 Quoted in Clayre, *Nature and Industrialization*, pp. 19–20.

12 Beds. R.O. QSR 25/1825/345. For the August and autumn peak of summary convictions see pp. 41, this volume.

13 Bushaway, *By Rite*, pp. 222–3.

14 *The Times*, 23 October 1795.

15 Beds. R.O. QSR 23/1817/423; QSR 23/1818/245 and 249; QSR 25/1823/304; QSR 1827/321.

16 **R. J. B. Knight**, 'Pilfering and theft from the dockyards at the time of the American War of Independence', *Mariner's Mirror*, **61** (1975), pp. 215–25; **Roger Morriss**, *The Royal Dockyards during the Revolutionary and Napoleonic Wars*, Leicester U.P., 1983, especially pp. 93–6; **John Rule**, *The Experience of Labour in Eighteenth-Century Industry*, Croom Helm, London, 1981, pp. 128–30.

17 A former colleague at the Open University recalls that during his boyhood in Plymouth in the Second World War, his next-door neighbour, who worked in the Royal Dockyards, successfully removed from the yard, piece by piece, a lathe. The lathe was then reassembled at his home.

18 Morriss, *The Royal Dockyards*, pp. 129–35.

19 **John Styles**, 'Embezzlement, industry and the law in England, 1500–1800', in **Maxine Berg**, **Pat Hudson** and **Michael Sonenscher** (eds), *Manufacture in Town and Country before the Factory*, Cambridge U.P., 1983, pp. 183–4; **Clive Emsley**, *British Society and the French Wars 1793–1815*, Macmillan, London, 1979, pp. 57–8, 120–1 and 151.

20 Rule, *Experience of Labour*, pp. 126–7 and 130–3; Styles, 'Embezzlement, industry and the law', p. 204.

21 **James Greenwood**, *The Seven Curses of London*, London, 1869 (reprinted, Basil Blackwell, Oxford, 1981), p. 109.

22 Rule, *Experience of Labour*, pp. 125–6 and 130; see also 'Conference Report', *Bulletin of the Society for the Study of Labour History*, **25** (1972), p. 13.

23 **Douglas Hay,** 'Manufacturers and the criminal law in the later eighteenth century: Crime and "Police" in South Staffordshire', *Past and Present Society Colloquium: Police and policing*, 1983, pp. 13–15; **David Philips,** *Crime and Authority in Victorian England*, Croom Helm, London, 1977, p. 182; 'Conference Report', *Bulletin of the Society for Labour History*, p. 7. As for the continuance of pilferage by industrial workers after the decline of outwork see the quotation from the Superintendent of K Division of the Metropolitan Police, p. 129, this volume, and **David Jones,** *Crime, Community, and Police in Nineteenth-Century Britain*, RKP, London, 1982, p. 157.

24 O.B.P. t17970111-48 (Hickson).

25 **Jennifer Davis,** 'Law breaking and law enforcement: The creation of a criminal class in mid-Victorian London', unpublished Ph.D., Boston College, 1984, p. 279.

26 Rule, *Experience of Labour*, pp. 127–8; see also Philips, *Crime and Authority*, pp. 182–4.

27 Leeds City Archives LC/QS 1/2 f. 117; Beds. R.O. QSR 22/1816/160 and 228–29; U.C.L. Chadwick MSS 11 answers to q. 10.

28 O.B.P. t18561124-13.

29 Davis, 'Law breaking and law enforcement', pp. 99–103.

30 **Patrick Colquhoun,** *A Treatise on the Police of the Metropolis*, 3rd edn, London, 1796, chapter 3 *passim*; *idem, A Treatise on the Commerce and Police of the River Thames*, London, 1800, chapter 2 *passim*; **Henry Mayhew,** *London Labour and the London Poor*, 4 vols, London, 1861–62, iv, pp. 366–70.

31 **Raphael Samuel** (ed.), *East End Underworld: Chapters in the life of Arthur Harding*, RKP, London, 1981, pp. 16–17.

32 Colquhoun, *A Treatise on the Police*, p. 64.

33 Davis, 'Law breaking and law enforcement', pp. 84–99.

34 P.P. 1877 (418) xi, *Select Committee on the House of Lords on Intemperance, Third Report*, pp. 8256–8.

35 P.P. 1839 (168) xix, *Royal Commission on Constabulary*, pp. 48–54.

36 **Harry Hanson,** *The Canal Boatmen 1760–1914*, Manchester U.P., 1975, p. 37.

37 **Jennifer Davis,** 'Criminal Prosecutions and their context in late Victorian London', paper presented to the Conference on the History of Law, Labour and Crime, at the University of Warwick, 15–18 September 1983, p. 7; **Anthony S. Wohl,** *Endangered Lives: Public health in Victorian Britain*, Dent, London, 1983, pp. 20–1.

38 Greenwood, *Seven Curses*, pp. 94–107; **Charles Booth,** *Life and Labour of the People of London, 2nd series, Industry* (5 vols) 1903, iii, p. 311.

39 **John P. Locker,** ' "Quiet thieves, quiet punishment": Private responses to the "respectable" offender, c.1850–1930', *C.H.S.*, 9, 1 (2005), pp. 9–31.

40 **S. A. Marglin,** 'What do bosses do? The origins and functions of hierarchy in capitalist production', *Review of Radical Political Economies*, 6 (1974), pp. 46–55.

41 **E. P. Thompson,** *Whigs and Hunters: The origin of the Black Act*, Allen Lane, London, 1975, p. 207; see also the paper by Peter Linebaugh in 'Conference Report', *Bulletin of the Society for Labour History*, pp. 11–15.

42 **P. C. Barrett,** 'Crime and punishment in a Lancashire industrial town: Law and social change in the borough of Wigan, 1800–50', unpublished M.Phil., Liverpool Polytechnic, 1980, pp. 84–6 and 191–5.

43 Philips, *Crime and Authority*, pp. 190–1.

44 Davis, 'Law breaking and law enforcement', pp. 267–70 and 283–4.

45 Davis, 'Criminal prosecutions', pp. 5–6; and see note 24.

46 **Peter Linebaugh,** *The London Hanged. Crime and Civil Society in the Eighteenth Century*, Allen Lane, London, 1991, p. 440.

47 **J. A. Sharpe,** *Crime in Early Modern England 1550–1750*, 2nd edn, Longman, London, 1999, p. 213. For the statutes which sought to control the outwork see Styles, 'Embezzlement, industry and the law', pp. 209–10.

48 Styles, 'Embezzlement, industry and the law', p. 188, and *passim*.

49 Hay, 'Manufacturers and the criminal law', p. 15. At the Labour History Society Conference on Industrial Crime one contributor noted from 'his own experience in the mining industry, [that] the most politically and industrially conscious workers were not sympathetic to pilfering, whereas the less conscious would steal a fellow worker's tools if they would filch something from an employer'. 'Conference report', *Bulletin of the Society for Labour History*, pp. 7–8.

50 Notts. R.O. QSD/1836; for a similar example, on this occasion of a confectioner marking money in his till and catching his shopman see OBP t17970111-27 (Bull).

51 **Stephen Humphries,** *Hooligans or Rebels? An oral history of working-class childhood and youth 1889–1939*, Basil Blackwell, Oxford, 1981, pp. 170–2.

52 Greenwood, *Seven Curses*, p. 97.

53 **Avril D. Leadley,** 'Some villains of the eighteenth-century market place', in **John Rule** (ed.), *Outside the Law: Studies in crime and order 1650–1850*, Exeter Papers in Economic History, no. 15, University of Exeter, 1982, p. 24.

54 Wilts. R.O. Stourhead Archive 383/955 Justice Book of R. C. Hoare 1785–1815.

55 Beds. R.O. QSR 18/1802/13; QSR 20/1808/170.

56 Greenwood, *Seven Curses*, pp. 101–2.

57 Wohl, *Endangered Lives*, p. 54.

58 **D. C. Woods**, 'The operations of the Master and Servants Act in the Black Country 1858–75', *Midland History*, vii (1982), pp. 93–115 (at p. 94); and see below pp. 156–7.

59 **George Robb**, *White-Collar Crime in Modern England: Financial fraud and business morality 1845–1929*, Cambridge U.P., 1992; for the estimate of fraudulent promotions see **H. A. Shannon**, 'The Limited Companies of 1866–83', *Economic History Review*, 4 (1933), pp. 290–316.

60 **Rob Sindall**, 'Middle-class crime in nineteenth-century England', *C.J.H.*, 4 (1983), pp. 23–40 (at p. 32); for more detail see **R. S. Sindall**, 'Aspects of middle-class crime in the nineteenth century', unpublished M.Phil., University of Leicester, 1974.

61 Beds. R.O. Whitbread MSS (uncatalogued) Magniac to Whitbread, 15 September and 12 October 1882.

62 **Gregory Anderson**, *Victorian Clerks*, Manchester U.P., 1976, pp. 35–6.

63 Robb, *White-Collar Crime*, pp. 138–42; **Rev. J. Stockwell Watts**, *The Biggest Crime of the Nineteenth Century and what the Churches say to it*, London, 1893.

64 Sindall, 'Middle-class crime', p. 34; see also in general Anderson, *Victorian Clerks*, and **Geoffrey Crossick**, 'The emergence of the lower-middle class in Britain: A discussion', in Geoffrey Crossick (ed.), *The Lower Middle Class in Britain*, Croom Helm, London, 1977.

65 **Alan Doig**, *Corruption and Misconduct in Contemporary British Politics*, Penguin, Harmondsworth, 1984, p. 69.

66 **Phil Fennell** and **Philip A. Thomas**, 'Corruption in England and Wales: An historical analysis', *International Journal of the Sociology of Law*, 11 (1983), pp. 167–89; **David Owen**, *The Government of Victorian London 1855–89*, Belknap Press, Cambridge, Mass., 1982, chapters 8 and 9.

67 **W. H. Watts**, 'Records of an old police court', *St. James's Magazine*, xii (1865), pp. 499–506 (at p. 506). On occasion, however, members of the new police were permitted to take gratuities and rewards. At the Nottinghamshire Epiphany Sessions in 1856, for example, three police constables from the county force were commended for apprehending a sheep-stealer and were rewarded out of county funds; one man received £3, the others £1 each 'which appears to this court to be a reasonable compensation for

their expenses, exertions and loss of time'. Notts. R.O. QSM 1856–60, adjournment sessions 7 March 1856.

68 Clive Emsley, *Policing and its Context 1750–1870*, Macmillan, London, 1973, pp. 128 and 159; Phillip Thurmond Smith, *Policing Victorian London: Political policing, public order, and the London Metropolitan Police*, Greenwood Press, Westport, Conn., 1985, pp. 53–4, 69 and 71; Manchester Police Museum, Watch Committee Minutes 1895 onwards, vol. 3, f. 83; Barbara Weinberger, 'Crime and police in the late nineteenth century: A case study from the Coventry area', unpublished M.A., University of Warwick, 1976, p. 34.

69 M. A. Crowther, *The Workhouse System 1834–1929: The history of an English social institution*, Methuen, London, 1983, pp. 118, 159–60, 216 and 241.

70 Beds. R.O. QSR 23/1818/528 and 529; QGV 10/4/128.

71 U.C.L. Chadwick MSS 16 'Police Memoranda etc. (1855–69)'. Printed return of cases of embezzlement and default by Poor Law administrators in the Metropolis 1853–59.

72 Davis, 'Law breaking and law enforcement', chapters 3 and 5.

CHAPTER 7

The criminal class and professional criminals

The use of the term the 'criminal class' was probably at its most common during the 1860s[1] but the idea of a criminal class and of professional criminals living, at least partly, by the proceeds of criminal behaviour was popular throughout the nineteenth century and also informed the work of several historians of criminality. While dubious about Engels's romantic notion that the most courageous members of the very poor became 'thieves and murderers' and waged 'open war against the middle classes', Kellow Chesney drew heavily on the work of investigators like Mayhew and revelled in the underworld slang of Victorian England to give his readers a glimpse of 'gonophs, footpads and the swell mob' and 'magsmen, macers and shofulmen'.[2]

A few men did get a lot of money from criminal behaviour, but those who made the greatest financial hauls were white-collar offenders who were never considered to be part of a criminal class; and while 'William Smith' of Baring Brothers' Liverpool house, or the embezzling nephew of the Mathesons, may have been considered as professional gentlemen, they were never considered as professional thieves. Similarly, fraudsters like the Bidwell brothers who, in January and February 1873, tricked the Bank of England out of £100,405 7s.3d., and who attracted enormous crowds on their arrest and removal to London, were rarely considered in the same breath as Bill Sikes.[3] Yet there were a few fraudsters from less well-to-do social groups that, from the mid-nineteenth century, were involved in various 'long-firm frauds' which generally involved ordering goods that were never paid for, but that were still sold on. Clerks, commercial travellers and various shopkeepers were often involved in such criminal transactions.[4]

Some individuals acting as receivers may have made reasonable profits. Yet it is doubtful whether any achieved the financial success of the

Bidwells or 'Smith'. It is difficult to know how many large-scale receivers existed, while the small-scale receiver is difficult to pin down. Policemen were concerned about pawnbrokers acting as receivers.[5] Some did so, though probably many more simply preferred not to ask questions, while others must have received stolen goods unknowingly. Pawnbrokers and, lower down the social scale, the proprietors of 'dolly shops' or 'leaving shops' were important figures to the urban working-class communities of the eighteenth and nineteenth centuries. They provided a vital financial service, and not simply to the casual labourers. Sometimes certain kinds of goods were left with the pawnbroker on a regular weekly basis – good clothes could be pawned during the week and redeemed for weekends after pay day. Many of the articles of clothing, bed linen, table linen and cutlery taken in a petty theft were hastened to a pawnbroker; but as several divisions of the Metropolitan Police reported to Chadwick and the Constabulary Commissioners, some petty thieves were caught precisely because of the vigilance of pawnbrokers.[6]

A variety of other kinds of dealer and retailer made profits from receiving. There were butchers and poulterers who received game from poachers and who sometimes organised the poaching gangs. Old clothes dealers, because of their trade, were suspect like pawnbrokers; so too were the owners of chandler's shops who might receive and resell whatever was purloined from ships by dockers, ships' crews or ship builders. There were scrap-metal dealers who asked no questions about small quantities offered to them for sale; and there were the grocers, like Harding's Aunt Liza, who received, repackaged and resold. It is unlikely that many of these receivers made significant profits or that many of them could, in any meaningful way, be considered as professional criminals. Rather many, perhaps most of them can be said to have been providing a service to the poorer working class.

Forms of criminal behaviour at the bottom of a network of illegal activity might also provide opportunities for the poor in a moment of need. Forged bank notes became a major problem in the early nineteenth century. The war with Revolutionary France created serious financial difficulties in the mid-1790s and, in February 1797, the Privy Council instructed the Bank of England to suspend cash payments. The simplicity of the new £1 and £2 bank notes that were issued following the suspension provided an opportunity to artisans in the small metal trades of Birmingham and Liverpool, who had enjoyed a sideline in false coinage, to branch out into forging bank notes. From the forgers at the top, a network spread out across the country for the circulation of the notes; the footsoldiers were the men and women, sometimes married or cohabiting couples, invariably poor, who uttered the notes in shops and pubs, at markets and fairs.[7]

From Elizabethan times at least there was concern that children were being taught to be professional criminals. Fagin's school for pickpockets appears to have had some basis in fact and it was confidently asserted that a child starting out as a 'gonoph' (street thief), if adept and well-trained, could rise to be a member of the exclusive group of professional pick-pockets known as the 'swell mob'.[8] But several points need to be made about pickpockets and their trade. First, rather than the offenders being in thrall to Fagin's, it seems probable that a considerable amount of pocket picking, especially by juveniles, was the result of opportunism.[9] Different styles of nineteenth-century fashion aided such offenders: a handkerchief poking from the back-pocket of a fashionable mid-century tailed coat was easy pickings. Arthur Harding noted how the bustle, which came in and out of women's fashion in the second half of the century, could have been designed with the thief's requirements in mind. Pickpockets worked best in crowds. Harding and his mates worked fairs, markets and races and moved round the country where their work took them.[10] What appears to have been a gang of travelling pickpockets was apprehended in Bedford-shire in October 1860 after Mary Mayne was robbed of a promissory note, value £5, two sovereigns and one half sovereign. The gang consisted of George Brown, a twenty-one-year-old hair-brush stainer born in Leicester; Henry James Green, alias James Middleton, aged twenty-three, a stocking weaver born in Dublin whose last residence was in Nottingham; his wife Jane Green, alias Elizabeth Lockery, aged twenty, also a stocking weaver born in Coventry; and William Jones, alias William Johnson, alias David Dunn, a twenty-four-year-old labourer from London. Both Henry Green and William Jones had previous convictions for picking pockets; Jones had been sentenced to seven years' transportation for such an offence at the Old Bailey in 1851 and had been released on licence in 1854.[11] The haul from Mary Mayne, split four ways, assuming it could be matched with similar hauls from the same crowd, may have provided the gang with a modest living. But it was estimated earlier in the century that a pocket-handkerchief thief would have to steal between twenty and thirty handker-chiefs in a week to be able to live off the booty.[12]

Burglary was another crime which most Hanoverian and Victo-rian commentators considered as a skill, the perpetrators of which were regarded as professional criminals. It was generally ignored that some individuals, especially children, who were charged with burglary, had merely taken what they could reach through a broken window.[13] Burglars, it was alleged, set out armed with jemmies and false keys. At least as early as 1783 burglary was being described in parliament as a 'science' with specially made instruments available for the practitioners. Detailed sketches of such instruments made their way into the pages of Victorian magazines, though whether certain tools were indeed 'house-breaking implements', or simply a carpenter's brace and bit, may have been purely within the perception of an arresting constable.[14] One or two burglars, however, equipped themselves with weapons which had only one use; press outrage and panic about armed burglars in the 1880s led to a revolver issue to a few metropolitan policemen on the more remote beats.[15]

During the 1860s, when reviewing the working of the old Marlborough Street Police Office, W. H. Watts could write:

There are now no professional highwaymen; there are no professional burglars; there are no localities given over absolutely to the outcasts of society; there are now no colonies of thieves who only live by thieving; no burglars or highwaymen who support existence solely by following out their penal trade. The old haunts of vice are broken up, and the old gangs of offenders have either died off or been utterly dispersed. If you see in the papers that 'burglars' have been captured, you will find, on enquiry, the culprits have mostly trades of their own; if a batch of pickpockets is taken, the chances are that you will discover they have a 'calling' besides that of picking pockets, at which they are able to, and do, maintain themselves when the 'honest fit' is upon them.[16]

It is difficult to be sure about whether Watts's view of the decline an old kind of full-time criminal was correct; probably not. The new police may have cleared some petty offenders from the streets, though these would not appear to have been the variety of criminals to whom Watts was referring. Moreover he was writing in the immediate aftermath of the publications of Mayhew and others who wrote in terms of a 'criminal class'. No accused individual ever stood before the Fieldings, Colquhoun or any other magistrate or judge and gave their trade or calling as burglar, highwayman or pickpocket. But Watts's comments point to some key questions about the eighteenth- and nineteenth-century professional criminal and criminal classes: For how much crime were these 'professionals' or this 'class' responsible? How many professionals were there? How big was the criminal class?

The statistics and the court records suggest that the overwhelming majority of thefts reported and prosecuted were opportunist and petty; most incidents of violence against the person involved people who were either related or who were known to each other. Professional criminals, in the sense of men who went out armed with tools for housebreaking and with weapons, and who committed more than one offence, might well have carried out the bigger robberies. Probably they committed these robberies as 'professionals' taking precautions and planning carefully, rather than yielding to momentary temptations; possibly fewer of them were arrested and prosecuted. Perhaps, as the new police grew in numbers and gained more experience, petty street thieves and opportunist thieves were at greater risk; this may have contributed to the proportionate increase in burglaries during the second half of the nineteenth century as those who were determined to profit from criminal behaviour recognised a need for better planning and organisation, though the problem here is that 'burglary' itself is an elastic term which could be stretched or slackened according to the discretion of prosecutor or police. In short, it would be impossible to prove that most thefts and most violence was the work of persons who indulged in criminal behaviour as a way of life.

The notion of a criminal class poses a rather different problem. As noted earlier, the criminal class described by Victorian commentators was largely synonymous with the poorer working class, particularly those who existed by casual labour as well as groups such as travelling showmen, the organisers of prize fights and so forth. Certainly some people in these social groups committed crimes: families, peer-group gangs – usually of young men – sometimes whole streets or villages had negative attitudes towards some aspects of the law, and towards the police in particular. James Waring, a sixteen-year-old sweep convicted, with two younger boys, of burglary at the Old Bailey in January 1797 used to pass his booty on to his mother who then took it to the pawn shop.[17] Listing the cases heard at the local Summer Assize in 1843 the *Bedford Mercury* singled out for comment the family of Thomas Smith, a seventeen-year-old stocking maker from Biggleswade who pleaded guilty to stealing a parcel from a coach:

The father of the prisoner has just completed his term of transportation; his mother has been in prison for a considerable time; his brother is transported; and three years ago the prisoner was also ordered to be transported, but was respited on account of his youth.[18]

Yet even communities with relatively negative attitudes towards the law and its representatives had not similar to those of other social groups. The Sheen family of Whitechapel were a notorious illustration of this. In 1827 William Sheen was acquitted twice on technicalities for beheading his illegitimate child. His subsequent career involved robbery and vicious drunken assaults, and he intimidated others with boasts of being a murderer. This in itself created tensions within the cluster of streets where William and other family members lived. Nor were the other family members paragons of virtue. His mother, Ann, allegedly ran a brothel and enticed children to work for her. Perhaps the most alarming thing about the Sheens was their dealings with local police constables, and they often acted as police witnesses in trials.[19]

Within several, perhaps most communities with a wariness of the law and its agents there were various groups, sometimes but not always with family ties, that engaged in criminal activity. Gwenda Morgan and Peter Rushton have suggested that three types of criminal organisation were to be found in eighteenth-century England. There were 'networks' containing individuals who played different roles such as thief or receiver and who linked with each other periodically. 'Groups' came together to undertake particular crimes but did not operate together regularly. And there were a few 'gangs' which had a more permanent organisation and which sometimes operated over long distances and over lengthy periods of time; again they had members who played distinct roles. Convicted gang members, both male and female, were among the most successful of the eighteenth-century transportees to avoid surveillance and servitude in America and to escape back to Britain. They may have had their own resources to purchase their freedom from ships' captains or else they drew on the assistance of friends in the colonies. But Morgan and Rushton also warn that the term 'gang' was used loosely and, whatever the notoriety of some such groups and the fears about them, they were probably only responsible for a tiny percentage of offending.[20] Similar criminal groups, based on families, friendships or community existed throughout the nineteenth century and beyond. At the end of the nineteenth and beginning of the twentieth centuries, Arthur Harding's East End gang picked pockets around the country and then began passing counterfeit money; subsequently they were available for hire as a gang of toughs and were, on one occasion, recruited to terrorise 'blackleg' printers.[21] Merthyr Tydfil's 'China' seems to have remained a criminal Alsatia for many years; and within the transient districts of other towns and cities could be found isolated individuals – wandering labourers, sometimes genuine vagrants who moved from one cheap lodging house to another, and if the worst came to the worst to street or hedgerow. Sometimes these individuals acquired exotic names like the 'Wolds Rangers' of the East Riding or the 'Rodneys' of South Staffordshire 'who go about without any settled residence, and who never work, but live by robbery, and sleep by the coke and engine fires which are numerous in this mining district'.[22] They were looked upon with suspicion by the respectable inhabitants whose streets or villages they dared to enter. The management of such people was increasingly taken over by the police; they were, in the modern sociological sense, 'police property'. Sometimes the wanderers and vagrants could be dangerous, sometimes they might steal, but it is not particularly helpful to lump them together with the Hardings, the Redmans of Houghton Conquest, the population of 'China' and the few criminal families and to conclude that, together, they all constituted a criminal class since the only common denominator is the breaking of, often very different, laws.

The term 'criminal class' was, indeed remains, a convenient one for insisting that most crime is something committed on law-abiding citizens by an alien group; and the more that historians probe the reality of a class passing criminal activity steadily from one generation to another, the more it is revealed to be spurious. A study of the railway town of Crewe from the 1880s to the 1940s, for example, suggests that a similar set of circumstances produced very different outcomes on different individuals and different groups. Within this complexity there was some, but no automatic intergenerational transmission of persistent offending. The culture of certain kinds of work could, when combined with alcohol and socialising, foster some criminal behaviour; but steady work could also lead to desistence. Marriage and settling down with a family, curiously, does not appear to have had much effect.[23]

There were individuals who enjoyed long careers of offending. Charlotte Walker, for example, was arrested at least thirty times during the last three decades of the eighteenth century. She was tried a dozen times at the Old Bailey but convicted only on the last occasion, and transported. She was a prostitute and a pickpocket; and she was intimidated by neither her accusers nor the court. Her daily existence, like that of so many of the poor in Hanoverian and Victorian England, was always precarious and fits with the general conclusions of wider studies that no clear distinction can be made between a dishonest criminal class and a poor but honest working class.[24] Simon Stevenson's analysis of those subject to the 'habitual criminals' legislation of 1869 and 1871 reveals how small the number of 'habituals' was; perhaps no more than 4,000 a year throughout the 1870s. Furthermore he suggests that it is very difficult to conceive of these individuals as either a class or a group of professionals readily and continually identifiable by their behaviour and integrating within some deviant familial lore. A few offenders adopted romantic names and posturings, but there does not appear to have been any specifically 'criminal' argot nor, in contrast to what many of the early criminologists believed, did they all go in for having tattoos. Most of the larcenies committed by these individuals involved goods of paltry value and criminal 'tools' were rarely used in the execution of their crimes. If the 'habitual criminal' did have unsavoury friends and acquaintances, often drawn from his peer group, he was also equally likely to have family support of a rather different kind with parents and sometimes wives urging him to more law-abiding and 'moral' behaviour.[25] A more recent study of serious, habitual criminals however suggests that they were less likely to be married than the usual offender, less likely to have children and more likely to be constantly on the move from place to place. Yet, like all offenders, even these rootless more serious 'habituals' stopped offending at some point in their lives, though this was often due to the long prison sentences awarded under harsh penal legislation.[26]

A criminal record led some men to be targeted by the police and, in many instances, men with criminal records had difficulty in finding work. The formal creation of the category of 'habitual criminals' by the Act of 1869 and the Prevention of Crimes Act 1871 probably contributed to such difficulties. Even Colquhoun recognised the problem of the newly released prisoner when he asked: '*Without friends, without character, and without the means of subsistence*, what are these unhappy mortals to do?'[27] The Victorians also recognised the problem. In January 1857 the Earl of Carnarvon and Henry Mayhew organised a meeting of eighty ticket-of-leave men in Holborn. They heard of their difficulties in finding employment and of harassment by the police.[28] A decade later James Greenwood expressed his doubts about the police supervision of ticket-of-leave men:

There are hundreds and thousands of men in London, and indeed in all great cities, who 'pick-up' a living somehow – anyhow, and who, though they are honest fellows, would find it difficult to account for, and bring evidence forward to show, how they were engaged last Monday, and again on Wednesday, and what they earned, and whom they earned it of. Such men 'job about', very often in localities that, in the case of a man under police supervision, to be seen there would be to rouse suspicions as to his intentions. For instance, many a shilling or sixpence is 'picked up' by men who have nothing better to do, by hanging round in railway stations and steamboat wharves, and looking out for passengers who have luggage they wish carried. But supposing that a man, a 'ticket-of-leave', was to resort to such a means of obtaining a livelihood, and that he was seen 'hanging about' such places day after day by a watchful

detective who knew who and what he was, – with what amount of
credibility would the authorities receive his statement that he was
'looking out for a chance to carry somebody's trunk or carpet-bag'![29]

The attempts of London's stipendiary magistrates to frustrate the supervision of habitual criminals by the Metropolitan Police may have stemmed partly from such a recognition; but the Convict Supervision Office organised within the Metropolitan Police in 1880 claimed, within a few years, to have solved many of the problems.[30] Voluntary attempts at a solution, such as the Discharged Prisoners' Aid Society established in 1857, were also attempted, with varying degrees of success.[31] Yet here again it must be emphasised that the largest number of offenders arrested and imprisoned were always drawn from the ranks of young men; and not all young men arrested for offences in their teens and twenties carried on with a criminal career into their thirties and forties. Parent-Duchâtelet and William Acton both noted that prostitution was a transitory stage for most women who followed the 'profession' during the nineteenth century; many women became prostitutes because of temporary economic hardship. Probably the same was true for those who committed the bulk of petty thefts brought before the courts during the eighteenth and nineteenth centuries; criminality, in the form of thefts committed by men from the poorer sections of the working class, was transitory behaviour, possibly fostered by economic hardship, probably encouraged by opportunity. Most thefts, and most crimes of violence, cannot be attributed to professional criminals; nor is it helpful to think of these offences as committed by a group that can, in any sense, be described as a separate class.

But if the 'reality' of a significant criminal class can be questioned, the texts which described the phenomenon, especially in the mid-Victorian years, are significant. These descriptions contributed to the construction of a reality for their readers. They revealed an organised, hierarchical social group which lacked any understanding of religious principles, social duty and virtue – in short a group which was ignorant of the key elements that Victorians liked to think underpinned their society. This gave the reader a sense of superiority over criminals, and a sense too that society was not responsible for the idle and vagrant who belonged to that class. Knowledge of the criminal class alleviated at least some of the uncertainty and fear about crime; and mid-Victorian commentators invariably stressed the watchfulness of the police whose particular expertise enabled them to identify criminals and check their depredations. At the same time, knowledge of the criminal class generated an urgency in the need to prevent juvenile offenders from becoming habitual criminals, and it contributed to a hardening of attitudes towards those defined as the latter.[32]

Notes

1 S. J. Stevenson, 'The "criminal class" in the mid-Victorian city: A study of policy conducted with special reference to the provisions of 34 and 35 Vict., c. 112 (1871) in Birmingham and East London in the early years of registration and supervision', unpublished D.Phil., Oxford University, 1983, p. 32 note 4.

2 Kellow Chesney, *The Victorian Underworld*, Harmondsworth, Penguin, 1970; the quotation from Engels', *The Condition of the Working Class in England in 1844* is on p. 99. Donald Thomas, *The Victorian Underworld*, London, John Murray, 1998, relies heavily and uncritically on Mayhew.

3 For the Bidwells see their autobiographies, Austin Bidwell, *From Wall Street to Newgate*, Hartford, CT, 1895 and George Bidwell, *Forging His Chains: The Autobiography of George Bidwell*, Hartford, CT, 1888. Both are discussed in Philip Priestley, *Victorian Prison Lives: English Prison Biography 1830–1914*, Methuen, London, 1985.

4 Heather Shore, *London's Criminal Underworlds, c.1720–1930: A Social and Cultural History*, Palgrave Macmillan, Houndmills, Basingstoke, 2015, pp. 130–40.

5 Patrick Colquhoun, *A Treatise on the Police of the Metropolis*, 3rd edn, London, 1796, p. 13 and chapter 8, *passim*. Colquhoun even proposed an act of parliament to control and supervise pawnbrokers and dealers in second-hand goods, see Sir Leon Radzinowicz, *A History of English Criminal Law*, 5 vols, Stevens, London, 1948–68, iii, Appendix 5.

6 U.C.L. Chadwick MSS 11 f. 23: E division response to q. 11; f. 25: R. division response to q. 11. For the importance of the nineteenth-century pawnbroker in working-class communities see Melanie Tebbutt, *Making Ends Meet: Pawnbroking and Working-Class Credit*, Leicester U.P., Leicester, 1983; for pawnbrokers as receivers and police informants see especially pp. 70 and 95–9. The fullest discussion of 'receiving' by pawnbrokers, 'dolly-shops', second-hand dealers as well as ordinary, legitimate tradesmen (like butchers or fishmongers buying pilfered paper to wrap their wares) is to be found in Jennifer Davis, 'Law breaking and law enforcement: The creation of a criminal class in mid-Victorian London', unpublished Ph.D., Boston College, 1984, chapter 2.

7 Randall McGowen, 'The Bank of England and the policing of forgery 1797–1821', *P and P*, 186 (2005), pp. 81–116; Deirdre Palk, *Gender, Crime*

and Judicial Discretion, 1780–1830, Boydell/Royal Historical Society, Woodbridge, 2006, chapter 5.

8 Chesney, *Victorian Underworld*, chapter 5, *passim*. For reference to a similar 'school' in Elizabethan London see **J. A. Sharpe**, *Crime in Early Modern England 1550–1750*, 2nd edn, Longman, London, 1999, p. 164.

9 **Heather Shore**, *Artful Dodgers: Youth and Crime in Early Victorian London*, Boydell/Royal Historical Society, Woodbridge, 1999, pp. 58–61.

10 **Raphael Samuel** (ed.), *East-End Underworld: Chapters in the Life of Arthur Harding*, RKP, London, 1981, p. 78.

11 Beds. R.O. QGV 10/4/23–26.

12 Shore, *Artful Dodgers*, p. 62.

13 **Charles M. De Motte**, 'The dark side of town: Crime in Manchester and Salford 1815–75', Ph.D., University of Kansas, 1977, p. 247.

14 *Gentleman's Magazine*, liii (1783), pp. 740–1. Several of the Victorian illustrations of housebreaking equipment are reproduced in Chesney, *Victorian Underworld*.

15 **Clive Emsley**, ' "The thump of wood on a swede turnip": Police violence in nineteenth-century England', *C.J.H.*, 6 (1985), pp. 125–49 (at pp. 136–41).

16 **W. H. Watts**, 'Records of an old police court', *St James's Magazine*, x (1864), pp. 458–65 (at p. 448).

17 OBP t17970111-9-10 (James Waring, Green, Milton and Elizabeth Waring).

18 *Bedford Mercury*, 22 July 1843.

19 Shore, *London's Criminal Underworlds*, chapter 5.

20 **Gwenda Morgan** and **Peter Rushton**, *Rogues, Thieves and the Rule of Law: The Problem of Crime in North-East England, 1718–1800*, U.C.L. Press, London, 1998, pp. 85–95; *idem*, 'Running away and returning home: The fate of English convicts in the American colonies', *C.H.S.*, 7 (2003), pp. 61–80.

21 Samuel (ed.), *East End Underworld*, pp. 78–80 and 121. For a general, wide reaching account see Shore, *London's Criminal Underworlds*.

22 *The Times*, 16 November 1850, quoting the *Derby Mercury*.

23 **Barry S. Godfrey**, **David J. Cox** and **Stephen D. Farrall**, *Criminal Lives: Family Life, Employment and Offending*, Clarendon Studies in Criminology, Oxford, 2007.

24 **Mary Clayton**, 'The life and crimes of Charlotte Walker, prostitute and pickpocket', *London Journal*, 33, 1 (2008), pp. 3–19; **David Philips**, *Crime and Authority in Victorian England*, Croom Helm, London, 1977; Davis, 'Law breaking and law enforcement'.

25 Stevenson, 'The "Criminal Class" in the mid-Victorian city', especially pp. 280, 284, 309, 311–31 and 355–61.

26 Barry S. Godfrey, David J. Cox and Stephen D. Farrall, *Serious Offenders: A Historical Study of Habitual Offenders*, Clarendon Studies in Criminology, Oxford, 2010.

27 Colquhoun, *Treatise on the Police*, p. 91.

28 Sean McConville, *English Local Prisons, 1860–1900: Next Only to Death*, Routledge, London, 1995, pp. 36–7.

29 James Greenwood, *The Seven Curses of London*, London, 1869, p. 125.

30 Stefan Petrow, *Policing Morals: The Metropolitan Police and the Home Office, 1870–1914*, Clarendon Press, Oxford, 1994, p. 79.

31 Priestley, *Victorian Prison Lives*, pp. 283 and 286 for prisoners' attitudes to the Prisoners' Aid Society.

32 Randall McGowen, 'Getting to know the criminal class in nineteenth-century England', *Nineteenth-Century Contexts*, 14 (1990), pp. 33–54.

CHAPTER 8

Prosecutors and the courts

There were significant changes in prosecution and court practice during the period 1750 to 1900. There were also significant changes in the kind of court environments in which criminal cases were heard. On occasions it was an act of parliament which heralded a change; sometimes, however, legislation simply formalised and sanctioned what had come to be practice; and many changes were gradual, almost imperceptible except over a long period.

The English legal system provides for any private citizen to initiate a prosecution. During the eighteenth century a few prosecutions were directed by the Treasury Solicitor, notably in coining offences; the assault on those responsible for forging and then uttering false money after 1797, however, was organised by the Bank of England. A few prosecutions were conducted by the Attorney General, principally cases of treason or sedition; but again the numbers remained small and during the 1790s, the period of the English 'reign of terror', the Crown Law Officers regularly refused to finance prosecutions for sedition and urged magistrates – not always successfully – to organise these locally. The overwhelming majority of criminal prosecutions, more than eighty per cent, were conducted by the victims of crimes or, rather less frequently, by private individuals acting on the victim's behalf; and, reflecting the dominance of the male in eighteenth- and nineteenth-century society, most prosecutors were men.[1]

Victims of a criminal offence had a variety of choices. They could let the matter drop, regarding it as too insignificant for a criminal prosecution. Sometimes, and especially in the earlier part of the period under consideration, an offender was dealt with by community action rather than by recourse to the law: a Jewish hawker, caught attempting to steal a ring from a young woman at Huntingdon races in 1753, was seized by a crowd and ducked in a horse pond.[2] However crowds, and individuals, could not be relied upon always to help a victim. Stories were reported in the courts of victims, in hot pursuit of thieves, being deliberately impeded either by individuals or by crowds.[3] Probably what happened in these instances was that individuals or crowds sided with the person who appeared to be the underdog. Arthur Harding recalled late-nineteenth-century crowds taking the part of children who, well aware of what they were doing and certain of getting popular support because of their tender years, openly stole from traders' carts and barrows or from shops and stalls.[4]

The occasional attack on, or 'rough musicing' of, a prosecutor is suggestive of communities which felt that certain offenders should not have been prosecuted, or at least should have been proceeded against on a lesser charge. In the summer of 1763 Mrs White, a Spitalfields victualler, prosecuted her servant, Cornelius Saunders, for theft after he had stumbled across her savings in her basement and decked himself out in new clothes. Saunders was found guilty and executed. Many inhabitants of Spitalfields were incensed; Saunders was well-known in the neighbourhood primarily, it seems, because he had been blind from birth. Mrs White's house was attacked by large crowds; her furniture and possessions were thrown out into the street and burned.[5] A rather more complex affair occurred in Bedfordshire half a century later. At the 1817 Summer Assizes, Thomas Flemings was prosecuted for raping fifteen-year-old Sarah Gardener. The girl had visited her sister at Tingrith village feast; on the way home she was frightened by a group of Irishmen and, in consequence, her sister asked Flemings to accompany her. It was during the two-mile walk to her parents' house in Ampthill that Flemings raped her. Flemings was found guilty and executed. He went to his death, according to the local newspaper, a true penitent:

he said he had never been guilty of any crime before, nor even summoned before a Magistrate on any occasion whatever; but he had neglected a place of worship and his Maker, which had brought him to that untimely end.

Sarah Gardener's parents then found themselves the objects of popular abuse; crowds of up to 200 gathered outside their house throwing stones, exhibiting effigies:

one dressed as a man another as a woman and another as a child [and] hallowing and charging the family with having hung the man and that they ought to be hung themselves.[6]

There is nothing in the surviving details of the Flemings-Gardener case to suggest why the prosecutors were so unpopular, but possibly there was a feeling that the charge of rape was being used rather too freely in Bedfordshire on flimsy evidence. Three rape cases had been brought before the Summer Assizes in 1815; one was thrown out by the Grand Jury, the other two resulted in acquittal. One of these acquittals led to a prosecution for conspiracy at the 1817 Lent Assizes, just five months before the Flemings-Gardener case. The Reverend Robert Woodward and his daughters Sarah and Susannah were indicted for conspiring to prosecute James Harris on a charge of rape and making Susannah pregnant. The Woodwards were found guilty; the daughters were each sentenced to one year's imprisonment and the Reverend Woodward was compelled by the bishop to resign his living – 'a degree of punishment' which, Woodward considered to be 'beyond what was in the contemplation of the Judge who passed sentence'.[7]

Violent hostility towards prosecutors and their witnesses in unpopular cases was not confined to the Georgian period. In Blackburn in November 1862, after the prosecution of four men for night poaching on the land of J. Butler Bowden, crowds turned on the gamekeepers who had given evidence as they left the town hall escorted by eight men from the Lancashire Constabulary. An estimated 400 people then marched on Bowden's house, Pleasington Hall, which they proceeded to stone until driven off by Bowden and his servants firing two or three shots over their heads. A troop of the 16th Lancers and members of the county constabulary were rushed into Blackburn to maintain order.[8] Traditional rough musicing, with all its folkloric paraphernalia, tended to fade away during the nineteenth century, though manifestations were not unknown in the great cities of mid-nineteenth-century England, and the Welsh variant, *ceffyl pren*, has been noted as late as the 1880s.[9]

If the offender was known to, or instantly apprehended by the victim, some personal retribution or private settlement could be sought, or offered, to avoid recourse to the law. Yet this was not necessarily the case however close the bonds were between individuals. The law could be used as a means of discipline within the family, as is revealed by cases of parents prosecuting their children for theft or urging other victims to prosecute them.[10] An agreement to come to some private settlement over a theft was compounding a felony and was itself against the law. In October 1794 Richard Wadeson, a tallow chandler of Worksop was indicted before the Nottinghamshire quarter sessions for a misdemeanour 'in compounding a felony with Marmaduke Littleover for feloniously stealing, taking and carrying away two pounds weight of candles the goods and chattles of the said Richard Wadeson'. The following January Wadeson appeared before the Court, submitted to the charge and was fined twenty shillings.[11] Offenders brought to court occasionally protested that the prosecutor had agreed to let matters be after a financial settlement; and depositions or statements in court suggest some offenders offered money to avoid prosecution. Thomas Richardson, a publican of Carnaby Street, prosecuted John Wilson at the Old Bailey in 1796 for the theft of two quart pewter pots and three pint pewter pots. Richardson testified in court that, when he confronted Wilson at the local watch-house after his arrest:

he made towards me, and said, I will give you ten or twenty pounds if you will not appear against me; I told him to offer me no money for I have suffered so much by pot stealers.[12]

George Burridge told the Bedfordshire quarter sessions in 1832:

I left my watch . . . hanging on the nail over the mantlepiece in my father's house at Steppingly between 7 and 8 in the morning. When I went home at 10 o'clock my watch was gone I have not seen it again. D[efendan]t when he was taken up said he would pay me for the watch and all expenses if I would settle it. I said I would if the magistrate would allow it.[13]

Other alternatives to prosecution continued to be exploited throughout the nineteenth century. Employers could, and often did, simply dismiss pilfering workmen; this, together with the threat that the offender would never be employed again was a tougher sanction than many courts could impose. Many victims were satisfied with the return of their stolen property and/or with the scare which they gave the accused by the very fact of involving the police; once property had been restored and the offender had been warned by police involvement, some victims declined to proceed with prosecutions, or else simply did not turn up for the trials.

Legally assaults were different from thefts in that they were not necessarily felonious. During the eighteenth century many cases of assault were settled with a financial payment made by the assailant to the victim. Magistrates could be involved in such settlements at petty sessions. At quarter sessions, if it was noted that agreement had been reached between the parties, the punishment imposed by the court could be nominal. In January 1766 at the Nottinghamshire Sessions, for example, William Wesson prosecuted Thomas Turner, a grocer of Derby, for assault; 'it appearing to the court that [the] prosecutor was satisfied', Turner was fined one penny and discharged.[14] But alleged agreements to make amends with a money payment could be as fraught with difficulties in assault cases as in larceny cases. At the Easter Sessions for Bedfordshire in 1833, Emily Crossley prosecuted Robert Wells for an assault after which she had suffered a miscarriage. Wells complained that 'the woman offered to make it up and did for 5/-'.[15] Such settlements continued to be sought in cases of assault throughout the nineteenth century. Moreover it seems that many working-class prosecutions for assault were part of continuing feuds between families or groups, with the law being employed as one way of the complainant achieving a measure of what he or she considered to be justice, but not necessarily bringing the affair to an end.[16]

Some victims of theft who reported their loss to constables or thief-takers, were prepared to pay a reward for the return of their property and to ignore prosecuting the offender. Corrupt and unscrupulous constables and thief-takers, working in league with thieves, were happy to fall in with these wishes, splitting the rewards with the offender.[17] Newspaper advertisements or handbills describing the stolen property and offering a reward were regularly employed by victims and not without success in both the recovery of goods, the identification of the offender and thus in his or her prosecution and conviction. The circulation of information about offences became central to the Fieldings' proposals for improving the system of policing. Some victims went to considerable personal lengths to pursue offenders and regain their property. In the summer of 1769 Richard Wallis, a baker, and William Thornton, a tallow chandler, spent several days chasing the men who had stolen their horses around the southern environs of London. After the theft of ten ferrets, a box, a spud, a dog and a gun, John Jeffries and Thomas Asplen pursued Samuel Colgrave for two days through the villages surrounding Bedford. They continued their pursuit into Huntingdonshire and Cambridgeshire, eventually running their quarry to earth in a Cambridge pub.[18] It was also possible for the victim to apply to a magistrate for a warrant to search a suspect's house or lodgings.[19] When an individual had gone to the effort and, like as not, the expense of an advertisement, of finding a constable or thief-taker, or of a personal pursuit, he or she was less likely to balk at the effort and expense of a prosecution. Once judicial agents, particularly magistrates, were involved there was more likelihood of a crime being taken to court; and a warrant for an arrest, generally entrusted to a constable meant, at least, a hearing before a magistrate once the suspect was apprehended.[20]

The number of offences which could be heard and resolved summarily before a single magistrate sitting informally in his parlour or in a local tavern, or before one or two magistrates sitting with rather more formality in petty sessions, increased during the eighteenth century as legislation altered penalties and consolidated existing laws. Summary offences included specific minor thefts such as embezzlement by textile workers, stealing wood or vegetables, as well as, most notoriously, certain poaching offences and, by the Combination Acts, trade union activity. The prosecutor had the opportunity to decide whether he wished to have the accused tried summarily or before a higher court; summary justice was prompt, but the penalties were less severe involving only a fine or a short period of imprisonment. If the prosecutor was determined to make an example he probably would opt for a higher court and it was also possible for magistrates to advise victims to prosecute in a higher court so as to make an example. In 1792 a Bedfordshire magistrate urged a draper of Biggleswade to prosecute the draper's servant at quarter sessions rather than letting the matter be resolved summarily; he explained to the clerk of the peace that it would have been possible to send the offending youth to the Bridewell for ten or fourteen days 'but as the practice of infidelity in servants is become so General and ought to be discountenanced as much as possible' he had recommended the draper 'to prosecute him as a Thief and if convicted to have him well flogged at Biggleswade Market with leave of the Court'.[21]

The legal guides for magistrates, like Richard Burn's *The Justice of the Peace and Parish Officer* which went through thirty editions between 1755 and 1845, stated that, unless the offence brought before him was one that could be tried summarily, in cases of felony, the magistrate had no alternative to committing the offender for trial in a higher court. In practice, however, often in consultation with the prosecutor, the magistrates employed wide discretion. Sometimes the accused was discharged for lack of evidence; and some magistrates rejected prosecutions, particularly some assault charges, if it appeared that they were brought out of spite. Richard Wyatt threw out Richard Wells's accusation that James Britton had threatened him with violence on the grounds that it was 'litigious, vexatious and frivolous'.[22] But even if there did seem a felony case to answer, magistrates often encouraged reconciliation and interpreted some theft accusations as disputes over ownership. During the 1740s William Hunt studiously avoided the word 'theft' when noting certain cases in his justice book.[23] Samuel Whitbread's notebooks, kept seventy years later, reveal him occasionally seeking to settle matters by correspondence, threats, and bringing parties together, rather than simply committing an offender to trial.[24] In those instances where magistrates persuaded the accuser to drop a charge they were not, at least in their own eyes, compounding the offence, rather they were effectively establishing that there had been no criminal offence in the first place. Some cases, especially assaults might be settled with a monetary payment from the accused to the victim. In poaching cases the accused could have proceedings against him dropped if he entered into a bond not to poach on the victim's land again. In other instances an apology inserted in a newspaper might suffice.[25] In wartime the accused could be recruited into the army or navy without the case going beyond the magistrate; this saved the accused from a possibly lengthy pre-trial imprisonment, and it saved the accuser the expense of a prosecution. In eighteenth-century Essex, at least, such a policy was also pursued in peacetime with the accused being encouraged to enlist in the East India Company's service.[26] Finally it is apparent that magistrates used their wide powers over vagrants, servants, or those who could be described as 'idle and disorderly' to imprison, or otherwise punish offenders guilty of minor crimes, particularly petty theft.

If it was decided to take the accused to a higher court the magistrate committed him, or her, for trial. Bail was very rarely given in larceny cases and committal generally meant the accused being put in gaol, often for several months before appearing in court – after all, with the exception of London and its environs, there were only four quarter sessions and only two assizes each year for the eighteenth and much of the nineteenth centuries. The magistrate also bound over the prosecutor and any witnesses to attend at the higher court. Still the prosecutor's discretion was not at an end. An indictment had to be prepared for the court; this was then submitted to the grand jury, together with any depositions, for a decision on whether or not there was sufficient cause for the case to proceed to a hearing before magistrates and a petty jury at quarter sessions, or judge and jury at assizes. The bill of indictment was generally prepared by the clerk of the peace, for quarter sessions, or the clerk of assizes. These clerks were solicitors, but very often in cases of theft their task was no more than taking a printed bill and filling in the names of the accused, the victim and the details of the offence; these details sometimes simply involved writing the word 'larceny' or 'felony'. A particularly determined, or particularly wealthy prosecutor, might employ his own, independent solicitor to prepare the bill of indictment in which case the bill could incorporate several separate counts to ensure that, if the accused escaped on one charge, he could be caught by another. Following an attempted robbery of his Soho Works in 1800 Matthew Boulton was determined to have the four accused executed on a charge of burglary. Boulton's son was most impressed with the eight-count indictment prepared by his father's solicitors: 'it appears to be formed like a swivel gun and may be directed to all points as circumstances require'.[27] Yet, during the eighteenth and early nineteenth centuries, prosecutorial discretion in the bill of indictment could also lead to an offence being downgraded so as to ensure that the accused did not face the most serious, generally capital, charge available. Joseph Stenson, a hatter, was prosecuted for theft at the Borough Sessions in Leeds in January 1801: he was accused of taking one canvas bag value two pence, 500 shilling pieces value threepence, 500 sixpenny pieces value two pence and one gold half guinea value one penny.[28] The total value of the money which Stenson was accused of stealing was £38.0.6d. but by downgrading its value to a mere sixpence he could be tried before the borough magistrates on a non-capital charge.

Several of the procedures outlined previously could be bypassed. A prosecutor could decide to proceed with a voluntary bill whereby a hearing before a magistrate and the entering into recognisances to appear and prosecute were avoided. In such a case the prosecutor went directly to the grand jury, and it was possible for all of the initial steps to be taken without the accused being aware of what was going on. The accused was even more disadvantaged by an *ex-officio* information which was filed by the Attorney General in the Court of King's Bench. This avoided both an initial hearing before a magistrate and the hearing before a grand jury. *Ex-officio* informations gave the Attorney General the opportunity of having the case heard before a carefully selected special jury, and even if the defendant was acquitted he could still be saddled with costs. Both voluntary bills and *ex-officio* informations were the exception rather than the rule; the latter, in particular, were rarely used and were confined to serious misdemeanours, often involving some form of sedition.[29]

The pursuit of offenders, going before magistrates and subsequent court appearances were time-consuming – there was no indication given beforehand of the point at which a trial would be heard at either quarter sessions or assizes and, in consequence, the prosecutor and his witnesses, after having travelled to the county town where a particular court was sitting, could have to wait for several days before their case was heard.[30] For members of the lower classes, however, time was money. Henry Fielding believed that the poor were often discouraged from prosecuting because of the expense. Besides the loss of a day or two's pay, there were also the fees: it cost two shillings for an indictment to be drawn up by the clerk of the court in Fielding's London,[31] and there was, in addition, the recognisance bond to appear in court. Local prosecution associations had been formed from the late seventeenth century. There were, perhaps, as many as a thousand of these societies at any one time; the greatest numbers appear to have been in the period immediately after 1780. Membership of the associations was generally in the region of twenty to fifty, with gentlemen and farmers predominating in rural areas, and tradesmen and small businesses in urban districts. The members paid a subscription to finance the pursuit and prosecution of anyone offending against one of their number; but they rarely assisted anyone who was not a paid-up member of the association and the poor man thus continued to remain largely dependent on his own resources.[32] Legislation of 1752 authorised the courts to pay expenses in felony cases if the prosecutor was poor and if the accused was convicted. An act of 1778 extended this provision to all prosecutors. Some courts, for the reasons given by the Nottinghamshire quarter sessions in October 1785, were prepared to pay expenses even if there was no conviction. The Nottinghamshire magistrates were concerned that 'many felonies' were compounded

and others not prosecuted for fear that the expenses of the prosecution should not be paid by the county, to prevent the like in future and for encouraging prosecutions against felons . . . it was ordered by the Court that an advertisement be inserted in the Nottingham paper signifying that in all future prosecutions for felonies the reasonable charges of the prosecutors and their witnesses should be paid by the county.[33]

The Leeds Borough Sessions commonly paid expenses at the turn of the century when an accused was acquitted but when the court considered that 'there was reasonable ground of prosecution'. In Essex it was even known for the quarter sessions to award expenses after a bill of indictment had been rejected by the Grand Jury.[34] The less well-to-do prosecutors profited most from this legislation and court practice, and the knowledge that expenses were likely to be paid even if a good case failed may have encouraged more poor men to prosecute. The evidence shows that 'labourers', servants, gardeners and husbandmen made up something like one-fifth of the prosecutors in larceny cases in the second half of the eighteenth century, with tradesmen and artisans accounting for about two-fifths.[35] Further legislation, culminating in Peel's Criminal Justice Act 1826, extended the provision of expenses to witnesses as well as prosecutors, and to certain misdemeanours (notably the more serious forms of assault) as well as felonies. Peel justified this extension on the grounds that, when expenses were not available 'you frequently close the avenues of justice in instances in which the poorest classes are the sufferers, and in which the public interest loudly demands reparation from the offender'.[36]

Besides the expense of, and time taken up by a prosecution Henry Fielding believed that some victims did not prosecute because of a misplaced
humanitarianism in not wanting to be the cause of someone being executed.[37]
Sir Samuel Romilly, Sir James Mackintosh and other reformers urged this
as a principal reason for bringing about a drastic reduction in the number
of capital statutes which existed under the eighteenth-century Bloody Code.
'Numerous and respectable witnesses' testified to the 1819 Select Committee on Criminal Laws 'that a great reluctance prevail[ed] to prosecute' in
some capital crimes and, unfortunately, this reluctance had 'had the effect of
producing immunity to such a degree, that it may be considered as among
the temptations to the commission of crimes'.[38] Mackintosh chaired most of
the committee's sessions and his influence coloured its conclusions; probably he also affected the choice of witnesses and the way in which they were
prodded for answers favourable to the reformers' agenda.

The manner in which some prosecutors reduced the value of stolen
property so as to reduce the charge, suggests that they thought very seriously about the likely outcome if they proceeded on a capital indictment.[39]
Yet when, in 1811, the metropolitan stipendiary magistrates were asked a
series of questions about the impact of Romilly's act removing capital punishment from the offence of stealing privately from a person (pickpocketing), the opinion was overwhelmingly that cost and inconvenience were
much greater deterrents to the prosecutor than capital punishment. The
Shadwell magistrates had found a reluctance to prosecute but believed that
this was because their jurisdiction bordered the Thames and victims in the
area were 'seafaring people who cannot attend properly to the prosecution
but are obliged to go to sea'. The Hatton Garden magistrates doubted
whether there had been reluctance to prosecute on account of capital punishment 'but a great deal . . . on account of the expense and trouble of
prosecuting especially where the property to be recovered is of little value'.
One of the stipendiaries from the Queen's Square office elaborated:

*The considerable sacrifice of time, the additional cost, nay the heavy
load of expense, the tiresomeness of attendance, and keeping witnesses
together, the too frequent petulancies etc etc in the many stages of
Judicature, and the many painful mortifications frequently endured from
examination, and the asperities of cross examination. But that the parties
are often deterred from the consideration of a higher description [?] of
punishment is not true.*[40]

These deterrents to prosecution continued well after the extension of
expenses for prosecutors and witnesses and well after the reduction of

capital statutes during the 1820s and 1830s. The Constabulary Commissioners were informed by the Metropolitan Police that 'the fear of ultimately having to prosecute deters many from giving information'.[41] Sometimes there was the problem of personal embarrassment as when clergymen or other gentlemen had their watches stolen while consorting with prostitutes;[42] and such embarrassment, particularly in the moral atmosphere of Victorian society, probably also dissuaded women from prosecuting in cases of indecent assault, rape or attempted rape.[43] A few individuals refused to prosecute from religious scruples,[44] or when they discovered that the offender was one of their own family, or a servant willing to make restitution.[45] Some victims were too frightened,[46] and in East Anglia, and probably elsewhere, incendiarism, or the threat, was used to dissuade both prosecutors and magistrates.[47] Other victims, together with their witnesses, were allegedly bribed:

[N]o doubt it often happens that between the committal and the
day of trial, the witness on whom the case rests is tampered with or
for some pecuniary gain (and in some cases not a small amount) his
testimony before the Grand Jury is quite different to what it was before
the Magistrate. This is a common practice with old Thieves who say
'Smother it before the Grand Jury' as they know they would stand but
little chance should it come into court. Hence the number of Bills ignored
without any one knowing the cause, the Grand Jury excepted.[48]

On some occasions the reasons why victims refused to give information and to prosecute remained a mystery to the police. When the police felt that they could identify deterrents these were, overwhelmingly, loss of time, general inconvenience, and expense:

Mr Lawrence, New Cut, Lambeth prosecuted a person for felony and a
short time afterwards another person robbed him. Mr L declined giving
him in charge stating that it was such an annoyance to be detained for so
long from business at the Police Office and again at the Sessions. Many
instances might be given.[49]
      Many instances have occurred where parties have wished to decline
prosecuting in consequence of loss of time. Many tradesmen preferring
the infliction of a summary punishment rather than attend the sessions.
Even after parties have been committed they have again been brought up
and summarily convicted at the instance of the party robbed.[50]
      In the neighbourhood of Wandsworth, Battersea and Barnes, the
market gardeners have declined prosecuting parties for robbing their

grounds from the expense attending conviction before a magistrate at
Wandsworth. Parties stealing fruit and vegetables are convicted in a
small sum and the other expenses . . . amounting sometimes altogether
to 7s. or 8. the party convicted is frequently sent to prison in default and
the expense falls upon the prosecutor besides his loss of time etc.[51]

Some nineteenth-century law reformers concluded from the reluctance
of some victims to prosecute that England needed a system of public prosecution similar to that used in Scotland and elsewhere in Europe. In 1826
Peel expressed sympathy for the idea believing that it would ensure a prosecution when necessary and prevent frivolous or vexatious prosecutions;
he suggested that much could be learned from Scottish practice.[52] During
the following decade, and again in the 1850s and the 1870s, proposals
were brought forward, even to the extent of bills being introduced in the
House of Commons, for such a system. Each time, for a variety of reasons,
the proposals were rejected. There was opposition from a powerful vested
interest in the shape of the growing profession of solicitors; they feared a
significant loss of income should the state take over prosecutions. There
was more general concern about the expense of a system of public prosecution and also of the growth of patronage that would accompany it.
Finally there were concerns that involvement by the state in prosecution
would lead to encroachments on personal and political liberties. A public
prosecutor, declared the Clerk of the Peace of Wigan, in the mid-1840s:

would have the power of refusing to proceed in cases where parties
thought there ought to be a prosecution, and this power might (and
particularly in cases of political excitement) cause a denial of justice.
I think that in all cases any man who has sustained injury, ought to be at
liberty to put the law in force, and not be deprived of his remedy through
the malice or caprice of a public prosecutor refusing to proceed, and
therefore leaving him without remedy. If this power is entrusted to a public
prosecutor, it will be a greater encroachment upon the right of a trial by
jury than any encroachment there has been, and these are not a few.[53]

As a result of such sentiments nineteenth-century legislation only marginally infringed on the rights of the private prosecutor. The Vexatious
Indictments Act 1859 limited the opportunities for bringing voluntary
bills for certain misdemeanours. A dozen or so other acts authorised only
specific inspectors or local authorities to prosecute for certain infringe-
ments, and limited the independent civilian prosecutor's discretion in cases
concerning excise offences, sedition, or other matters involving sensitive

domestic or international affairs. A Director of Public Prosecutions was first appointed in 1879, but for nearly thirty years the position was almost entirely advisory.[54]

Yet, while no nineteenth-century legislation had any dramatic impact on the system of prosecution by private individuals, there was a very significant, if gradual, change brought about with the development of the new police. In certain circumstances, before the establishment of police forces, it could be difficult to find a prosecutor. Joseph Radcliffe, a magistrate of the West Riding, was not prepared to finance the prosecution of Joseph Jubson for seditious words in 1803; after all, he protested to the Home Secretary, the offence was not personal to him. In 1824 Essex magistrates were unwilling to organise and finance the prosecution of people who had attacked an informer; they remembered an earlier prosecution which had resulted in them being saddled with a solicitor's bill for £200.[55] The new police could take on such prosecutions and, gradually, they extended this role beyond these instances. The increasing role of the police as prosecutors from the middle of the nineteenth century has been largely ignored by historians and there has been no detailed study, even on a regional basis, of precisely how, when and why the police came to predominate as prosecutors.[56] Constables and local law officers had always had a role in prosecuting misdemeanours such as vagrancy and petty street offences. When the new police forces were established the incidence of arrests for these kinds of offences generally increased; at the same time acts of parliament relating to the police and local government bye-laws consolidated and extended the policeman's role in this area. Private individuals could bring prosecutions under police acts, and Charles Dickens expressed satisfaction in having prosecuted a young woman for bad language in the street under a Metropolitan Police Act.[57] But, overwhelmingly, the police dominated the prosecution of offences against public order, public decency and public safety. Such offences were usually processed by the police courts or petty sessions. Probably the step from prosecuting these petty offenders to prosecuting petty thieves was not seen as a particularly great one by the new police as they grew in confidence and professionalism.

In 1855 an experienced attorney, William Foote, informed the Select Committee on Public Prosecutors that he considered the prosecution of offenders as:

part of the policeman's duty; it certainly is part of his duty to trace out and detect crime, and if his duty is to trace out and detect crime, it is his duty to trace out the evidence to support the charge.[58]

If, as was repeatedly stated, the key role of the new police was the prevention of crime, what better way to prevent crime than to arrest and ensure the conviction of its perpetrators? Policemen, like their contemporaries, tended to think of crime as something committed by a criminal class; a perception encouraged by the requirement that they submit annual statistics of 'known criminals' in their district along with the figures of crimes reported and arrests made. At the same time it seems probable that the new police were sucked into acting as prosecutors from their early years because of the poverty of some of the victims of theft. The Superintendent of B Division of the Metropolitan Police explained to the Constabulary Commissioners that on one occasion arresting police constables had been obliged to pay for a bill of indictment since the two prosecutors in the case were too poor.[59] It may be significant that in several cases in mid-nineteenth-century Bedfordshire in which the police acted as prosecutor, or joint prosecutor, the victim, or other joint prosecutor, was a woman. Once the police began to step in as prosecutors in cases where the victim was poor or a 'weaker vessel', it was logical that they should step in on other occasions when the victim was simply reluctant. But it is not simply the case that the new police were drawn in as prosecutors because of the poverty or 'weakness' of the victims. Evidence from Lancashire suggests that, from the creation of its constabulary in 1840, senior police officers were considered as akin to public prosecutors, while the clerk of the peace conducted all prosecutions. The Home Office was doubtful as to the legality of this, and the Crown Law Officers advised that neither police officers nor anyone else should be bound over to prosecute when the injured party was unwilling to act;[60] but it is unclear whether the practice was terminated. In 1846 the Nottinghamshire Constabulary preferred three out of 118 indictments at the quarter sessions; another one was preferred by an old-style parish constable. Ten years later the police preferred twenty-two out of 166, with two other indictments preferred by parish constables. In 1866 there were ninety-five indictments at the quarter sessions, of which forty-seven were preferred by the police. These Nottinghamshire cases do not readily reveal much in the way of common characteristics suggesting why some, rather than others, were taken on by the police. Nor was the increase in the number of cases prosecuted by the Nottinghamshire Police either a steady linear progression or precisely parallel with the pattern elsewhere; in London, at least until 1880s, the private prosecutor seems to have dominated.[61]

For victims it probably seemed logical and preferable to hand over prosecutions to the police who increasingly claimed to be the experts in the 'war' against crime. It was particularly preferable since, even though the prosecutor's expenses might be reimbursed, he could still be out of pocket with some costs, or was at least fearful of such.[62] It was noted previously that the market gardeners of south London were reluctant to prosecute for petty thefts of their produce in case they were saddled with costs when the convicted offender was too poor to pay these as well as a fine. In 1844 a poor man was charged before Oxfordshire magistrates with stealing turnips. He was found guilty and sentenced to pay a fine of two shillings, a further two shillings, being the value of the turnips, and eleven shillings, being the costs of the magistrates' clerk. The man, who confessed that want had driven him to commit the theft in the first place, could not pay and was committed to prison. The magistrates then instructed the prosecutor to pay the clerk's costs. Naturally the man protested:

[he] said he did not understand why he should be saddled with such expenses for merely discharging his duty towards himself and the public, and added something about its being much cheaper letting the thief off with his booty, than seek for punishment for the offence.

The newspaper reporting the case declared such instances to be commonplace.[63]

There remains much work to be done into the role of private individuals and local communities in prosecuting or otherwise enforcing the law as they understood it.[64] Not everyone was keen to see the police acting as prosecutors. The legal profession was the most obvious group here, protesting that policemen were not properly trained for such a task, and that they might seek to put over evidence in a partial manner to ensure conviction. There were also stories reported to the mid-century Select Committee on Public Prosecutors of policemen supplementing their low wages by engineering malicious or trivial prosecutions to win the costs which the courts awarded, and sometimes sharing these with disreputable solicitors.[65] In the long term, however, the police assumption of the role of prosecutor may have brought them closer to the working class – as much, if not more, the victims of petty crime as any other group – and helped to foster that police legitimacy which appeared unique to England from roughly the middle of the nineteenth century to the middle of the twentieth.

From 1750 to 1850, and probably even later, most of the cases brought before assizes and quarter sessions were characterised by a face-to-face confrontation between the prosecutor and the accused. Occasionally the accused said nothing, or made very little response to the charge.[66] They had, after all, had little time or opportunity to prepare a defence while incarcerated in the squalid gaols of the period. They were denied access to depositions and to the names of prosecution witnesses; and even the charges against them could be changed at the last minute.[67] Sometimes the accused attempted to blacken the prosecutor's name: 'I hope your Lordships will examine this woman well', protested eighteen-year-old James Angas when he faced his principal accuser at the Old Bailey in April 1797, 'for she has transported several, and wants to make a property of me; she transported her own son'. Sixty years later Mary Ann Harriet Forbes, aged sixteen, was prosecuted by her master for stealing his property after which, without notice, she had left his employ. In court she protested that she had left after he had seized her round the waist, kissed her, and told her to 'pull the bed down'. Unfortunately she had made no similar complaint to the arresting police constable, and the court did not believe her.[68] More often than not, however, the defence consisted simply of a denial of the charge and a succession of character witnesses.

The confrontation between prosecutor and accused gradually disappeared during the nineteenth century as, increasingly, it was replaced by a confrontation between lawyers acting for both the prosecution and the defence. The legal profession, like many others grew in numbers during the nineteenth century, and while its standards of training remained minimal, legal practitioners of all types jealously preserved and advanced their boasted expertise. Part of this preservation of expertise involved a rigorous demarcation of their sphere of influence. The courts, with their ritual and tradition, were one such sphere; and as the century progressed the non-initiated public were required, more and more, to depend upon, and to pay for, the expert barrister and solicitor when they entered the courts.[69]

During the seventeenth century prosecuting counsel rarely appeared in the criminal courts, and only then in cases such as treason. Defence counsel were even more rare, appearing only in complex misdemeanour cases, notably those involving civil or regulatory matters such as liability for the upkeep of roads. The theory was that the accused had no need of counsel since the burden of proof was on the prosecution and the accused was a greater expert on the truth, or otherwise, of what was alleged against him or her, than any lawyer. The trial judge was expected to assist the accused with legal advice when necessary, though the speed of trials and the apparent indifference of many judges suggest that the expectation was rarely met in practice. Concern for the weakness of the accused's position began to be expressed with reference to treason prosecutions towards the end of the century and defence counsel were permitted by the Treason Act of 1696. The *Old Bailey Proceedings* began recording the rare appearances by prosecution counsel in other criminal cases during the second decade of the eighteenth century, most notably in murder cases. By the end of the century such appearances were more common, but were by no means the rule; generally speaking prosecuting counsel appear to have been employed primarily in cases where the victims were particularly aggrieved, where the case was difficult, or where the defence was employing counsel and it was feared that this might lead to acquittal. The prosecutors who employed counsel were clearly going out of their way to ensure that the case was conducted correctly and that the verdict was satisfactory; associations for the prosecution of felons appear, perhaps understandably, to have been significant among the employers of counsel. By the 1840s the employment of such counsel seems to have been widespread, particularly at assizes, and was also to be found at quarter sessions. Indeed, the lack of prosecution counsel at the Bedfordshire Lent Assizes for 1844 prompted two outbursts from Sir John Pattison, the presiding judge. He interrupted one case to enquire:

why there were no counsel for the prosecution, and observed that it was a disgrace to the county to impose upon the Judge the necessity of acting as a counsel against the prisoner ('an unseemly position' added his Lordship, with emphasis) besides the additional trouble which it entails upon the judge.

Then, when the case against a tramp for stealing a shawl was called, 'his lordship said, "There is no counsel I suppose?" and upon the clerk of the arraigns replying in the negative, added, "Ah! Bedford's so poor it can't afford them".'[70]

Defence counsel, according to the evidence of the *Old Bailey Proceedings*, began to make very rare appearances in ordinary criminal trials during the 1730s, but for the eighteenth and the early part of the nineteenth centuries their role was not strictly defined and the extent of their participation seems to have varied from one assize circuit to another. Both the accused and his or her counsel could cross-examine witnesses. What defence counsel could not do, until legislation in 1836, was sum up the defence for the benefit of the jury. Judges may have begun to allow counsel to appear for the accused because of the concern about the weakness of the accused's position; this concern also led to a greater querying of hearsay and circumstantial evidence as the eighteenth century progressed, and confessions were often rejected, especially if there was the slightest hint of them being extracted under duress. At the same time, even during the reforming years of the 1830s, a Solicitor General could voice concern that 'improper acquittal' could result from a barrister's eloquence, while another M.P. feared:

that if Counsel were allowed to both prisoner and prosecutor, it would have no better result than giving rise to trials of professional skill. The prosecutor in most cases being the richer, would have the advantage, since it might naturally be supposed that he could obtain the best professional aid.[71]

Some contemporaries suggested that the Prisoner's Counsel Act 1836 favoured professional thieves who could afford counsel, at the expense of poor prosecutors who could not. Yet a limited analysis of the employment of counsel suggests that overwhelmingly it was prosecutors who hired counsel rather than defendants[72] and throughout the nineteenth century the accused probably remained at a disadvantage.

It was not until the end of the nineteenth century that the accused in criminal proceedings was allowed to give evidence on oath. Two decades of heated debate preceded the Criminal Evidence Act 1898: on one side it was insisted that the accused's ability to give sworn evidence on his own behalf would reduce the number of innocent persons convicted as well as abolish anomalies and bring criminal law in line with civil law; on the other side it was alleged that such a change would disadvantage the nervous, foster perjury and, perhaps most serious, transform the judge from an impartial observer to a bullying French-style inquisitor.[73] It is, of course, impossible to assess how far the accused was disadvantaged by being unable to give sworn evidence, but financial considerations unquestionably limited his options. There were no expenses allowed for the accused; travelling to court as a witness for a defendant could cost an individual expenses for the journey; time spent in court, or waiting to be called, also cost money. Defence counsel cost money. Except in cases of murder there was no provision for legal aid for a defendant, otherwise the cheapest counsel available was through the system known as 'dock briefs' by which the defendant could pay one guinea, plus a clerk's fee, and obtain the service of a barrister without the mediation, and expense, of a solicitor. Barristers were obliged to accept 'dock briefs' but the overall standard of those who undertook criminal work was regarded as inferior. Money was one key incentive for the more able barristers to concentrate on civil business; in the 1840s it was estimated that earnings from the latter were ten times greater than earnings from criminal business. In 1851 it was argued in the *Law Times* that the state had a duty to allow or assign counsel to prisoners who could not afford them, but it was not until the

Poor Prisoner's Defence Act 1903 that any significant move was made in this direction.[74]

As trials at assizes and quarter sessions increasingly became contests between lawyers, so judges and juries played less of a central role and, in addition, trials became much longer and more formal. One legal historian has suggested that these changes led to some negative results. The increasing appearance of defence counsel meant increasing silence on the part of the accused and new burdens of proof being required from the prosecution; the focus, in turn, became the contest between legal adversaries rather than a system designed to seek the truth.[75] The increasing length and formality of trials, however, had its positive side. During the eighteenth and early nineteenth centuries most criminal trials were over in a matter of minutes; they rarely seem to have taken as long as an hour. Often the jurors did not leave the courtroom to deliberate, but simply went into a huddle, and not a particularly refined huddle. Towards the end of the eighteenth century Martin Madan condemned the practice of courts meeting during the afternoon following a lengthy break for food and drink. It was the drink which created the problems according to Madan; sometimes the judge had to spend an hour bringing the court to order:

and when this is done, drunkeness is too frequently apparent, where it ought of all things to be avoided, I mean, in jurymen and witnesses. The heat of the court, joined to the fumes of the liquor, has laid many an honest juryman into a calm and profound sleep, and sometimes it has been no small trouble for his fellows to jog him into the verdict – even where the wretch's life has depended on the event!

Madan claimed to have witnessed such incidents personally; and it was not only jurors who were said to be the worse for drink. A press report of an 1844 assize graphically describes a jury huddling in the court to discuss the verdict.

After a few minutes noisy consultation a portion of the jury turned round and said they were divided, as 'one or two old men wouldn't fall in with the others', whereupon the 'one or two old men' nodded their heads sagaciously, and in a manner to indicate that they had 'a reason for it'.[76]

Jurors served for an entire session of the court and were often drawn from men who had served before, even quite recently; jurors were thus often old hands who well understood the procedures and the tasks expected of them. Moreover the evidence of the *Old Bailey Proceedings* suggests that while jurors were in harmony with, and deferential towards the judge,

OLD BAILEY JUSTICE AFTER DINNER.

'Old Bailey Justice After Dinner'
The cartoon is a reflection on the suggestion made in November 1844 by Sir James Graham, the Home
Secretary, that Old Bailey judges should finish the day's business before adjourning for dinner. (TopFoto)

they were not simply passive auditors but asked questions and, on occasions, stated their reasons for a verdict. In January 1766, for example, an
Old Bailey jury acquitted Brian Swinney on a charge of highway robbery
and 'declared that they had a very bad opinion of the prosecutor'.[77] Sometimes, during the supremacy of the Bloody Code, juries brought in verdicts
reducing the value of property stolen to bring the accused out of range of
a capital statute; such behaviour was connived at, or often directed, by the
judge. There could be an exchange of views with the judge if he queried a
jury's verdict, and it was not unknown for a judge to reinstruct a jury and
to request it to deliberate again should it have returned a verdict which
he believed to be incorrect. Some judges exerted much greater influence
over juries than others. Lord Mansfield drew the fire of John Wilkes's
supporters for brow-beating and bullying juries; such behaviour probably
disadvantaged the accused and it appears that when Mansfield was on

the bench there were marginally more convictions than usual.[78] Interplay between the magistrates and the jurors at quarter sessions was probably much the same, but the paucity of evidence remaining for such proceedings makes any detailed analysis difficult if not impossible.

The right to a trial by a jury of his peers was lauded as one of the key rights of the free-born Englishman. Yet it is probably the case that, even during the eighteenth century, the most common experience of the law and of courts, for the bulk of the people, was the magistrate sitting alone, or with one or two colleagues more formally in petty sessions. Justice in these instances was administered summarily and while, during the eighteenth and nineteenth centuries, juries gradually became less and less active participants in the higher courts, so did new legislation bring more and more cases within the remit of the magistrates acting without a jury. Considerable concern was expressed about this development. Sir William Blackstone condemned summary jurisdiction as 'fundamentally opposed to the spirit of our constitution'. In 1772 the *London Chronicle* condemned a new Game Act which established summary jurisdiction in certain poaching offences and thus undermined 'the great Bulwark of an Englishman's Rights, the Trial by Jury'. Over half a century later *The Times* expressed similar regrets in a wide-ranging review of the activities of magistrates.[79] But requirements that justice be speedy and that it put the minimum burden on the prosecutor's time and pocket, were paramount.

Technically summary jurisdiction in the eighteenth and early nineteenth centuries only covered misdemeanours; felonies had to be tried on indictment before a jury. The spread of summary jurisdiction, however, increasingly blurred the distinction as legislation gave the prosecutor greater discretion in how he wanted to proceed against an offender and also what kind of punishment he wanted; punishments under summary jurisdiction were limited to either a fine, a whipping, or, at most, a few months' imprisonment. An employer wanting to prosecute the organisers or perpetrators of industrial action could use summary jurisdiction. From the early eighteenth century a number of acts had been passed relating to separate trades, each of which prohibited workers in that trade from combining to improve their wages or conditions. The Combination Act of 1799, and the amending legislation of the following year, consolidated these acts and enabled employers to take men involved in what were called 'combinations in restraint of trade' before magistrates in petty sessions. The acts were only enforced spasmodically and were repealed in 1824. Punishment, as in other summary offences, was minor. However, if an employer wanted to inflict a terrible example he could opt for a prosecution on indictment at a higher court on a charge of larceny, if the offence was the appropriation of materials, or on a charge of conspiracy, if the offence involved some kind of strike activity; in both such instances the punishment could be transportation. Similarly the increase of summary jurisdiction in poaching offences gave the prosecutor a wide choice: he could choose between the new summary jurisdiction, the more serious prosecution on indictment, and even a civil suit by which the plaintiff sued for half of the fine to be imposed and, if he won, he also collected twice the cost of the prosecution.[80]

As these examples of summary jurisdiction suggest, certain of the increasing summary categories were delicate ones for the relationships between social groups. From the late seventeenth until well into the nineteenth century, the Game Laws provoked considerable anxiety and outcry. These laws manifestly preserved the privileges of sporting gentlemen possessed of wealth and property. Many magistrates were such gentlemen, or were closely involved with such, and concern developed about partiality in Game Law cases before summary tribunals. This concern culminated in the petition of John Deller presented to parliament in 1823 in the midst of the early nineteenth-century debates on law reform. Deller was a Hampshire farmer whose farm was bounded in part by land belonging to the Duke of Buckingham. He had been brought before the Duke on a complaint from two of the Duke's gamekeepers for coursing hares on his own farm. Deller protested that the hares had done between £30 and £60 damage, but this did not prevent the Duke from fining him £5 and warning him that any impertinence would lead to the stocks or to gaol. Subsequently Deller brought a complaint against one of the Duke's servants for entering upon his land with three dogs, but two clerical justices had continually postponed the hearing while binding Deller over for assault:

[Y]our humble petitioner has heard much talk about the liberty and property of Englishmen; but . . . to his plain understanding, a state of slavery so complete as that in which he has the misfortune to live, cannot be found in any other country in the world.[81]

Yet, whatever the mythology and the occasional instance of cases like Deller's, Game Law offences do not seem to have dominated eighteenth-century summary tribunals. Furthermore the most sober recent study of the workings of these laws concludes that, especially after the 1750s 'openly biased tribunals were less common than the game laws' critics have assumed'.[82]

The Combination Acts have a notoriety akin to that of the Game Laws, yet there has never been a detailed analysis of their use; indeed, given the paucity of evidence surviving from summary tribunals, probably there cannot be. Similarly the trade-specific predecessors of the Combination Acts have received little serious attention and, again, the lack of evidence militates against detailed statistical assessments.[83] The poor man and the employee probably did have the cards stacked against them in eighteenth- and early nineteenth-century summary tribunals; but there were magistrates who sympathised with them and who were especially critical of the employers who used illegal truck payments.[84] Furthermore partly through public pressure, but also no doubt because the ruling class believed the rhetoric of the law's impartiality, magistrates were keen to demonstrate their impartiality. In 1824 the *Kent and Essex Mercury* condemned an Essex magistrate who prosecuted a waggoner for obstruction and inflicted an on-the-spot fine of ten shillings.[85] Ten years later West Country newspapers were highly critical of a Devon magistrate who, after having been fined £5 for violently assaulting his children's nurse, went into an adjacent room to try another assault case.[86] But such incidents appear exceptional and the outcry which they provoked reinforces this assumption. There was a tradition, clearly apparent in the eighteenth century, that magistrates should not try cases in which they had a personal concern;[87] and when they stepped down from the bench they could not be sure that colleagues and friends would find in their favour.[88] The problem is, of course, assessing the extent to which economic and social class, and/or class prejudice displaced a magistrate's impartiality. During the eighteenth century some magistrates enforcing labour legislation were employers in the industries concerned. This was especially true in big manufacturing boroughs, like Norwich, but could also be true in rural manufacturing areas, like Wiltshire. In early nineteenth-century Wigan magistrates linked with local industry appear to have administered justice with relative impartiality, except in cases of industrial theft; but after the Municipal Corporations Act political and sectarian partiality became apparent.[89] Across the Pennines in West Yorkshire some manufacturers in the woollen and worsted trades held summary hearings in their homes or factories, and showed no qualms about judging their own employees on charges of embezzlement.[90] In the various jurisdictions of the Black Country during the second quarter of the nineteenth century there was a change in the composition of the magistracy in the as industrial entrepreneurs began to dominate over landowners; this change was accompanied by increasing activity in prosecuting for industrial theft and in seeking to control the workforce by means of the Master and Servant Act. It has been suggested that while, in comparison with the size of the labour force, prosecutions under the Master and

Servant Act in the third quarter of the century were small in number, they were not confined to exceptional cases. In fact the Act appears to have been regarded as an essential weapon for controlling labour.[91] However changes in the magistracy were quite different in neighbouring Warwickshire where landed gentry displaced clergy on the bench to become the dominant group and where, during industrial troubles, notably those in the mines during the 1840s, most magistrates had no direct interest.[92] Finally it is also probable that the increasing appointment of professional lawyers as stipendiaries and as recorders to supervise the part-time magistrates, particularly at borough sessions, checked the most blatant abuses.

The relaxed, relatively informal magistrates' tribunals of the eighteenth century had little place in the increasingly urbanised England of the nineteenth century with its emphasis on decorum and bureaucratic formality. The system of magistrates sitting singly or in petty sessions was not spread uniformly throughout eighteenth-century England; while petty sessions met in Hampshire and Dorset for example, none appears to have met in Berkshire.[93] Populous urban districts had difficulty in finding gentlemen of the first rank to act as magistrates and 'trading justices' had begun to appear in and around the metropolis during the seventeenth century. These were gentlemen, generally of modest property, who could be relied upon to act in these urban districts for the sake of the fees which they could collect for resolving petty disputes and for granting and signing particular documents. From the beginning of the eighteenth century the 'trading justices' of the Kent parishes bordering London were far busier than the justices of rural Kent; they were looked down upon by their country cousins because they took fees, and some of them became justifiably notorious but, manifestly, they were fulfilling a need.[94] The Bow Street magistrates' office grew out of the trading justice system, though from the mid-eighteenth century the magistrates here, notably Henry and later Sir John Fielding, received money from the Treasury rather than relying on fees. The system of stipendiary magistrates established for London in 1792, primarily as a police measure, created a more general, and more formal precedent for the way in which magistrates adjudicated lesser offences. In 1839, ten years after the creation of the Metropolitan Police, the stipendiary magistrates of London lost their police role and their offices were transformed into the Metropolitan Police Courts, vividly described for the *Illustrated London News* by Angus Reach:

In Bagnigge Wells road . . . that glaring and dusty summer thoroughfare, stands a large pile of buildings, generally ornamented by numerous lounging policemen, and further diversified and adorned by crowds of

*shabby-looking people, a vast proportion whereof may be observed to
have their personal appearance improved by such additional attractions
as are contributed by blackened eyes, plastered-up foreheads, and noses
with broken bridges.*

*The buildings form the Clerkenwell Police Court and its
appurtenances; the lounging constables are the guardians of last night's
peace, waiting to prefer charges against its disturbers; the maltreated
gentry about are the sufferers – some of them, perhaps, the active, as well
as passive partakers in the constant drunken rows which such districts as
Clerkenwell – a favoured abode of those unfortunate helots of the hod,
generally complimented as the 'low Irish' – naturally furnish, from day to
day, for police adjudication.*

*We enter – we traverse a long, dirty passage: the passages leading to
Police Courts are always dirty – the walls are always greasy – glazed, so
to speak, by the constant friction of frowsy rags. A turn to the left – a
push at a swinging door – and we stand in the midst of a similar crowd
to that which we left outside, to that which we passed in the lobby – the
disreputable public of a Police Court.*

*The room is a larger one than most of the 'Worthy Magistrates' are
blessed with – in fact, a handsome, airy, wainscotted apartment. You
glance at once towards the judicial armchair, and see it faced and flanked
by the usual Police Court arrangements – a square, open box in the
centre, bounded, so to speak, on one side by the bench, on the others by
the particular boxes occupied by Clerks, Police Inspectors, Reporters,
Barristers, and last, not least, Culprits. The part of the room not taken
up by these pens and boxes, forms the locus standi for that portion
of the enlightened public who come to improve their tempers by the
contemplation of the placid equanimity of a Greenwood – or to see how
perfectly even the balance of justice, as between a private individual and
a policeman, can be held by a Combe.[95]*

By the middle of the century there were thirteen such courts in London
with twenty-three magistrates like Messrs Combe and Greenwood, dis-
pensing justice in cases of misdemeanour such as common assault, drunk
and disorderly, gambling, suspicious behaviour, unlawful possession and
vagrancy. Justice in these courts was speedy with little time available for
deliberation; at the beginning of the twentieth century Edward Carpenter
reckoned that cases took 'on an average say three minutes to dispose of'.[96]
At the same time, and in keeping with the notion that the law was impartial, these magistrates were also charged with providing 'a system of poor

Clerkenwell Police Court, 1847
The magistrate, wearing the top hat, is Mr Greenwood, described by Angus Reach as 'a Yorkshireman –
a hard, tetchy, irritable, high-dried Whig. The *Times* and the *Examiner*, in particular, have kept a sharp
look out upon him; and his decisions have given rise to many a bitter article.' © Illustrated London
News Ltd/Mary Evans

man's justice' which could 'encourage in the common people a habit of
looking to the law for protection'. There is no question but that many of
them took this charge seriously, and that they sometimes used their power
and authority to conform to popular conceptions of justice rather than to
the strict letter of the law.[97]

A few fast-growing provincial urban districts began contemplating the
appointment of stipendiary magistrates from the moment they appeared
in London; but the first such appointments were not made until the early
nineteenth century and it was not until 1835 that legislation made it possible for any borough that so wished to appoint a stipendiary. The arguments in favour of stipendiaries were manifold. Many of the fastest growing
urban-industrial sprawls had no resident magistrate since they were not
incorporated boroughs and county magistrates, even with property in the
town, were often reluctant to commit themselves to the time necessary for

6 (1981), pp. 155–84; *idem*, 'Repression, "terror" and the rule of law in England during the decade of the French Revolution,' *E.H.R.*, C (1985), pp. 801–25.

2 *Northampton Mercury*, 6 and 13 August 1753.

3 George Rudé, *Criminal and Victim: Crime and Society in Early Nineteenth-Century England*, Clarendon Press, Oxford, 1985, pp. 59–60. Rudé cites four examples; the first three (from 1810, 1820 and 1830 respectively) were instances of the victim being impeded in his pursuit of the offender; in the fourth instance (from 1840) the victim was helped.
   Rudé asks: 'does this denote a change in popular attitudes towards criminal and victim?' Obviously it will take far more than four examples to prove anything like this, and it should also be remembered that the hue and cry had a long pedigree.

4 Raphael Samuel (ed.), *East End Underworld: Chapters in the Life of Arthur Harding*, RKP, London, 1981, pp. 43–5.

5 Peter Linebaugh, 'The Tyburn riot against the surgeons', in Douglas Hay, Peter Linebaugh *et al.* (eds), *Albion's Fatal Tree: Crime and Society in Eighteenth-Century England*, Allen Lane, 1975, pp. 107–8.

6 *Huntingdon, Bedford and Cambridge Gazette*, 2 and 16 August 1817; Beds. R.O. QSR 23/1817/230–31.

7 *Huntingdon, Bedford and Cambridge Gazette*, 15 and 22 July 1815, 22 March 1817; Beds. R.O. QSR 23/1817/508.

8 HO 45.7323. My thanks to Professor John Bohstedt for this reference.

9 David Jones, *Crime in Nineteenth-Century Wales*, University of Wales Press, Cardiff, 1992, pp. 11–12; for an example of charivari or rough music in mid-nineteenth-century Liverpool see *Liverpool Mercury*, 12 November 1855, though the cause appears to have been sexual transgression rather than crime.

10 In June 1847, for example, Ann Wood, a widow of Edingley, Nottinghamshire, left her house in the care of one of her daughters. In the mother's absence a second daughter stole several articles of clothing together with some money and then ran off. She was eventually arrested in Derbyshire by a police constable. Notts. R.O. QSD/1847. See also Jennifer Davis, 'Prosecutions and their context: The use of the criminal law in late nineteenth-century London', in Douglas Hay and Francis Snyder (eds), *Policing and Prosecution in Britain 1750–1850*, Oxford U.P., Oxford, 1989, pp. 415–16.

11 Notts. R.O. QSM 1788–96; East Retford 10 October 1794 and 16 January 1795.

12 OBP t17961130–43.

13 Beds. R.O. PM 2629, Notebook of Francis Pym (1832–34); see also Beds. RO. QSR 1830/34.

14 Notts. R.O. QSM 1761–67; Nottingham 13 January 1766.

15 Beds. R.O. PM 2629, Notebook of Pym.

16 Davis, 'Law breaking and law enforcement', pp. 307–10.

17 John Styles, 'Sir John Fielding and the problem of criminal investigation in eighteenth-century England', *T.R.H.S.*, 5th series, 33 (1983), pp. 127–50; *idem*, 'Print and policing: Crime advertising in eighteenth-century provincial England', in **Hay** and **Snyder** (eds), *Policing and Prosecution*; **Gwenda Morgan** and **Peter Rushton**, *Rogues, Thieves and the Rule of Law: The Problem of Law Enforcement in North-East England, 1718–1800*, U.C.L. Press, London, 1998, p. 38.
    In 1827 John Pilstow, a shopkeeper of Northampton, stopped at a Woburn Inn on his way to London. During the night he was robbed. He promptly had some handbills printed offering a £1 reward for the arrest of a suspect; the handbills led directly to an arrest two days after the robbery, in Leicester. Beds. R.O. QSR 1827/295.

18 **Elizabeth Silverthorne** (ed.), *Deposition Book of Richard Wyatt J.P. 1767–76*, Surrey Records Society, vol. xxx, 1978, nos 64–7; Beds. R.O. QSR 1830/495.

19 Wilts. R.O. Stourhead Archive, 383/955 Justice Book of R. C. Hoare 1785–1815 has several examples of warrants issued on suspicion, for example: '21 Feby [1795] Granted a Warrant on Information of Giles Jupe of Mere to search the houses of Edmund Williams, Thomas Herridge, Hugh Deverill, Edward Mills, John Miles and Edward Avery, for wood stolen from the coppice of Deverill Longwood.'
    Wood was found in the possession of Herridge and Mills, and acting summarily Hoare fined them both 10s.
    For an example leading to a more serious charge see OBP t180101114-5 (Hannam) for a warrant issued to Richard Jones, a soap and perfume manufacturer of Shoreditch, to search the lodgings of his former foreman whom he rightly suspected of pilfering large quantities of goods to set up in the trade on his own account.

20 Beds. R.O. 25/1822/610 contains a letter from a magistrate, the Revd Orlebar Smith, suggesting that a certain Sinfield be indicted for felony. Sinfield had gone to Smith for a warrant accusing William Pilgrim of stealing his watch. He had then used the warrant to frighten Pilgrim into returning the watch and to paying Sinfield 30s. in compensation; the business completed to his satisfaction, Sinfield had then, illegally, destroyed the warrant.

21 Beds. R.O. QSR 17/1792/119.

22 Silverthorne (ed.), *Deposition Book of Richard Wyatt*, no. 207.

23 **Elizabeth Crittal** (ed.), *The Justicing Notebook of William Hunt 1744–49*, Wiltshire Record Society, vol. xxxvii, 1982, pp. 13–14.

47 John E. Archer, '*By a Flash and a Scare.*' *Arson, Animal Maiming and Poaching in East Anglia, 1815–1870*, Clarendon Press, Oxford, 1990, pp. 145–7.

48 U.C.L. Chadwick MSS 11 ff. 50–1: G division response to q. 22, and see also ff. 47–8 responses to q. 21.

49 U.C.L. Chadwick MSS 11 f. 41: C division response to q. 17; there were similar responses from other divisions.

50 U.C.L. Chadwick MSS 11 f. 39: L division response to q. 16.

51 U.C.L. Chadwick MSS 11 f. 44: V division response to q. 19. As late as the 1880s many of the same reasons were being given as deterring prosecutions in Wales, even in cases of arson. (Jones, 'Welsh and crime', p. 88 and note 22.)

52 *Hansard*, new series xiv (1826), col. 1232.

53 Quoted in Hay, 'Controlling the English prosecutor', p. 176.

54 Hay, 'Controlling the English prosecutor', pp. 178–9 lists fourteen acts, excluding the Vexatious Indictments Act, passed between 1791 and 1888 which infringed the discretion of the private prosecutor.

55 Emsley, 'Aspect of Pitt's "terror"', pp. 161–2; Gyford, '"Men of Bad Character"', pp. 18–19.

56 Clive Emsley and Robert D. Storch, 'Prosecution and the police in England since 1700', *Bulletin of the International Association for the History of Crime and Criminal Justice*, 18 (1993), pp. 45–57. See also David Philips, *Crime and Authority in Victorian England*, Croom Helm, London, 1977, pp. 101 and 123–4.

57 Charles Dickens, 'The Ruffian', in *The Uncommercial Traveller*; also *idem*, footnote to 'Stories for the first of April', *Miscellaneous Papers* (first published in *Household Words*).

58 *P.P.* 1854–55 (481) xii, *Select Committee on Public Prosecutors*, q. 2929.

59 U.C.L. Chadwick MSS 11 f. 36.

60 HO 45.2742, Yarker to Grey, 6 September 1849; HO 48.41, Law Officers' Opinion, 7 November 1849.

61 In 1859, for example, of the ninety-two indictments brought before the Nottinghamshire quarter sessions, the police preferred only fourteen and a parish constable one. For the limited number of prosecutions by the police in London see Davis, 'Law breaking and law enforcement', p. 195.

62 *The Times*, 11 September 1856, for a letter from a Cornish attorney (following similar complaints from Devon and Yorkshire), critical of the paucity of costs allowed by Cornish magistrates and instancing a respectable tradesman who, in order to prosecute a serious case of felony, had to travel fifty miles and spend three nights in a hotel, for all of which he was allowed one guinea in expenses.

63 *Bedford Mercury*, 30 March 1844, quoting *The Globe*.

64 David C. Churchill, 'Rethinking the state monopolisation thesis: The historiography of policing and criminal justice in nineteenth-century England', *CHS*, **18**, 1 (2014), pp. 131–52 (at pp. 143–5).

65 Emsley and Storch, 'Prosecution and the police', pp. 51–6.

66 In six of the twelve cases brought before the Bedfordshire Epiphany Sessions for 1832 the Chairman of the bench noted 'Defence says nothing'. Beds. R.O. PM 2629, Notebook of Pym.

67 For a general description of the plight of the accused in court see **V. A. C. Gatrell**, *The Hanging Tree: Execution and the English People, 1780–1868*, Clarendon Press, Oxford, 1994, pp. 537–8.

68 OBP t17970426-23 (Angas) and t18570511-600 (Forbes); see also Rudé, *Criminal and Victim*, pp. 58–9.

69 For the development of the legal profession at the Old Bailey see **Allyson N. May**, *The Bar and the Old Bailey*, University of North Carolina Press, Durham, NC, 2003.

70 *Bedford Mercury*, 23 March 1844.

71 *Hansard*, 3rd series xvi (1833), cols 1202–3.

72 Philips, *Crime and Authority*, pp. 104–5.

73 **Graham Parker**, 'The prisoner in the box – the making of the Criminal Evidence Act', in **J. A. Guy** and **H. G. Beale** (eds), *Law and Social Change in British History*, Royal Historical Society, London, 1984.

74 **A. H. Manchester**, *A Modern Legal History of England and Wales 1750–1950*, Butterworths, London, 1980, p. 100; **Brian Abel-Smith** and **Robert Stevens**, *Lawyers and the Courts: A Sociological Study of the English Legal System 1750–1965*, Heinemann, London, 1967, pp. 32 and 135–6.
   It is worth noting that a form of legal aid had existed for the accused in Scotland since the late Middle Ages.

75 **John H. Langbein**, *The Origins of Adversary Criminal Trial*, Oxford U.P., Oxford, 2003, pp. 342–3.

76 **Martin Madan**, *Thoughts on Executive Justice*, London, 1785, pp. 143–4; *Bedford Mercury*, 23 March 1844. See also Gatrell, *The Hanging Tree*, pp. 529–41.

77 OBP t17660116–2.

78 King, *Crime, Justice and Discretion*, p. 224.

79 For Blackstone and the eighteenth-century debate on summary jurisdiction see **Norma Landau**, *The Justices of the Peace 1679–1760*, University of California Press, Berkeley and Los Angeles, CA, 1984, pp. 343–5; *London Chronicle*, 12 March 1772; *The Times*, 4 May 1829.

80 Munsche, *Gentlemen and Poachers*, chapters 1 and 4 *passim*.

81 *Hansard*, new series viii (1823), cols 1292–8.

82 Munsche, *Gentlemen and Poachers*, p. 162; while noting that game offenders were probably punished more severely, King found a far greater incidence of wood, fruit and vegetable theft brought before summary jurisdiction in eighteenth-century Essex (*Crime, Justice and Discretion*, pp. 99–103).

83 **John Styles**, 'Embezzlement, industry and the law in England 1500–1800', in **Maxine Berg, Pat Hudson** and **Michael Sonenscher** (eds), *Manufacture in Town and Country Before the Factory*, Cambridge U.P., Cambridge, 1983, pp. 200–4.

84 **R. E. Swift**, 'Crime, law and order in two English towns during the early nineteenth century: The experience of Exeter and Wolverhampton 1815–56', unpublished Ph.D., University of Birmingham, 1981, pp. 329–30.

85 *Kent and Essex Mercury*, 27 January 1824, quoted in Gyford, ' "Men of Bad Character" ', p. 24.

86 Swift, 'Crime, law and order', pp. 125–6.

87 Landau, *Justices of the Peace*, pp. 356–8; Silverthorne (ed.), *Deposition Book of Richard Wyatt*, p. x and nos 108–10.

88 Francis Pym recorded stepping down from chairmanship of the Bedfordshire bench at the Midsummer Sessions in 1833 when Samuel Barnes was tried for a larceny in stealing wood from Pym's land. He also recorded 'verdict of *acquitted* on the ground that it was trespass and not a felony'. Beds. R.O. PM2629.

89 **P. C. Barrett**, 'Crime and punishment in a Lancashire industrial town: Law and social change in the borough of Wigan, 1800–50', unpublished M.Phil., Liverpool Polytechnic, 1980, pp. 84–6 and 88–98.

90 **Barry Godfrey**, 'Judicial impartiality and the use of criminal law against labour: The sentencing of workplace appropriators in Northern England, 1840–1880', *C.H.S.*, 3 (1999), pp. 57–72 (at p. 66).

91 **D. C. Woods**, 'The operation of the Master and Servants Act in the Black Country 1858–75', *Midland History*, vii (1982), pp. 93–115.

92 **R. Quinault**, 'The Warwickshire country magistracy and public order, c. 1830–70', in **John Stevenson** and **Roland Quinault** (eds), *Popular Protest and Public Order: Six Studies in British History, 1790–1820*, Allen and Unwin, London, 1974, pp. 189, 207.

93 **Olwen Hufton**, 'Crime in pre-industrial Europe', *Newsletter of the International Association for the History of Crime and Criminal Justice*, 4 (1981), p. 15.

94 Landau, *Justices of the Peace*, chapter 6.

95 *Illustrated London News*, 22 May 1847, p. 332. Charles Dickens gave a far less attractive picture with his portrayal of Mr Fang (based on the notorious Mr Laing of Hatton Garden) in *Oliver Twist*, chapter xi.

96 **Edward Carpenter**, *Prisons, Police and Punishment*, London, 1905, p. 70.

97 **Jennifer Davis**, ' "A poor man's system of justice": The London police courts in the second half of the nineteenth century', *H.J.*, **27** (1984), pp. 309–35: quotations at p. 315. See also *idem*, 'Law breaking and law enforcement', pp. 297–8.

98 *Hansard*, new series xviii (1828), cols 166–7; *The Times*, 4 May 1829.

99 *Hansard*, 3rd series lii (1840), col. 652.

100 *Bedford Mercury*, 11 February 1843.

101 *Hansard*, 3rd series xc (1847), cols 430–8, and xcii (1847), col. 38.

102 *Hansard*, 3rd series xcii (1847), col. 46.

103 *Hansard*, 3rd series cxxxvi (1855), col. 1871, cxxxvii (1855), col. 1168, and cxxxix (1855), cols 1867, 2018.

104 Abel-Smith and Stevens, *Lawyers and the Courts*, p. 31.

105 Philips, *Crime and Authority*, pp. 132–4.
    Reference to the quarter sessions minute books of both Beds. and Notts. shows the dramatic decline in cases brought before these courts in the second half of the century. At the Epiphany Sessions in the middle years of the century, for example, the counties were hearing, on average, about twenty and between thirty and forty cases respectively; by the late 1890s these numbers had fallen, generally, to less than half a dozen in both instances. At the same time the number of cases heard summarily was soaring; at the Epiphany Sessions by the mid-1860s Beds. was recording around fifty and Notts. around one hundred cases under the Criminal Justice Act, with another half dozen or so under the Juvenile Offenders Act. In addition they were also filing, respectively, around 150 and around 300 other summary convictions for assault, drink offences, malicious damage, game offences, highway offences, vagrancy, etc.

106 *Hansard*, 3rd series ccxliii (1879), cols 1099 and 110–13, and ccxlvii (1879), col. 1703.

107 Abel-Smith and Stevens, *Lawyers and the Courts*, pp. 31–2; **David Bentley**, *English Criminal Justice in the Nineteenth Century*, London, Hambledon Press, 1998, p. 20.

108 *Hansard*, new series vi (1822), col. 1320.

109 Abel-Smith and Stevens, *Lawyers and the Courts*, pp. 31–2.

CHAPTER 9

Detection and prevention: the old police and the new

The period 1750–1900 witnessed a marked increase in the number of professionals employed in England and Wales to combat crime. The line taken by an old school of police historians, leaning heavily on the arguments of early nineteenth-century police reformers, was that the old system of police was inadequate and ineffective. Recognition of this situation, the story went, led Sir Robert Peel, as Home Secretary, to establish the Metropolitan Police in London in 1829. The Municipal Corporations Act 1835 spread the new system of police into provincial boroughs. The Rural Constabulary Act 1839 enabled counties, or parts of counties, to establish similar, effective police forces. The County and Borough Police Act 1856 capped this legislation making the new police obligatory for all local authorities. This was a Whig interpretation. It was rooted in the idea of progress and looked back from an idealised contemporary model assuming that this was the model which far-sighted reformers and politicians of the late eighteenth and nineteenth centuries had in mind. The first serious academic critics of the Whig view emphasised how the duties of the new police were in keeping with the control requirements of a new capitalist society. More recent research has drawn attention to developments during the eighteenth century and to continuities between the old police and the new.[1]

For most of the eighteenth century in England, as elsewhere in Europe, the word 'police' was applied, not to an institution but to the management and government of a particular piece of territory, particularly a town or city. In England the idea of a uniformed body of policemen patrolling the streets to prevent crime and disorder was anathema. Such a force smacked of the absolutism of continental states. The models for such police forces were to be found in the organisation commanded by the *lieutenant général de police* in Paris, and in the military police, the *maréchaussée*, which patrolled the main roads of provincial France. The fact that these mod-els were French, in itself, was sufficient to make many eighteenth-century English gentlemen consider them as inimical to English liberty. Policing in eighteenth-century England was perceived as a local government task, and like other areas of local government it depended upon local men being selected, or voluntarily coming forward, to serve in an official capacity, but generally for a limited period, part-time, and usually unpaid.[2]

The constables of eighteenth-century England were neither a preven-tive nor a detective police. The high constables of counties were often men of some social standing. These were selected in a variety of ways, depending on traditional local practice. They had a variety of tasks, the most important of which was supervision of the collection of the county rates. In respect of crime, they had an obligation to pursue any felonies reported to them, and this might involve primitive detective work as when, in 1818, John Shaw, high constable of the hundred of Redbornstoke in Bedfordshire found a footprint near the hiding place of some stolen wine and was subsequently able to fit a shoe to it.[3] The high constables had supervision of the petty constables. The latter were men of less social sig-nificance; again they were selected in a variety of ways depending upon local custom. The petty constable's tasks were many and varied, and he was allowed expenses and fees. The pursuit of offenders was often under-taken by victims, as described in the preceding chapter; but the constable was charged with making arrests. He was also required to serve warrants, to move offenders from place to place – either transporting a vagrant out of the parish, or taking an accused party to court; he might even have to accommodate offenders, temporarily, in his home. Such tasks were bur-densome; if a man had a trade, any time spent on constable's duties could cost him business. Occasionally the tasks brought threats and sometimes actual violence, as a glance at any eighteenth- or early nineteenth- century newspaper or run of quarter sessions indictments will show. In 1817, for example, Constable Henry Thompson of Ruardean in Gloucestershire was shot dead by William Turner after he had arrested the latter's wife in pos-session of stolen wheat. A more typical example occurred one Saturday evening in the late summer of 1827 when Thomas Franklin, the constable of Leighton Buzzard, was called to a public house where a quarrel had led to blows. William Smith, a butcher, who was to go to Franklin's aid, described what happened as he was walking past the pub:

I saw Thomas Franklin . . . coming out . . . backwards. John Brandon . . . was opposite and close to the constable. I saw the said John

Brandon strike the said constable twice 'bang full in the face' the blows knocked the constable down on his back John Brandon fell down with him. Sarah Adams . . . got on top of the constable and jostled his head against the ground. . . . The constable appeared very much hurt and his face was all over blood.[4]

Brandon and Adams were both indicted for assault.

Yet whatever the burdens and dangers there were men prepared to take on the post of constable full time, and some acted with vigour. William Payne who was a carpenter by trade provides an example of an enthusiastic constable keen to enforce morality as well as apprehend criminal offenders. He acted out of a sense of civic duty and was highly regarded by those living in his district of London who shared his perspectives. Elsewhere, in return for an initial payment some individuals agreed to act in place of men selected as constables and then sought to earn their living through the fees. There was nothing especially new in this; Elbow, the simple constable in Shakespeare's *Measure for Measure*, was described as acting in this way. Of course the fact that some men were prepared to take on the tasks of constable full time does not mean that they were, necessarily, any good at the job. Many parish constables probably were as bad and as uncommitted to their tasks as the police reformers made out. But others, like Payne, were competent and were relied upon; a serious analysis of the men who fulfilled this role during the eighteenth and early nineteenth centuries is long overdue.[5]

Preventive policing in eighteenth-century England was largely confined to urban areas where watches patrolled the streets after dark. Shakespeare provided a comic example with the watchmen who act under the bumbling Dogberry and Verges in *Much Ado About Nothing*. The problem is that too often these fictional, comic characters have been taken as representatives of a reality spanning the period from the Tudors to the late Hanoverians because they fit so well with the police reformers' condemnations of the old system of policing.[6] In fact eighteenth- and early nineteenth-century watchmen have been as poorly researched as the constables, and it is becoming increasingly clear that in some metropolitan parishes there were determined attempts to ensure that the night watch was competent and capable a hundred years before the Metropolitan Police took to the streets.[7] Some watchmen knew their job. They were fully prepared to stop men on suspicion, and their suspicions could prove valid; one night towards the end of 1796 John Wilson was picked up on suspicion by two London watchmen; he was taken to the Hanover Square parish watch-house where he was searched by a constable and found to have five pewter pots concealed about his person; the pots had been taken from a pub in Carnaby Street and Wilson was subsequently tried and convicted at the Old Bailey. Indeed evidence from an Old Bailey burglary trial twenty years later suggests watchmen in some parts of the metropolis were behaving in the active and observant way which, according to the Whig historians, was introduced only with the new Metropolitan Police:

On the night of the 12th December, I was calling four o'clock in the morning; I came by Mr. Levy's house, in Wentworth-street; I saw the prisoner standing in the court there; I did not know him before, I thought he might live in the court; I went up the court, and took particular notice of his dress, as I passed him; I went on, and returned again; I missed him; I went up the court, and saw Levy's side door was open, it is in the court; I returned to my box, and in a few minutes, the prisoner came by my box; I stepped out, and called to him, he stopped, and I crossed over to him, and asked him what he did at the house round the corner – he said 'what house', and seemed strange. I asked him, what he had got upon him, his pockets appeared full, and bulky – he said, 'nothing at all', and that he was a different character to what I took him to be . . . Levy's house is considered a receiving house. I have been on that beat fifteen months.

The watchman found stolen lace hidden in the prisoner's hat, and took him into custody.[8] The Select Committee enquiring into the police of the metropolis in 1828 heard largely complimentary comments on the watches in Marylebone, St James's, and St George's Hanover Square. The majority of these watchmen appear to have been ex-soldiers, 'stout tall fellows', according to the inspector in St James's 'not exceeding forty years of age'.[9] This is not to argue that the watch was not in need of reform, but rather that the traditional image of the 'Charlie' as old, decrepit and, like as not drunk or asleep when needed, is a generalisation often wide of the mark.

Provincial magistrates might be found who were interested in detecting and apprehending offenders, and they were prepared to go to considerable trouble and expense in so doing.[10] But if a victim could not follow up an offence in person, with friends, or by advertisement, the only other recourse – apart from a visit in rural areas to the cunning man – was to a thief-taker. Until the establishment of a special group of thief-takers in the office of the Bow Street magistrates in the middle of the eighteenth century, the thief-takers were private individuals. They lived off the rewards from the courts for bringing offenders to justice, and the rewards from victims who paid to get property returned.[11] Both kinds of reward were liable to abuse. The reputation of the thief-takers is low primarily because of the notorious career of Jonathan Wild, the self-appointed 'Thief-taker General of Great Britain and Ireland' who was exposed, in 1725, as a receiver of stolen goods who kept himself in the thief-taking business by the occasional sacrifice of a thief on the gallows. The Stephen McDaniel affair which blew up some thirty years later was less far-reaching, but re-emphasised the dangers of rewarding thief-takers by results when the result, as like as not, was an innocent body swinging from the gallows.[12] Yet not all pre-police thief-takers were like Wild and McDaniel, especially the semi-official detectives like Richard Green who combined his detective work with being keeper of the lock-up at Knott Hill, Manchester, and John and Daniel Forrester who worked in the City of London from 1817 to 1857.[13]

It was the metropolis which witnessed the major developments and the major proposals for police reform during the eighteenth century; both the square mile of the City of London proper, which had its own police system organised under the Lord Mayor and the City Marshals, and the sprawls of the City of Westminster, urban Middlesex and, south of the Thames, urban Surrey.[14] The best-known architects of these developments and proposals were the Fieldings who established the group of paid thief-takers – the celebrated Bow Street Runners – in the 1750s, and who, after some abortive starts, organised paid patrols of part-time constables circulating the central thoroughfares and the main roads into the metropolis from evening until midnight. By the end of the century the Bow Street Patrol consisted of sixty-eight men divided into thirteen parties. Sir John Fielding drew up plans for a centralised police for London with five or six separate police offices under the overall supervision of Bow Street. This central office, he argued, could act as a clearing house for information about different crimes and different offenders; detailed information and descriptions, readily available to different peace officers, were regarded by the Fieldings as central in the 'war' against crime. Sir John's proposals for a systematised and centralised police in London came to nothing during his lifetime, but they influenced the abortive legislation of the 1780s and the Middlesex Justice Act 1792.

In 1772 and 1773 Sir John circulated the clerks of the peace of all the English and Welsh counties with his General Preventative Plan. His idea was to make the Bow Street Office a central clearing house for information about serious crimes and offenders encompassing the whole country. He wanted provincial magistrates to supply Bow Street with details of offenders and offences, gaolers to supply descriptions of those committed to their custody via the assize calendars already received in his office, and both officials and members of the public to give descriptions of stolen horses. The proposal was well received and, from the autumn of 1773 with government backing to the tune of £400 per annum, this information was collected in Bow Street, collated and circulated in the form of a newspaper, *The Hue and Cry*. The extent to which the circulation of information in this way improved the clear-up rate cannot be ascertained, for one thing there is no data on which to base a measurement of the situation beforehand, yet it appears to have contributed to some arrests.

In February 1775 Fielding circulated a further set of proposals. These were far more radical, recommending what would have amounted to a system of paid professional policemen. Fielding recommended that high constables be resident on the main roads for at least one hundred miles distance from London. They were to display a board announcing their office outside their home, to undertake the pursuit of offenders, to keep a horse for these pursuits and to be paid a salary. In addition, the number of petty constables was to be increased. The proposals were received coolly. This probably reflected reluctance on the part of the county benches to reorganise the tasks of their constables, especially when high constables were men of some standing who would have balked at being simply the pursuers of common felons. Probably also the magistrates could see little value in the proposals for their own localities; provincial England was not the urban sprawl of London with its apparently disproportionate amount of serious crime. Local constables could handle the vagrants on the roads; there were few highway robberies in the provinces and seemingly few fugitives moving along the roads from one district to another. What appeared of value for London to suppress the city's unique crime problem, had little value beyond.[15]

Yet whatever the concerns of men like Fielding about crime in eighteenth-century London, the fear of a French system of police was at least as great. A bill brought before parliament in 1785 proposed dividing the entire metropolis into nine police divisions each with three stipendiary magistrates and twenty-five constables; it foundered partly on the fear that a system of regular police was alien to England, and partly because of the hostility of the City of London which mustered its powerful parliamentary lobby to protect its independent jurisdiction. When, seven years later, the Middlesex Justice Bill was introduced, the territory of the Lord Mayor and his Marshals was studiously omitted. The legislation of 1792 established seven police offices, six north of the Thames – Queen's Square, Westminster; Great Marlborough Street; Hatton Garden, Shoreditch; Whitechapel; Shadwell – and one south of the river in Southwark. Each office had three stipendiary magistrates and six constables. Among the first of the magistrates was Colquhoun who poured a steady stream of voluminous letters in miniscule writing in the direction of different offices of state; many of these letters urged various reforms and improvements.[16] Attempts to spread the system failed, probably because of expense, but in 1798 Colquhoun was instrumental in the creation of the Thames Police Office at Wapping with, ultimately, three stipendiaries and one hundred constables to police the river. The system of stipendiary magistrates and their constables working alongside the Bow Street Patrol, and the various parish constables and watches (Table 9.1), with the City jealously guarding its separate jurisdiction, saw London into the new century. The stipendiary magistrates and some of their constables rapidly assumed the role of experts on crime to be consulted when ministers or parliament, pressurised by reformers like Romilly and Mackintosh or by events like the Ratcliffe Highway murders, mounted enquiries into aspects of crime and policing in London. In February 1811 a circular was sent to the police offices requesting the magistrates' opinions on whether the recent abolition of the death penalty for picking pockets had led to any change in the incidence of the crime, of prosecutions for the crime, or convictions.[17] Magistrates and constables became regular witnesses before parliamentary committees. Some of the constables, like George Ruthven and John Townsend of Bow Street, acquired formidable reputations as detectives; the assistance of such Bow Street officers was often sought by provincial authorities faced with a spate of robberies, a gang of poachers or a difficult murder. Yet the concerns about 'blood money' continued. Most of the constables had underworld informants known as 'Noses',[18] and on occasions links with the underworld became rather too friendly. Even Bow Street officers were suspended and occasionally prosecuted for compounding, or for conspiring with offenders whom they subsequently brought before the courts on capital charges so as to claim the reward.[19]

The revelations of corruption, the scare created by the Ratcliffe Highway murders, the publication of statistics giving a public picture of crime, the reports of crowd behaviour in revolutionary Paris which aggravated fearful recollections of the Gordon Riots, combined with the writings of men like Colquhoun to make gentlemen of property concerned about the policing of London. Yet parliamentary committee after parliamentary committee was reluctant to recommend a completely new police system; a centralised system still appeared inimicable to English liberty, it was something peculiarly French, and under Napoleon the police system of the old enemy had achieved an authoritarian model of even more alarming proportions.

TABLE 9.1 *Watchmen, patrols, superintendents and beadles acting in the jurisdiction of the Police Magistrates, Union Hall, Southwark, 1 January 1812*

Parish or district	Population	Number of beadles/superintendents	Number of watchmen	Number of 'patrols'	Total police
Christchurch, Southwark	11,050	1	23	–	24
St George, Southwark	27,967	1	17	2	20
St John, Southwark	8,370	1	14	–	15
St Olave, Southwark	7,917	1	16	–	17
St Thomas, Southwark	1,466†	–	2 (private watch)	–	2
St Saviour's Southwark	15,349	1	11	–	12
St Saviour's Clink Libery	–	2	–	14	16
Manor of Hatcham				Patrolled by Bow Street Patrol	
Bermondsey	19,530	1	13	–	14
Camberwell		1	16	3	20
Dulwich	11,309‡	–	2	1 (horseman paid by subscription)	3
Peckham		1	7	2	10
Clapham Town	5,083§	1	14	2	17
Clapham Road		–	10	2	12
Lambeth	41,644		Patrolled by Surrey Watch, some private watchmen, numbers unknown		–
Newington	23,853	1	24	2	27
Rotherhithe	12,114	1	14	6	21
Streatham	2,729	1	2	6	9
Surrey Watch	–	1	42	2 (horsemen)	45

Source: Based on information in HO 42.114.29, and population statistics drawn from the 1811 census
The area of urban Surrey covered by the magistrates at Union Hall was the largest jurisdiction of the seven police offices established in 1792; from the centre in the borough of Southwark it ran about five miles south-west up the Thames to Clapham, four miles east downstream to Rotherhithe, and six miles due south to Streatham
† Includes the 'population' of St Thomas's and Guy's Hospitals
‡ Population of the Parish of Camberwell, which included Dulwich and Peckham
§ Population of Clapham Parish

Early in 1822 Robert Peel became Home Secretary. He was determined to reform and revise the criminal code and he considered the establishment of a preventive police as integral to this. His involvement in the creation of the Police Preservation Force when Chief Secretary for Ireland during the preceding decade, had convinced him of the utility of police reform. He and other liberal, reforming Tories did not consider that police were a threat to English liberty. Peel's police reforms were centred on London and, initially, on the expanding Bow Street establishment; in 1805 a horse patrol had been established and in 1821 a dismounted night patrol. In the summer of 1822 Peel set up a force of twenty-four men as the Bow Street day patrol. These men, mainly ex-soldiers, wore a uniform of blue coat and red waistcoat – hence their nickname of 'redbreasts'; they patrolled the main streets of the centre of the metropolis between 9 a.m. and 7 p.m. In 1828 Peel set up a new parliamentary committee into the police of London; and many of the men appointed shared his ideas. The committee recommended the creation of a centralised, uniformed, preventive police for London, and in the following year Peel skilfully guided the legislation establishing the Metropolitan Police through parliament; he carefully avoided a confrontation with the City by omitting the square mile from the jurisdiction of his new force.

The view of the Whig police historians was that 1829 was the turning point. They considered that the new Metropolitan Police checked crime and disorder, provided a model for the rest of the country and, indeed, for the rest of the world. The reformers, from the Fieldings to Colquhoun, and on to Peel and the first two commissioners of the Metropolitan Police, Colonel Charles Rowan and Richard Mayne, were portrayed as far-sighted men; those who opposed the reforms as un-English or who criticised the police as a military body, as 'gendarmes', were perceived as myopic, foolish, or worse. The creation of a police force of 3,000 uniformed men answerable directly to a minister of state was, indeed, something new and something possibly deserving the adjective 'revolutionary' in the English context. But the new police force, with its uniformed men and hierarchical structure, was not a logical extension of the developments originating with the Fieldings. It is debatable whether the new police provided, overnight, a new level of efficiency in the struggle against crime. Moreover the point noted earlier with reference to provincial magistrates' reluctance to adopt Fielding's proposal in 1775, might also help to explain the opposition to change in the provinces over the next few decades: what relevance did this metropolitan model have for the rest of the country?

The police reform clauses of the Municipal Corporations Act 1835 appear to have been included, not so much from any recognised success of the metropolitan model, but because municipal policing had always been the preserve of local government, and if the entire system of municipal government was to be reformed and rationalised, then it was logical, indeed necessary, to include municipal policing. Some boroughs appear to have had disciplined and fairly efficient police systems at their disposal before the act. Indeed, much of the Bank of England's relatively successful campaign against false money had depended on the use of the existing police arrangements.[20] What was singularly absent was any degree of uniformity. The 1835 act required boroughs to establish watch committees which, in turn, were to appoint police forces. Yet while watch committees generally appear to have been set up fairly quickly, many boroughs were dilatory in fulfilling the statutory obligations relating to police forces; of the 178 boroughs mentioned in the 1835 act, only one hundred could claim to have police forces by the beginning of 1838, and fifteen years later at least six still had no force.[21] In some boroughs the creation of police merely meant that various town functionaries like the sword bearer, the beadle and the watchmen simply donned uniforms and began to be called policemen. The nine policemen of the borough of Bedford appointed in January 1836 included the mayor's sergeant, the bellman and the beadle; and the old system of one group of men to patrol by day and another by night was maintained into the 1850s. The division of day and night police was similarly maintained in Exeter and Nottingham where the new police were also largely recruited from the old.[22] In towns without charters local worthies had long been developing police systems to their own needs. Some had their own lighting and watching committees established through private acts of parliament. The Lighting and Watching Act passed by parliament in 1833 provided an umbrella under which urban districts could set up such committees without any special legislation. A private act had enabled Wolverhampton to establish a watch in 1814; a police force was established in the town in 1837, eleven years before incorporation. The worthies of Wolverhampton recruited Richard Castle, a sergeant of the Metropolitan Police, to command their new force; but half of the twelve-man force were veterans of the watch.[23] In 1838 the leading residents of Horncastle in Lincolnshire, with a population of just under 4,500, determined to establish a police force under the terms provided by the Lighting and Watching Act 1833. They approached the commissioners of the Metropolitan Police for a possible chief policeman, but were informed that no member of that force would go to Horncastle for less than 30s. a week. In the event they were lucky enough to find a local man who had served in London and who was willing to act for 16s. a week. The new police of Horncastle consisted of two men.[24] The market town of Hudder-sfield, now at the centre of a booming textile trade, was different again. It established a watch committee under its own Improvement Act of 1848. It kept the town bailiff as head of police, but recruited a man from Ripon to command its night constables and an ex-soldier and serving member of the Manchester Police as his sergeant. The three day constables were former parochial employees, one of whom had been responsible for the town gaol while the other two were noted for their activity in pursuing offenders.[25]

The desire for men from the Metropolitan Police to command the new borough forces has been interpreted as a desire to follow the London model. Up to a point this may be true: the municipal authorities of early-nineteenth-century England wanted value for money; the Metropolitan Police acquired a reputation for efficiency and consequently a chief police-man with experience of London policing was to be valued precisely because of this experience. But the actual practices of policing did not always owe much to a metropolitan model; the division between day police and night police, which in Huddersfield and elsewhere continued sometimes into the 1860s, was a legacy of traditional policing. The relationship between policemen and the municipal authorities was also different. The Metropoli-tan Police were responsible directly to the Home Secretary. This was a mat-ter of concern and annoyance to ratepayers in metropolitan parishes during the early years of the police. As they saw it, they were having to pay for a force over which they had no control; and this was an issue that was to recur throughout the century and beyond.[26] Elsewhere municipal ratepay-ers financed municipal police forces, and they had no intention of allowing anyone outside the locality, not even the Home Secretary, to give orders to their police. Municipal governments, through their watch committees, kept firm control of their policemen, and the relationship was very much that of master and servant with the policemen occasionally required to perform tasks which would never have been required of any Metropolitan police constable.[27] Again this reflected the continuation of 'pre-police' traditions.

Lord Grey's Whig government contemplated a bill for the creation of a national police system between October 1831 and June 1832. The discussions were prompted by the Reform Bill crisis and by fears gener-ated by a succession of economic disorders. The proposal lapsed as the unrest subsided; the government apparently concluded that the need was no longer pressing, and that without obvious need it would be difficult to get such legislation through parliament because of possible constitutional fears and, above all perhaps, because of the cost of such a measure.[28] Four years later, however, in 1836, the Whigs turned their mind specifically to the policing of the counties, appointing the Royal Commission on a Rural Constabulary. Three men served as commissioners: Edwin Chadwick, Colonel Charles Rowan of the Metropolitan Police, and Charles Shaw Lefevre, an M.P. who had only recently served on the Royal Commission on County Rates. Chadwick was largely responsible for writing the report. His Benthamite notions of centralisation and his desire for close links between rural police and the new poor law organisation were not shared by his fellow commissioners, though all three men agreed on much else. The aspects of centralisation recommended in the report, published in March 1839, provoked hostility and disquiet. Rowan was amazed and suggested to Chadwick that one way of avoiding the supposed:

danger to the liberties of the country would be to give the power absolutely of dismissal to the magistrates. Thus if the Secretary of State should take it into his head to endeavour to enslave a whole country (which is not at all [illegible] likely, after paying 20 million to enfranchise the niggers) by sending six or seven additional Police Constables 'armed with a bare bodkin' into that county, the magistrates might, seeing the immency [sic] of the danger, immediately dismiss the said six dangerous individuals and thus frustrate the base attempt. It is impossible to maintain gravity on the subject.

He concluded with a sentence prefiguring the thinking of the Whig police historians: 'What a pity it is that all men who are not Rogues should be fools.'[29]

Melbourne's government was too weak to attempt such a contentious reform as a national constabulary even if it had so wished. Moreover it seems that the Home Secretary, Lord John Russell, and interested cabinet colleagues never contemplated anything other than permissive legislation with the new county forces firmly under local control. The Royal Commission's recommendation that the Treasury pay one-quarter of the cost of rural constabularies and that the Metropolitan Police train and appoint their members was not included in the Rural Constabulary Bill that swept through parliament in the summer of 1839. Alongside it were bills to establish police forces in Birmingham, Bolton and Manchester. Chartist activity provided the government with the opportunity for legislation, particularly in the case of the three urban police acts. The Rural Constabulary Act enabled any county that so wished to authorise the appropriate rate and to establish its own police force.

Two crucial points in the origins and early workings of this legislation have been too little emphasised. First, the Royal Commission's investigations revealed that provincial England during the 1830s was not unpoliced, and that such policing as there was did not always depend upon the old constable system. In 1829 parliament had authorised the creation of a county police system in Cheshire. The Cheshire Police were not centralised under a single chief constable but were based on the hundred or petty sessional division; each hundred was supervised by a paid high constable who maintained close communication with the local magistrates. The system was amended slightly by act of parliament in 1852. Edwin Corbett, the vice-chairman of the Cheshire quarter sessions, informed the 1853 Select Committee on Police that he did 'not think it possible for any police force to work better than it does' and that the London Metropolitan Police was 'more completely organised than we should be able to establish in the rural districts'.[30] Elsewhere, sometimes established under the Lighting and Watching Act 1833, there were small, professional police forces functioning under local magistrates and/or local gentlemen. Some of these were financed out of a local rate, others by subscription. The second point is that the quarter sessions' debates over whether or not to implement the legislation in 1839 and 1840 did not divide simply into those who wanted a new, county-wide constabulary and those who wanted to maintain the old system. Some conservative backwoodsmen wanted the preservation of the old parish system, but these were a minority. Some still condemned the idea of a uniformed constabulary as un-English. More concern, however, was expressed about cost. Some magistrates were uneasy about the power to raise new rates which the legislation gave them; unlike the borough magistrates, those in the counties were unelected and unrepresentative. There were others who felt that police reform was desirable, but they preferred smaller forces under immediate local control, rather than constabularies which would cover whole counties.[31] There is discrepancy in the figures, but of the fifty-four provincial counties in England and Wales (that is excluding Middlesex and dividing Yorkshire into its three constituent ridings) only two-thirds had established new constabularies by the mid-1850s, and in nine instances these 'county' forces were confined to one or two divisions or hundreds within the county.[32]

The forces established under the 1839 act and amending legislation of 1840 were not based on any one simple model drawn from the London experience. Men who had served in new police forces were recruited by the counties, particularly for the more senior positions. But men were also recruited from the old police: Henry Goddard, the first chief constable of Northamptonshire, was a former Bow Street officer; two long-serving constables from the old police, William Craig from Stowbridge and James Kings from Bromsgrove, were appointed superintendents in the new Worcester-shire Force.[33] Gloucestershire magistrates had employed Metropolitan Police officers for temporary emergencies during the 1830s, but when it came to establishing a county force in 1839, they turned to the Irish model; the first chief constable, Anthony Lefroy, brought thirteen men with him from Ireland as a cadre for the 250-man Gloucestershire force. Other counties also looked to Ireland.[34] Like the borough police, the new county constabularies remained firmly under local control; but the relationship between the magistrates on the police committees and their police forces differed from the master-servant relationship of most boroughs. The chief constables of counties were, generally speaking, of more genteel origin than their borough counterparts. There was, in addition, a significant presence of military officers among them, and this presence increased as the century wore on: seven out of the twenty-three chief constables appointed to English counties before 1856 had army or naval experience; twenty-two out of the twenty-four appointed between 1856 and 1880 had such experience. The perception of the police as a kind of soldiery informed much of the thinking behind the County and Borough Police Act 1856 and, both before and after this legislation, several chief constables were eager for their men to receive military training so that they might act as auxiliaries to the army in case of invasion. Many magistrates perceived their county constabularies as the first line of defence against an internal enemy which, in cases of popular disorder, led to them being deployed in a military fashion.[35]

Those counties which did not take advantage of the 1839 act did not leave their police systems unchanged. Some districts organised patrols under the Lighting and Watching Act 1833, and some used the enabling legislation of the Parish Constables Act 1842. The latter reaffirmed the old system of local policing and selection of parish constables; it also autho-rised the recruitment of paid, superintending constables to oversee the par-ish constables of a petty sessional division. For many, including persons in those counties where rural constabularies had been established, the act was a godsend. It offered a policing system which was cheaper and which seemed better suited to the needs of a rural society. In Nottinghamshire, for example, the quarter sessions received 224 petitions from different groups of ratepayers urging that the new constabulary be disbanded. Among these petitions was one from the parish of Harworth which expresses clearly and fully the sentiments of the dissatisfied ratepayers:

*The parish of Harworth has paid during the last year upwards of 21.. 9..
2 pounds [sic] as their quota of the expenses incurred by the maintenance*

of [the County Constabulary], without discovering they have received
any benefit whatever. And legislation has provided for a considerable
increase of parish constables (men who know all the suspicious
characters in the neighbourhood and who are specially interested in
keeping a good look-out and in whom their neighbours can place
implicit confidence) the Ratepayers and other Inhabitants of the Parish
of Harworth respectfully request the Magistrates will take their case into
their most serious consideration.[36]

In the event none of the new constabularies was disbanded, though
many were reduced in size and the old parish constable system continued
to be developed and refined. In 1850 amending legislation extended the
provisions of the 1842 act and the provisions were adopted by a total of
fourteen counties. The new lease of life injected into the old system was
popular not only because it was cheaper than a full-blown county constabulary but also because it kept control of the police within the smaller,
traditional units of parishes and petty sessional divisions.

Even the best of the Whig historians wrote off the superintending constables as a failure, yet the evidence given to the 1853 Select Committee
on Police suggests that there was satisfaction in counties where they were
established. Lieutenant Colonel Henry Morgan Clifford M.P., chairman of
the Herefordshire quarter sessions, insisted that they were 'quite sufficient;
the diminution of crime is very great'. Sir Robert Sheffield Bart., chairman of the quarter sessions for the parts of Lindsey, Lincolnshire, believed
that the system worked well; he was not sure what the long-term impact
was going to be on crime, but 'certainly the county looks to the superintendents very much as protectors', and they had reduced the number of
vagrants. Richard Healey, the Chief Constable of the Hundred of Aveland
in the parts of Kesteven, Lincolnshire, was of the opinion that the creation of a rural constabulary would be very unpopular in his district: 'the
farmers . . . and the ratepayers are exceedingly well satisfied with things
as they are'. Maurice Sawbey, a former police magistrate, and a county
magistrate for Buckinghamshire, Middlesex and Surrey, urged that a rural
constabulary be established in Buckinghamshire, but he had to admit that
the ratepayers did not complain about any threat to their property and
seemed satisfied with the protection which they received from the superintending constable system. On the other hand William Hamilton, one of
the superintending constables in Buckinghamshire and a veteran of sixteen
years' service in the Irish Constabulary and the Lancashire and the Essex
constabularies, was highly critical of the superintending constable system,

and particularly of the parish constables who served under him; David Smith, another veteran of the Essex force and a superintending constable in Oxfordshire was similarly critical. But George Carrington, a Buckinghamshire magistrate, was not surprised:

I think those men naturally wish for the discipline of a regular force; but that is their opinion, and I am only giving mine. The man who was examined from our county gave me a general idea, before he came to the Committee, what he was going to say; he came to me afterwards, and told me that he was asked whether he could say it was efficient; he said, he thought he could not say so. He has told me that some of the [parish] constables are efficient men, and ready to act with him; of course not so ready to act as men whom he might dismiss at a moment's notice. What he said was, 'I can lead them, but I cannot drive them'.

Carrington wished to see how the system developed in Buckinghamshire, but he felt that it would be perfectly adequate for the preservation of the peace and the protection of property.[37] The superintending constables, however, were swept away by the County and Borough Police Act 1856 which made the new, uniformed police obligatory.

The County and Borough Police Act stemmed from a variety of beliefs and concerns. Palmerston, briefly Home Secretary in 1852 and 1853, was convinced of the need for reform. He seems to have accepted the criticisms of the patchwork system of policing the demands for uniformity and rationalisation. The Select Committee which he established, and which met in 1853, lacked the reforming fervour of a Chadwick at the helm, but, nevertheless, stacked the evidence in favour of consolidation and a uniform system across the country. The desire for new legislation was also fostered by the belief that a reformed police would assume some kind of auxiliary military role. In addition there were fears brought about first, by the virtual end of transportation, which threatened that more 'habitual criminals' would be discharged from prison on to the highways and byways, and second, by the fear of brutalised soldiers demobilised following the Crimean War. Yet the legislation eventually steered through parliament by Palmerston's successor at the Home Office, Sir George Grey, was a compromise. The initial plans to amalgamate the smaller borough forces and five small county forces with their larger neighbours provoked an outcry and were dropped. The police forces of provincial England and Wales remained under local control, but the new legislation imposed some basic standards and uniformity, notably with the creation of a national system of supervision by the three Inspectors of Constabulary; and there was also a greater degree of central government involvement thanks to the Treasury's agreement to pay one-quarter the cost of pay and clothing for forces declared 'efficient' by the inspectors. Twenty years later the grant was increased to one-half and greater pressure was put on the smaller boroughs to amalgamate with their surrounding county force.

In spite of the urgings of some reformers and chief constables, notably Admiral MacHardy the Chief Constable of Essex, the police were not trained as military auxiliaries. Their tasks, however, were many and varied. The continuing 'servant' role of many borough policemen led to them acting as collectors of market tolls, poor law relieving officers, and the local fire brigade. Emergencies stretched manpower; following disorders and an alleged spate of pickpocketing in the summer of 1867, the Home Secretary lamented to the Commons that some 300–400 members of the Metropolitan Police were having to be employed to keep cattle plague out of the city.[38] The Metropolitan Police, county forces and the largest urban forces were often called upon as riot squads to assist outside their districts; the smaller borough forces were too small to cope with large crowds. But the maintenance of public order did not just mean riot control; from their creation the new police were employed to clamp down on those working-class leisure activities which offended middle-class sensibility.[39] Order, in its broadest sense, also meant keeping the traffic moving and keeping the streets tidy and safe. In October 1841, for example, the Bedford Watch Committee expressed its concern to the Chief Constable about harrows, ploughs and other articles exposed for sale on Market Hill, and left there after dark when they became a danger to pedestrians. In Manchester during the 1890s the Watch Committee and Chief Constable were vexed by the traffic problems ranging from ice-cream stalls to 'scorching' cyclists, and to school children throwing fireworks near horses on the run-up to Guy Fawkes' Day.[40]

Yet in spite of this variety of tasks, crime was perceived as the *raison d'être* for the new police. The Fieldings, Colquhoun and Peel had all argued that a preventive police was essential in the struggle to combat crime in the metropolis. The *New Police Instructions* published in September 1829 announced: 'It should be understood at the outset, that the object to be attained is "the prevention of crime".'[41] It was crime – its amount and its seriousness – rather than any of the other tasks that fell to policemen, which dominated the debates in quarter sessions over whether or not to establish a constabulary during 1839 and 1840. Once formed, the county forces had their preventive role emphasised in the instructions drafted by chief constables. Lefroy in Gloucestershire used, word for word, the London formulation quoted previously; Gilbert Hogg, in Staffordshire, informed his men that: 'It should be understood that the principal object to be attained is the *prevention of crime*.'[42] The reformers had great hopes of prevention; the regular patrols of the police constable, the impersonal agent of the law, would, it was hoped, deter potential malefactors. So confident of success was Sir Richard Mayne, Rowan's fellow commissioner, that in 1834 he suggested to a parliamentary committee the possibility of reducing the number of police in London in one or two years when 'the present race of thieves, who may be called the schoolmasters, are sent abroad, as we hope they soon will be, and the rising generation will become better'. Almost forty years later the Chief Constable of Chester boasted that, in just under a decade, he had successfully removed from his district the forty-seven known thieves and depredators:

There is, I am afraid, a widely spread feeling that, as there always have been criminals in society, so there always must be. I am not entirely of that opinion. Given the power, I really see no great difficulty, if not in stamping out professional criminals, at least in reducing their numbers very materially, especially in a comparatively small place such as Chester.[43]

It is impossible to measure prevention accurately. Whig historians, like the police reformers, lauded the new system and asserted its success. But contemporary newspapers often carried complaints that police were not to be found when they were needed either to prevent crime or to help victims seize offenders. One night in April 1844 William Radley Mott had his pocket picked in Brighton and the *Brighton Gazette* reported that 'he searched the town from Steyne to Ship Street without being able to find a single policeman to take the rascal into custody'. Twenty-four years later, worthies of London's East End protested that Metropolitan policemen were spending too much time warning children not to play with their hoops in the street and protecting the wealthy of the West End. According to the *East London Observer*: 'In the leading thoroughfares outrages of all kinds are perpetrated – frequently in broad daylight – and to look for a policeman is out of the question.' 'Where are the Police?' demanded *The Times* in 1875 following a warehouse robbery in High Holborn which must have taken the perpetrators two or three hours. On the other hand some petty offenders were foolish enough to attempt crimes under the eyes of watchful, uniformed policemen – like John Mason and Richard Kidd who, in November 1836, tried to pick a pocket in Blackfriars in full view of P.C. Charles Goff; and some street robberies were committed within calling distance of the beat policeman who was able to assist the victim and catch an offender – as when P.C. William Cottle caught James Adams running away after the attack on a merchant seaman in Shadwell in April 1857.[44] The more critical and thoughtful historians of crime and policing have suggested that the new police contributed to the statistical decline of theft and violence in the second half of the nineteenth century.[45] It seems reasonable to acknowledge that the physical presence of uniformed policemen on the streets did deter some petty theft from shops, stalls or individuals. But empirical evidence of the situation with and without police is impossible to come by. The proposal of a Bedfordshire magistrate in 1844 to remove the county force from two divisions of the county and to measure the result, was rejected by his fellows on the county bench; contemporary experiments and research suggests that the removal of police patrols makes little difference to the level of reported crime yet it is probably equally true to say that policing does have some impact in keeping crime to a certain base-line level.[46]

A police constable could not report to his superiors and, at the top of the hierarchy, a chief constable could not report to his Watch Committee or County Police Committee, that their activities had prevented a particular number of crimes over a given period. However the new police could demonstrate their worth by publishing the statistics of arrests. Except where there was a positive identification of a thief or of a violent offender, the easiest arrests to make were those for petty public order offences. Such offences as begging, drunk and disorderly, drunk and incapable, illegal street selling and soliciting were generally committed in the street and were often observed by the beat policeman. Moreover the removal of the drunk, the nomadic street seller, the prostitute or the vagrant was popular with the respectable Victorians who perceived these individuals as members of the dangerous or criminal classes. The early years of new police forces saw an increase in the statistics for these offences.

Yet if success could be claimed for the new police in dealing with some of the behaviour of the criminal class, there were crimes about which a uniformed constable patrolling an urban or a rural beat could do little. After all individual beats could be large; in London, in 1870, the average daytime beat was seven-and-a-half miles, the average night-time beat was about two miles;[47] in rural districts beats could be very much larger and villages without a resident constable might rarely see one. Major crimes in urban areas often, if not generally, took place behind closed doors and closed windows. If, for example, burglars could observe a police constable pass on his beat and then enter a property, especially when the

patrols. There was concern that the new police should not be reminiscent of a 'Continental Spy system', and the recollection of the spies and secret agents employed against British Jacobins and Regency Radicals remained painful. For the first decade of their existence the Metropolitan Police functioned side by side with the old London Police Offices, each with its complement of plain-clothes constables; indeed, some men left the Metropolitan Police to take up the better-paid position of constable under the stipendiary magistrates.[50] The policing tasks of the stipendiaries' offices, together with their constables, were abolished in 1839. Three years later, with some reluctance, Rowan and Mayne were forced to admit the need for, and to appoint, a small group of full-time detectives. Concerns about European spy systems, together with fears that men in plain-clothes were much more susceptible to corruption, meant that this body was increased only slowly over the next twenty-five years – from eight men to fifteen. Even those who praised the old police office constables to the detriment of the new police could unwittingly indicate dangers inherent in the detective system. W. H. Watts, for example, argued during the 1860s that the new police had been singularly unsuccessful against burglars and robbers, and that while the developing detective system was an improvement on uniformed constables periodically adopting disguises, it remained inferior.

One reason is, that the old officers were generally of a better class, had more general experience, possessed larger funds, and were permitted a wider field of action, being sure to have the protection of their own magistrates if, in the capturing or ferreting out of offenders, they overstepped those strict limits which it might be conceived were proper for a police officer to observe.[51]

Following hard on the failure of the Metropolitan Police in intelligence gathering during the Fenian outrages of 1867, full-time divisional detectives were established in 1869. Nine years later, after the exposure of four detective inspectors for involvement in an international swindling racket, the divisional detectives were centralised into the Criminal Investigation Department under a young former army officer and barrister, Howard Vincent, who brought himself to government notice with a report on the detectives of the Paris Police. By the mid-1880s Vincent's department had grown from 250 to 800 men.[52]

The *modus operandi* of the new detectives, indeed of the new police in general, when it came to investigating offences and pursuing offenders, was not greatly different from the more conscientious and determined of their predecessors. Policemen in plain-clothes watched and followed suspicious characters, sometimes with reward as when constables George Legge and Samuel Evans followed two young men who were gazing into jewellers' shops in Cheapside; the suspects 'watched the [uniformed] policeman on the beat away', and then attempted a smash-and-grab raid.[53] Policemen in uniform on their beats stopped suspicious characters, as the best of the old watchmen had done, again sometimes with success;[54] and until the developments of fingerprinting and forensic science, detection still often simply involved matching a suspect's shoes to footprints at the scene of the crime, perhaps with the occasional refinement of digging such footprints up, preserving them between boards and presenting them in court as evidence.[55] The telegraphic communications, photographic records of offenders and centralised record-keeping which began to be developed and used towards the end of the nineteenth century can be seen as technical aids to the kind of information gathering, circulation and storage urged by Sir John Fielding. Finally the occasional revelations of both uniformed and detective policemen profiting from links with a criminal underworld demonstrate that the new police did not sweep away all the abuses of the old.[56]

The uniformed police constable received only a modicum of training – much of it military-style drill – before being put on his beat. Few of the early recruits seem to have conceived of the police as a career; many appear to have volunteered to tide themselves over a period of unemployment. Of course some stayed in the police, sometimes prospering; a few transferred to another force to gain promotion. But while the pay may have been regular, unlike the pay in many working-class occupations, it was not high. Moreover there were niggling restrictions on the constables' ability to make money on the side. A constable in Northamptonshire protested to a local M.P. in 1880 that his pay was less than that of a farm labourer; in addition there was:

the ban on police keeping dogs, fowls, or more than two pigs, neither of which must be a brood sow. To supplement the family income I am not permitted to take in a lodger; nor can I sell the produce from my garden.

Others protested that, unlike the wife of a rural worker, the country policeman's wife was forbidden to keep a cow. Equally, unlike the wife of an urban worker, the urban policeman's wife could not run a small shop and, in many instances, she was forbidden from undertaking any form of paid employment.[57] Even if a man was eligible, before 1887 policemen were denied the vote for fear of political partiality.[58] The constables worked long hours in all weathers; more than one-quarter of the men pensioned for disability from the Metropolitan Police between 1840 and 1860

THE LONDON

POLICEMAN.

"EXCEPT THE LORD KEEP THE CITY, THE WATCHMAN WAKETH BUT IN VAIN."

No. 9.   SATURDAY, AUGUST 24, 1833.   PRICE ONE PENNY.

THE POLICE INSPECTOR.

Intercepted Correspondence.

[The following letter from Paul Pry, Esq., amateur inspector of the P division of the police force to Mr. Thomas, ex-superintendent of the A division, has been forwarded to us by the gentleman who supplies "The Times" with the Miguelite correspondence.]

Dear Thomas—

I have been down Prince's Street, and find that Mrs. Andrews is still in the habit of pumping into the milk-pails at six precisely every morning; some people insinuate that her milk is too blue and not true blue, but I suppose it is only to make her pails clean. The servant at No 4, continues to correspond with the butcher boy, and Mrs. Jenkins at No. 6, has not settled her baker's bill for the last three weeks. She says she expects a letter from Mr. J., but people *do* say J. is in the Fleet Prison. Sad goings on in Downshire-street—Tom Coddle has died of the cholera, and the first floor lodger at No. 16 always

brings home a girl with him. It is given out that he is newly married, but lord bless you, they are too loving for married folk. That sweet girl, Jenny Ginnum's, still keeps on her fascinating ways—I take a peep at her every night as she goes to bed in the down-stairs parlour floor—nice girl that, Tommy; people do say that it is not for nothing she goes to the Horse Guard Barracks. How do you get on at Manchester? People here keep a sharp look-out upon us, and several of the publicans have refused to bribe us to allow them to keep open at night. Popay is discharged (for a week or so, but mum's the word), and the public are pacified,—wait until Parliament is shut up and then we will slap away at the rascals again; meantime, my dear little man, believe me, to remain yours,

PAUL PRY, P. Division.

Excuse haste, for the house-keeper at No. 49, intimates that her dinner is ready at two.

The policeman as spy

There was concern that the new police would be used to spy on people. The revelations that Police Sergeant William Popay had participated in radical meetings in 1833 led to an inquiry by a parliamentary select committee. The particular concern was of men working in plain-clothes, though the cartoonist here envisaged uniformed men peering through windows at young women.

suffered from chest and rheumatic complaints.[59] Discipline was harsh and enforced by fine, demotion or dismissal. These conditions and regulations contributed to an enormous turnover of manpower. They also provoked dissatisfaction leading to petitions and strikes within some forces.[60] The complaints found a national focus in the *Police Service Advertiser* first published in February 1866 which urged improvements in pay, conditions and pensions. 'Probably', it lamented, 'no public servant is so ill-used by his employer as the policeman'.[61]

The *Police Service Advertiser* helped to develop the idea of the ordinary policeman as a professional, yet the idea of police as professionals and, consequently, as experts in the war against crime was fostered early on by the demands of the government and the legislature. Like the magistrates and constables from the London Police Offices, senior officers, first from the Metropolitan Police and then from other forces, were called upon to give evidence to committees and commissions. As noted previously the Royal Commission on a Rural Constabulary received and published lists of known criminals prepared by local forces, and from 1857 all forces were required to prepare such details for the annual Judicial Statistics; the definition of 'known criminals', however, was left to the discretion of the individual police forces. This requirement fed upon itself to reinforce the perception among policemen, their political masters and commentators on criminality, that a criminal class existed. At the same time the labelling of individuals as criminals, and of the districts in which they lived as criminal, could become self-fulfilling by propelling first-time offenders into further crime since they were now stigmatised, and by urging any 'respectable' families to do their best to move out of a stigmatised neighbourhood. Labelling as a 'criminal' might not even have occurred as the result of an initial offence. Gilbert Hogg advised his men that arrest on suspicion was one means of ensuring the principal object – prevention; the constable could, therefore, arrest an individual:

whom, from his situation and character, the law judges to be likely to commit some felony, and whom [the constable] has just cause to suspect is about to do so. . . . Though no charge be made, yet if the constable suspect a person to have committed a felony, he should arrest him; and if he have reasonable grounds, founded on fact, for his suspicion, he will be justified, even though it should afterwards appear that no felony was committed.[62]

Woolly directives of this sort were open to abuse, and not always deliberately given that the constable on the beat had so little training. Occasionally constables were criticised by magistrates and the objects of their suspicion were promptly released, but this was not always the case. Two men were arrested and charged with the garotte robbery of James Pilkington M.P. The police had no direct evidence against them other than information which they claimed to have received; but the accused, both ex-ticket-of-leave holders, were sentenced to three months' imprisonment each as suspicious characters.[63] Perhaps the labelling process only affected a minority of offenders and turned only a few into recidivists or 'professional' criminals, but it gradually enhanced the professionalism of the police by giving them an identifiable enemy to observe, catalogue and, when appropriate, to arrest for the good of society.

Rowan put it to a select committee that 'we look upon it that we are watching St James's and other places while we are watching St Giles and bad places in general'.[64] It was among the poorer working class in these 'bad places' that persons were to be found indulging in the boisterous popular culture which so offended Victorian sensibilities and which the police were directed to control. In the same places, and from the same groups, were to be found the street-traders who were 'moved on', the men on the tramp and the seasonal workers suspected of being criminals simply because they were on the roads; Chadwick, and several other witnesses to the Select Committee of 1853 urged the value of a centralised, uniformed constabulary for bringing about a significant decline in vagrancy – 'a great source of crime . . . they begin by being vagrants, and they end by becoming thieves'.[65] It was from among these groups in general that, it appears, the police found 'suspicious persons'; and in garrison towns from the mid-1860s to the mid-1880s it was young women from the working class who might be stopped and questioned on suspicion of being prostitutes under the Contagious Diseases Acts. The new police might also be felt as a pressure by members of the working class who broke their contracts and thus, under the provision of the master and servant legislation, were subject to criminal prosecution, as well as by workers taking strike action who sought to dissuade police-protected 'blacklegs' from working. Yet the new police were not simply a pressure on the working class. Police constables woke up workingmen in the morning to enable them to get to work on time or to be first in the queue for the distribution of casual work. They could be called in or used as a potential threat against an obstreperous neighbour even in a notoriously 'criminal' quarter like Jennings Buildings in Kensington. When all else had failed a distraught parent might summon a constable to deal with a difficult child; thus in March 1871 P.C. Alexander Hennessy of the Metropolitan Police was called upon to arrest Catherine Driscol, aged fourteen and a half, charged with stealing clothing by her mother.[66] Lost children were also reported to, and found by, the new police; indeed some children from the poorer districts may deliberately have got themselves lost, or been encouraged so to do by their parents, since, in the police station, they might enjoy a period of play with a few toys and a slice of bread and jam.[67] Assisting in the domestication and disciplining of the working class may have been one role imposed upon the police – both old and new. But many working-class radicals were sympathetic to domestication and discipline. Moreover, the system of beat policing, which was central to the new police, was designed for the prevention of crime; what men understood by crime was essentially theft and, to a lesser extent, assault and the working class were as much, if not more, the victims of crime than their social superiors. Working-class victims could, and did, use the police in the same way as victims from other social classes.

Notes

1 Among the most significant of the Whig police histories are **Charles Reith**, *The Police Idea*, Oxford U.P., Oxford, 1938; *British Police and the Democratic Ideal*, Oxford U.P., Oxford, 1943; **Sir Leon Radzinowicz**, *A History of English Criminal Law*, 5 vols, Stevens, London, 1948–69; **T. A. Critchley**, *A History of Police In England and Wales*, 2nd edn, Constable, London, 1978.

    Critics of the Whig interpretation include most notably **Allan Silver**, 'The demand for order in civil society', in **D. J. Bordua** (ed.), *The Police: Six Sociological Essays*, Wiley, New York, 1967; **Robert D. Storch**, 'The policeman as domestic missionary: Urban discipline and popular culture in Northern England, 1850–80', *Journal of Social History* (Summer 1976), pp. 481–509; 'The plague of blue locusts: Police reform and popular resistance in Northern England, 1840–57', *International Review of Social History*, **xx** (1975), pp. 61–90.

    The most recent interpretations which address the Whig/revisionist debate are **Clive Emsley**, *The English Police: A Political and Social History*, 2nd edn, Longman, London, 1996; *idem, The Great British Bobby: A History of British Policing From the 18th Century to the Present*, revised edn., Quercus, London, 2010; and **David Taylor**, *The New Police in Nineteenth-Century England: Crime, Conflict and Control*, Manchester U.P., Manchester, 1997.

2 For the concept of police and the Anglo-French comparison, see **Clive Emsley**, *Crime, Police and Penal Policy: European Experiences 1750–1940*, Oxford U.P., Oxford, 2007, pp. 61–73 and 105–13.

3 Beds. R.O. QSR 23/299; for a similar 'detection' by the Constable of Ampthill see *ibid.*, QSR 1827/316.

4 Bryan Jerrard, 'Early policing methods in Gloucestershire', *Transactions of the Bristol and Gloucestershire Archaeological Society*, **c** (1982), pp. 221–40 (at p. 227): Beds. R.O. QSR 1827/338.

5 Joanna Innes, 'The Protestant Carpenter – William Payne of Bell Yard (c. 1718–82); the life and times of a London informing constable', in Joanna Innes (ed.), *Inferior Politics: Social Problems and Social Policies in Eighteenth-Century Britain*, Oxford University Press, Oxford, 2009. See also Emsley, *Great British Bobby*, pp. 26–9 and **Francis M. Dodsworth**, ' "Civic" police and the condition of liberty: The rationality of governance in eighteenth-century England', *Social History*, **29** (2004), pp. 199–216.

6 Emsley, *English Police*, pp. 10–13. The point generally ignored in Whig police history about Dogberry, Verges and their watchmen is that they do catch the villains.

7 **Elaine A. Reynolds**, *Before the Bobbies: The Night Watch and Police Reform in Metropolitan London, 1720–1830*, Macmillan, London, 1998.

8 OBP t17961130–43. Patrick McCarty (apparently a watchman, though this is not stated) was less fortunate than the men who detained Wilson when, a few months after their success, he stopped William Gore who had 37 lbs of lead in his possession. Gore was indicted but was acquitted at the Old Bailey as no-one knew to whom the lead belonged. OBP t17970215–49 (Gore). OBP t18170115–77 (Lawrence).

9 P.P. 1828 (533), vi, *Police of the Metropolis*, pp. 25–6, 60, 92–3, 123–4 and 126.

10 One of the best examples is John Hewitt, a magistrate based in Coventry, who corresponded with officials as far apart as London and Newcastle in his pursuit of a criminal gang. See **Gwenda Morgan** and **Peter Rushton**, *Rogues, Thieves and the Rule of Law: The Problem of Law Enforcement in North-East England 1718–1800*, U.C.L. Press, London, 1998, pp. 43–4 and 89–90.

11 An act of 1692 was the first significant reward statute promising £40 to anyone apprehending and successfully prosecuting a highwayman. This was followed over the next half-century by a series of statutes promising similar financial reward or sometimes 'Tyburn Tickets' which exempted their holders from parish or ward office. See **John H. Langbein**, 'Shaping the eighteenth-century criminal trial: A view from the Ryder sources', *University of Chicago Law Review*, **50** (1983), pp. 1–136 (at pp. 106–10); Radzinowicz, *Criminal Law*, ii, pp. 155–61 especially.

12 **Gerald Howson**, *Thief-Taker General: The Rise and Fall of Jonathan Wild*, Hutchinson, London, 1970; **Ruth Paley**, 'Thief-takers in London in the age of the McDaniel gang, c. 1745–1754', in **Douglas Hay** and **Francis Snyder** (eds) *Policing and Prosecution in Britain, 1750–1850*, Oxford U.P., Oxford, 1989.

13 J. J. Tobias, *Crime and Police in England 1700–1900*, Gill and Macmillan, Dublin, 1979, pp. 54–6; *idem, Prince of Fences: The Life and Times of Ikey Solomons*, Valentine Mitchell, London, 1974, p. 31.

14 Reynolds, *Before the Bobbies*; **J. M. Beattie**, *Policing and Punishment in London, 1660–1750: Urban Crime and the Limits of Terror*, Oxford U.P., Oxford, 2001; **Andrew T. Harris**, *Crime and Legal Authority in London c.1780–1840*, Ohio State University Press, Ohio Columbus, 2004.

15 **John Styles**, 'Sir John Fielding and the problem of criminal investigation in eighteenth-century England', *T.R.H.S.*, 5th series, 33 (1983), pp. 127–49.

16 Radzinowicz, *Criminal Law* has references to Colquhoun's letters in the Home Office files. The failed London Police Bill of 1786 was taken over and modified by the Irish Law Officers and, as a result, professional magistrates and police were established in Dublin. Six years later, as the new London stipendiaries were being appointed, a campaign against the Dublin Police was gaining momentum. The Dublin Police system was condemned as expensive and inefficient, and the policemen themselves were criticised as brutal and oppressive. In 1795 the system was dismantled and magistrates elected by the Lord Mayor and the Corporation replaced the stipendiaries. See **Stanley H. Palmer**, *Police and Protest in England and Ireland, 1780–1850*, Cambridge U.P., Cambridge, 1988, chapters 3ii and 4ii, *passim*. Policing in Edinburgh developed under a series of acts of parliament establishing lighting and watching commissioners. By the early nineteenth century the Edinburgh Police – one superintendent, or captain-lieutenant, three lieutenants, a sergeant-major, two dozen sergeants and about 200 watchmen – seem closer to a Parisian-style police than anything English. The lieutenants, for example, took turns at supervising night duty and had strict instructions on daytime tasks which began before breakfast with the supervision of scavengers, and involved checking streets and lanes, inspecting pavements, removing 'nuisances', ordering repairs to unsafe structures and visiting lodging houses on the look-out for suspicious characters. (See Edinburgh R.O. Minute Book of Watching Committee March 1820 to February 1827, ff. 25–32.) However when the force was reorganised in 1843 William Haining, the Superintendent, applied to the Commissioners of the Metropolitan Police for a man to serve as one of the Lieutenants and to assist in the reorganisation. W. F. N. Smith, from the Greenwich Division, subsequently moved to Edinburgh (Edinburgh R.O. Minute Book of Watching Committee April 1839 to June 1844 ff. 172–3).

17 HO 42.114.

18 The best studies of Bow Street are **David J. Cox**, *A Certain Share of Low Cunning: A History of the Bow Street Runners, 1792–1839*, Willan Publishing, 2010, and **J. M. Beattie**, *The First English Detectives: The Bow Street Runners and the Policing of London, 1750–1840*, Oxford U.P., Oxford, 2012.

19 See e.g. *The Times*, 23 and 25 September 1816 for the affair of Constable George Vaughan; *The Times*, 24, 27 February and 30 March 1818 for the affair of Constable Thomas Limbrick; Tobias, *Prince of Fences*, pp. 53–4 for the affair of Bow Street Constable Bishop who, in 1828, agreed, for a reward, to get back property stolen from a jeweller, and eventually returned the property less £50-worth of jewels.

20 Randall McGowen, 'The Bank of England and the policing of forgery 1797–1821', *P and P*, **186** (2005), pp. 81–116.

21 Jenifer Hart, 'Reform of the borough police, 1835–56', *E.H.R.*, **LXX** (1955), pp. 411–27 (at pp. 414–16).

22 Beds. R.O. Bedford Borough Records: Watch Committee Minutes B 3/1 f. 3; **R. E. Swift**, 'Crime, law and order in two English towns during the early nineteenth century: The experience of Exeter and Wolverhampton 1815–56', unpublished Ph.D., University of Birmingham, 1981, p. 142; **Geoffry G. Everitt**, 'The development of law and order in Nottingham', unpublished M.A., University of Sussex, 1971, copy in Notts. R.O. at M24, 550; see also **John Field**, 'Police, power and community, in a provincial English town: Portsmouth, 1815–75', in **Victor Bailey** (ed.), *Policing and Punishment in Nineteenth-Century Britain*, Croom Helm, London, 1981, pp. 48–9; **B. C. Jerrard**, 'The Gloucestershire constabulary in the nineteenth century', unpublished M.Litt., University of Bristol, 1977, pp. 40–2.

23 Swift, 'Crime, law and order', pp. 358, 368, 381.

24 **B. J. Davey**, *Lawless and Immoral: Policing a Country Town 1838–57*, Leicester University Press, Leicester, 1983, p. 55.

25 **David Taylor**, *Beerhouses, Brothels and Bobbies: Policing by Consent in Huddersfield and the Huddersfield District in the Mid-Nineteenth Century*, Huddersfield University Press, Huddersfield, 2016.

26 Emsley, *English Police*, pp. 26–7 and 85–6; U.C.L. Chadwick MSS 16, Police Memoranda etc. (1880–90) for a draft 'Bill for Placing the Police of the Metropolis under the Control of the Ratepayers, February 1889'.

27 **Carolyn Steedman**, *Policing and the Victorian Community: The Formation of English Provincial Police Forces 1856–80*, RKP, London, 1984, pp. 15–16, 39, 53–5; Emsley, *English Police*, pp. 82–4.

28 **David Philips** and **Robert D. Storch**, 'Whigs and Coppers: The Grey Ministry's National Police Scheme, 1832', *Historical Research*, **lxvii** (1994), pp. 75–90.

29 U.C.L. Chadwick MSS 1722/70–1, Rowan to Chadwick 26 May 1839. The government had emancipated slaves in the British Empire, with £20 million paid in compensation to slave owners, in 1833. For a detailed analysis of the 1839 legislation see **David Philips** and **Robert D. Storch**, *Policing Provincial England 1829–1856: The Politics of Reform*, Leicester U.P., London, 1999.

mirror image of each other. In the Whig interpretation the humanitarian and progressive nature of penal reform fits with the humanitarian and progressive requirements of the consensual society that they saw as emerging in the early nineteenth century. In the revisionist account there is a fit between the new system of prison and punishment and the control requirements of the developing capitalist system.

There was a range of punishments available to judges and magistrates when passing sentence during the eighteenth century. The most serious offences against persons and property tried at assizes or at the Old Bailey were punishable by death; the legacy of the Middle Ages also left one or two borough sessions with the authority to impose a capital sentence[2] but county quarter sessions had no such power. Execution was usually by hanging; the more grisly punishments inflicted on the offender's body were rarely used in the mid-eighteenth century though traitors could still be sentenced to death by beheading, drawing and quartering, and until 1790, women found guilty of high or petty treason (which included coining) could be burned at the stake. The lesser forms of mutilation which were not part of a capital sentence, such as burning in the hand, were also declining. Whipping remained a common punishment for petty offences. The offender, male or female, was stripped to the waist and flogged along a public street or at a fixed whipping post. The judiciary introduced private whipping from the middle of the eighteenth century, and this was given statutory approval in 1779. The public whipping of women was abolished in 1817, but for men the punishment continued until the mid-1830s.

Individuals convicted of some capital offences could escape the death penalty by pleading benefit of clergy. This was a left-over from the right of clerics to be tried before ecclesiastical courts alone which, by the mid-seventeenth century, had been extended to men and women who were not clerics but who could demonstrate basic literacy. The courts had begun to clamp down on benefit of clergy in the early eighteenth century and many of the capital statutes passed during the century were declared specifically to be non-clergiable, yet the right to plead benefit of clergy in some offences remained until Peel's rationalisation of the criminal law in the 1820s. Conviction on a capital charge did not automatically lead to a death sentence, or, at least, did not automatically lead to an execution. Even though in the century following the Glorious Revolution of 1688 many more capital statutes found their way on to the statute book, there was considerable debate about, and interest in, secondary punishments. Two alternatives dominated this debate: prison and transportation.

Custodial confinement in some form of institution went back at least to the Middle Ages and was always available as an option for eighteenth-century judges and magistrates. Eighteenth-century gaols held the accused before trial; some petty offenders were sentenced to short periods in gaol, in particular those who were perceived to be on the slippery slope to perdition and therefore in need of correction – the disorderly, the idle, the vagrant and even some described simply as 'pilfering persons'. The more well-to-do among the lesser offenders might be punished with a fine, the less well-to-do with a whipping sometimes, to give maximum emphasis to the punishment, at the scene of the offence.[3] Both the pillory and the stocks also remained available: the pillory for serious public crimes such as fraud, cheating, some sexual offences, sedition and libel; the stocks for petty local offences, indeed the use of the stocks continued at least until the middle of the nineteenth century.[4] No-one seriously suggested extending the use of the pillory or the stocks, but perceived crime waves prompted suggestions for the severe physical punishment of offenders. More importantly in the late seventeenth and early eighteenth centuries the various merits of prison and transportation were rehearsed and experiments were made in the desire to find a satisfactory secondary punishment. The Transportation Act 1718 more or less resolved the matter for roughly fifty years. Transportation provided for the removal out of the kingdom of those offenders who, for a variety of reasons – their youth, the actual nature of their offence, the fact that it was a first-time offence – were not considered to be deserving of the death penalty but something more than a whipping and a discharge. The sentence was generally for periods of seven or fourteen years; sometimes it was for life. Transportation across the Atlantic began to lose favour in the middle years of the century and was effectively ended by the outbreak of the war for American independence, however the courts continued to pass sentences of transportation and some expedient had to be found to cope with the offenders so sentenced. In 1751 a committee of the House of Commons had proposed hard labour in the Royal Dockyards as a suitable alternative to transportation, but this was not taken up except as a temporary solution to the difficulties created by the American war. In the years between the Declaration of Independence and the departure, in 1787, of the first 778 convicts for the new penal colony of Botany Bay, the government took over the management of a large number of convicted felons within the kingdom as those sentenced to transportation were incarcerated in old, rotting ships – the hulks – and set to work dredging rivers or labouring in the naval dockyards. The appalling state of the hulks gave the reformers yet more ammunition in their campaign to establish well-regulated prisons, designed to reform offenders, as the principal, and much expanded secondary, punishment in the criminal justice system.[5]

One of the key errors of many historians, both Whig and revisionist, has been to take the eighteenth-century Bloody Code at a face value based on modern perceptions of the law; thus they have assumed that the increase in capital statutes during the eighteenth century was a meaningful one. In reality the new capital legislation of the eighteenth century generally defined offences in a very narrow way and often made reference to a specific institution or piece of property only; as a consequence the number of prosecutions likely to follow the passing of a capital statute was tiny. Destroying Westminster Bridge was the same kind of offence as destroying Fulham Bridge, but each offence had its own capital statute. Peel made much of such legislation when, in 1826, he proposed his rationalisation of the law relating to felony. There were, he explained, twenty statutes concerning the protection of trees from theft and wilful damage; the legislation for the prevention of stealing or destroying madder roots and for the preservation of hollies, thorns and quicksets in forests was tacked on, respectively, to acts relating first, primarily to sugar brought from the Americas and second, to customs duties. 'If an offence were committed in some corner of the land,' protested Peel:

a law sprang up to prevent the repetition, not of the species of crime to which it belonged, but of the single and specific act of which there had been reason to complain.[6]

Matters had rarely been that simple, nevertheless Peel was right in drawing attention to the fact that eighteenth-century parliaments did not legislate for species of crime. While there were efforts to consolidate the vagrancy laws and the game laws, eighteenth-century legislators had never attempted to codify capital legislation; they did not think in terms of general codification or going back to first principles.

More important, perhaps, in any assessment of the Bloody Code is to recognise that the majority of those executed during the eighteenth century were prosecuted under legislation which went back to the Tudors and Stuarts. Furthermore there were far more executions during the late sixteenth and early seventeenth centuries than during the eighteenth; and one or two offences ceased to be capital: at least two Jacobite pamphleteers were executed for sedition, but at the end of the eighteenth century Jacobin pamphleteers, if convicted, even at worst were rarely sentenced to more than two years in gaol.[7] Figure 10.1, based on figures in the appendices of

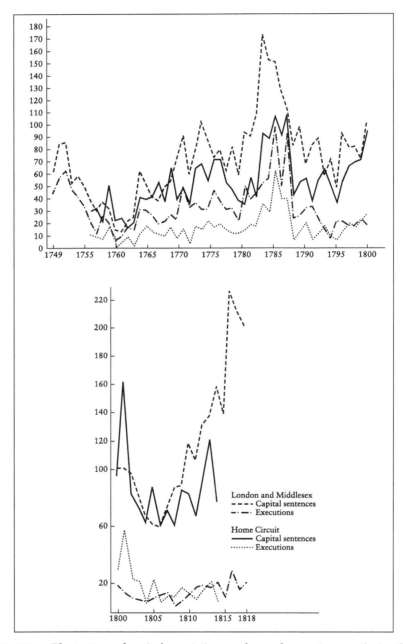

FIG 10.1 *The pattern of capital convictions and actual executions on Assize Circuits, 1749–1819*

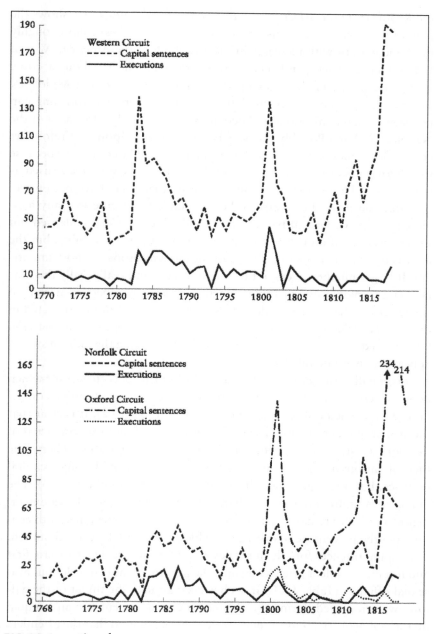

FIG 10.1 *continued*

the *Report from the Select Committee on Criminal Laws 1819*, shows the pattern of capital convictions and actual executions. These follow roughly the same pattern with increases in the aftermath of the American War of Independence, when gentlemen were expressing concern about a crime wave, and in the famine year of 1801, though London and Middlesex saw no marked increase on the latter occasion. There is a widening gap between capital convictions and actual executions in the aftermath of the Napoleonic Wars. Possibly this was because the promptings of reformers critical of the Bloody Code were having an effect on the courts and because the alternatives of transportation and the penitentiary were recognised as readily available. At the same time, however, there may have been a recognition that it would simply not be acceptable to execute so many individuals. V. A. C. Gatrell has argued that the Bloody Code collapsed not simply because of an increase in humanitarianism and sensibility, but the increasing numbers of successful prosecutions was probably more important. If larger numbers were not to be executed – and realistically this was neither acceptable nor possible – then increasing numbers convicted of capital crimes had to be pardoned. Ninety per cent of those convicted in the post-Napoleonic War period were pardoned, as opposed to between fifty and sixty per cent in earlier years. This was making the judicial system appear an unsustainable lottery.[8]

It is equally instructive to see what were the principal offences for which persons were executed (Table 10.1) and what percentage of capital convictions were carried out for the major offences (Table 10.2). It is clear that the largest number of capital sentences were passed on those convicted of the more serious kinds of theft, namely burglary and highway robbery. The theft of various animals – cattle, horses and sheep – could bring a capital sentence, but it was also more likely to bring a reprieve (Table 10.3). The numbers capitally convicted on charges of burglary and, to a lesser extent, highway robbery remained high into the early years of the nineteenth century, but the percentage of executions which were actually carried out fell. The capital offences for which reprieves were most rarely given were, first and foremost, violent offences against the person, notably murder but also sexual offences (Table 10.4). If, as has been argued, the threat of the gallows was employed during the eighteenth century to enforce an unequal division of property, it must, nevertheless, be recognised that the offenders least likely to escape the gallows were those guilty of offences against the persons of others. There is one significant exception to this; to modern eyes the most startling figures are probably those of the percentage executed out of those convicted for forgery. The offence was made capital in

1729 (2 Geo. II c. 25) following disquiet aroused by the South Sea Bubble affair and a succession of subsequent frauds. The new legislation swept up members of the lower classes who forged documents to obtain the prize money or the earnings of seamen, but it was aimed principally at forgers from the respectable classes, people who rarely appeared as defendants in the courts and especially not on capital charges. The old punishment had been the humiliation of the pillory. The use of the gallows to punish this offence, as Randall McGowen has forcefully argued, addressed the whole community and made a significant public statement about behaviour that threatened to destroy commerce and the production of wealth by under-mining a system in which paper credit was becoming more and more important. The offence was not seen in purely economic terms, rather it was a question of morality and upholding norms that made economic and social life possible. The judiciary, as well as the parliament that passed the new legislation, thought in this way. Judges sustained prosecutions in spite of procedural difficulties which could have brought them to a halt, and rejected appeals for pardon which, in the normal course of events, they probably would have forwarded given the social origins of the defendant.[9]

It is probably significant that the peak year for convictions for sheep-stealing on all three circuits was the famine year of 1801: forty-four convicted, of whom three were executed on the Home Circuit; twenty-four convicted, of whom four were executed on the Norfolk Circuit; and forty convicted, of whom sixteen were executed on the Western Circuit.

Crowds massed around pillories and gallows in both London and the assize towns. Public punishment was theatre. In as much as the ruling class or the state had devised such punishment it was didactic theatre: the gallows and the pillory were to provide lessons and warnings for would-be transgressors. But for the crowds, drawn from all social groups, the proceedings appear to have been melodrama of the rudest sort: at one extreme there could be villains to jeer and abuse, at the other there were unfortunates to be cheered and cherished. The crowd had a positive role to play at the pillory; under the watchful eye of a sheriff or other law officer, it was authorised to pelt the offender with fruit, vegetables, eggs, dung and so forth. But increasingly the manner in which the crowd played its role did not fit the prepared text of the authorities. Pilloried offenders, to whom the crowd had taken a dislike, were cruelly treated; some lost eyes, some died as a result of their treatment. But others became popular heroes, and their time in the pillory became a moment of triumph. John Williams, for example, a bookseller, fell foul of authority for selling both prints which ridiculed the Earl of Bute and a reprint of John Wilkes's *North Briton*. His

TABLE 10.1 *Principal offences for which persons were executed, 1755–1814*

	London and Middlesex*		Home Circuit	Western Circuit	Norfolk Circuit
	(a)	(b)			
1755–1764					
Total executed	162	191	96		
Burglary	18 (11.1%)	23 (12.0%)	17 (17.7%)		
Forgery	24 (14.8%)	28 (14.6%)	4 (4.1%)		
Highway robbery	58 (35.8%)	65 (34.0%)	28 (29.1%)		
Murder	17 (10.4%)	26 (13.6%)	23 (23.9%)		
Horse stealing	6 (3.7%)		6 (6.2%)		
Housebreaking			1 (1.0%)		
Sheep-stealing			3 (3.1%)		
1765–1774					
Total executed	278	303	139	43†	33‡
Burglary	86 (30.9%)	53 (17.4%)	24 (17.9%)	8 (18.6%)	14 (42.4%)
Forgery	20 (7.1%)	19 (6.2%)	3 (2.1%)	1 (2.3%)	1 (3.0%)
Highway robbery	79 (78.4%)	57 (18.8%)	63 (45.3%)	11 (25.5%)	7 (21.2%)
Murder	29 (10.4%)	30 (9.9%)	14 (10.0%)	14 (32.5%)	
Horse stealing	2 (1.0%)		7 (5.0%)	1 (2.3%)	1 (3.0%)
Housebreaking	3 (1.0%)		6 (4.3%)		1 (3.0%)
Sheep-stealing			1 (0.7%)	2 (4.6%)	1 (3.0%)
1775–1784					
Total executed	414		197	85	67
Burglary	108 (26.6%)		56 (28.4%)	18 (21.1%)	30 (44.7%)
Forgery	21 (5.0%)		3 (1.5%)		4 (5.9%)
Highway robbery	124 (29.9%)		87 (44.1 %)	29 (34.1%)	12 (17.9%)

Murder	17 (4.1%)	20 (10.1%)	23 (27.0%)	4 (5.9%)
Horse stealing	1 (0.2%)	9 (4.5%)	3 (3.5%)	3 (4.4%)
Housebreaking	6 (1.4%)	5 (2.5%)	2 (2.3%)	2 (2.9%)
Sheep-stealing		2 (1.0%)	5 (5.8%)	5 (7.4%)
1785–1794				
Total executed	375	234	180	126
Burglary	103 (27.4%)	54 (23.0%)	30 (23.8%)	3 (2.3%)
Forgery	27 (7.2%)	1 (0.4%)	3 (1.6%)	
Highway robbery	121 (32.2%)		96 (41.0%)	36 (20.0%)
Murder	18 (4.8%)	9 (3.8%)	24 (13.3%)	23 (18.2%)
Horse stealing	12 (3.2%)	23 (9.8%)	27 (15.0%)	14 (11.1%)
Housebreaking	12 (3.2%)	12 (5.1%)	10 (5.5%)	4 (3.1%)
Sheep-stealing	2 (0.5%)	6 (2.5%)	12 (6.6%)	6 (4.7%)
1795–1804				
Total executed	142	217	160	78
Burglary	23 (16.1%)	48 (22.1%)	34 (21.2%)	16 (20.5%)
Forgery	40 (28.1%)	4 (1.8%)	11 (6.8%)	2 (2.5%)
Highway robbery	22 (15.4%)	58 (26.7%)	25 (15.6%)	15 (19.2%)
Murder	18 (12.6%)	14 (6.4%)	25 (15.6%)	4 (5.1%)
Horse stealing	3 (2.1%)	17 (7.8%)	15 (9.3%)	15 (19.2%)
Housebreaking	2 (1.4%)	8 (3.6%)	4 (2.5%)	1 (1.2%)
Sheep-stealing		10 (4.6%)	19 (11.8%)	9 (11.5%)

continued

TABLE 10.1 *continued*

	London and Middlesex* (a)	(b)	Home Circuit	Western Circuit	Norfolk Circuit
1805–1814					
Total executed		137	142	82	39
Burglary		24 (17.5%)	30 (21.1%)	13 (15.8%)	6 (15.3%)
Forgery		44 (32.1%)	13 (9.1%)	22 (26.8%)	3 (7.6%)
Highway robbery		13 (9.4%)	12 (8.4%)	7 (8.5%)	1 (2.5%)
Murder		21 (15.3%)	21 (14.7%)	20 (24.3%)	9 (23.0%)
Horse stealing			11 (7.7%)	4 (4.8%)	6 (15.3%)
Housebreaking			8 (5.6%)		
Sheep-stealing			13 (9.1%)	5 (6.0%)	2 (5.1%)

* There are two separate returns for London and Middlesex in the appendices for the 1819 Report from the Select Committee on Criminal Laws. Column (a) is based on the more detailed figures in Appendix No. 5; column (b) is based upon Appendix No. 2
† Figures for 1770 to 1774 only
‡ Figures for 1768 to 1774 only

TABLE 10.2 *Capital convictions and executions for principal offences, 1775–1815*

	London and Middlesex			Home Circuit			Western Circuit			Norfolk Circuit		
	Convicted	*Executed*	*Executed as percentage convicted*	*Convicted*	*Executed*	*Executed as percentage convicted*	*Convicted*	*Executed*	*Executed as percentage convicted*	*Convicted*	*Executed*	*Executed as percentage convicted*
1775–1784												
Burglary	185	108	58.3%	115	56	48.6%	99	18	18.0%	73	30	41.0%
Forgery	37	21	57.7%	4	3	75.0%	14	–	–	4	4	100.0%
Highway robbery	318	124	38.9%	227	87	38.3%	158	29	18.3%	35	12	34.2%
Murder	18	17	94.4%	25	20	80.0%	30	23	76.6%	4	4	100.0%
1785–1794												
Burglary	220	103	44.2%	120	54	45.0%	139	51	36.6%	79	30	37.9%
Forgery	38	27	71.0%	2	1	50.0%	32	3	9.3%	3	3	100.0%
Highway robbery	309	121	39.1%	224	96	42.8%	111	36	32.4%	50	31	62.0%
Murder	19	18	94.7%	11	9	81.8%	25	24	96.0%	23	23	100.0%
1795–1804												
Burglary	168	23	13.6%	176	48	27.2%	130	34	26.1%	56	16	28.5%
Forgery	61	40	65.5%	9	4	44.4%	20	11	55.0%	2	2	100.0%
Highway robbery	127	22	17.3%	134	58	43.2%	84	25	29.7%	42	15	35.7%
Murder	20	18	90.0%	17	14	82.3%	26	25	96.1%	4	4	100.0%

continued

TABLE 10.2 continued

	London and Middlesex			Home Circuit			Western Circuit			Norfolk Circuit		
	Convicted	Executed	Executed as percentage convicted	Convicted	Executed	Executed as percentage convicted	Convicted	Executed	Executed as percentage convicted	Convicted	Executed	Executed as percentage convicted
1804–1815*												
Burglary	226	18	7.9%	158	30	18.9%	118	13	11.0%	53	6	11.3%
Forgery	84	47	55.9%	17	13	76.4%	30	22	73.3%	9	3	33.3%
Highway robbery	196	17	8.6%	62	12	19.3%	39	7	17.9%	16	1	6.2%
Murder	26	26	100.0%	26	21	80.7%	28	20	71.4%	9	9	100.0%

* London and Middlesex figures, 1812–1818
Source: Constructed from tables in the Report from the Select Committee on Criminal Laws, 1819

TABLE 10.3 *Capital convictions for animal theft*

	Convictions	Executions	Executions as a percentage of convictions
Home Circuit, 1755–1814			
Cattle theft	42	7	16.6%
Horse theft	549	73	13.2%
Sheep theft	381	35	9.1%
Norfolk Circuit, 1768–1818			
Cattle theft	37	4	10.8%
Horse theft	267	36	13.4%
Sheep theft	278	25	8.9%
Western Circuit, 1770–1818			
Cattle theft	98	15	15.3%
Horse theft	355	50	14.0%
Sheep theft	457	48	10.5%

Source: Constructed from tables in the Report from the Select Committee on Criminal Laws, 1819

TABLE 10.4 *Capital convictions for sexual offences*

	Convictions	Executions	Executions as a percentage of convictions
London and Middlesex			
1756–1804			
Rape	19	11	57.8%
Sodomy	9	5	55.5%
1812–1818			
Rape	3	2	66.6%
Sodomy	4	4	100.0%
Home Circuit			
1755–1814			
Rape	38	18	47.3%
Buggery	14	12	85.7%
Norfolk Circuit			
1768–1818			
Rape*	15	11	73.3%
Buggery and sodomy	4	3	75.0%
Western Circuit			
1770–1818			
Rape‡	29	20	68.9%
Carnally knowing an infant under 10 years	4	3	75.0%
Sodomy	7	4	57.0%

* Includes two cases of rape committed on infants
‡ There is a discrepancy in the figures between the annual totals for the Western Circuit and the overall figures for particular offences given in Appendix 9 and Appendix 10 of the 1819 Report. The figures given here are for the offence totals in Appendix 10; the annual figures, given in Appendix 9, when totalled come to 26 convictions and 17 executions. The discrepancy appears to be for the period 1810–18
Source: Constructed from tables in the Report from the Select Committee on Criminal Laws, 1819

hour in the pillory in February 1765 only aggravated the government's discomfiture, however, since, rather than pelting him with anything that came to hand, the crowd cheered him and raised a collection for him amounting to £200. The situation became such that from roughly the middle of the eighteenth century, the pillory was used less and less to punish cases of sedition where the crowd's sympathy might be with the offender. As a result, a greater proportion of those sentenced to the pillory were unpopular with the crowd and were savagely pelted and ill-treated. This, in turn, aggravated concerns about crowd behaviour in the public space around the pillory.[10]

The crowd did not have such a defined, participatory role at public executions. Here it was very much the audience, yet it still made its views felt. It generally execrated the hangman when the offender was not a murderer or when it felt that he or she was being executed unjustly. Members of the crowd sympathised most with those with whom they could readily identify; thus respectable people recorded being particularly shaken by the execution of someone from their own social class, a forger, for example, like the Reverend William Dodd in 1777. But the majority in the crowd was plebeian, and it appears to have been particularly approving when the victim came from a higher social class. Until executions were established immediately outside prisons – as they were from 1783 in London with the erection of the new drop at Newgate – the journey to the scaffold could begin the tumult and reveal the crowd's attitude. In August 1754 Mary Smith was executed at Tyburn for robbing a three-year-old girl. The *General Evening Post* reported that:

instead of Pity and Prayers, generally used on these Occasions [the crowd] especially the Females, vented bitter Execrations as the Cart went along; particularly a poor Woman in Oxford Road, who, to show her Indignation to the Criminal, held up a Child in her Arms, which this Wretch had stripped, rejoiced in her Punishment, and seemed pleased to exhibit a remarkable Proof of her offence.[11]

On occasions the condemned behaved with the kind of penitential decorum that suited the authorities' requirements for the didactic theatre of punishment; they ascribed their ruin to drink or 'to the Association of lewd Women, who drove them to unlawful Courses, in order to escape the Extravagances of these Daughters of Plunder'.[12] Even if the condemned was not penitent, enterprising printers provided cheap handbills with appropriate 'last dying words' or doggerels illustrating his or her moral decline. Some of the capitally convicted refused to play the game and insisted that they did not deserve death:

James Holt, the Smuggler, behaved very penitently, but did not seem convinced that his Sentence was just, or that Smuggling merited Death. Amongst his last words were, 'It is very hard to be hanged for Smuggling'.[13]

Others struggled with the executioner or, probably fortified with strong drink, affected an air of heroic nonchalance. Penitence, protest or non-chalance might further help to shape the responses of the crowd. So too might a botched execution, or the decision to convey the body of an executed felon to a surgeon for dissection. Crowds strongly objected to the latter, particularly when the condemned had made 'a good end' or when the popular feeling was that he or she did not deserve to be executed. Yet as Elizabeth Hurren has recently shown, the prospect of dissection played on the mind and behaviour of the crowd in a variety of different ways.[14]

If, for most of the eighteenth century, the Bloody Code was not actually increasing the numbers of those being executed, nevertheless there does appear to have been an increase in judicial violence. The Murder Act of 1752 extended gibbeting and dissection as the judiciary began to introduce private whipping. It seems probable that plebeian crowds regarded this as a violation of accepted norms, as the law failing to reflect popular ideas of culpability and justice, and as evidence of a contempt for popular culture. At the same time, the growth of the press meant greater publicity for executions which, in all probability, led to greater crowds. Larger crowds, and plebeian frustration, provoked greater turmoil around the scaffold. Well before the end of the century the authorities had lost control of the pillory and they began to fear that they were also losing control of 'the hanging tree'.[15] There was disquiet that the crowds were not learning the appropriate lessons and that they were not behaving as they should; this was linked to an increasing distrust of crowds, and also to an almost wilful misapprehension that the crowds who assembled to watch executions were uniformly plebeian. Concerns about the behaviour at executions, together with demands for a better regulated system of intermediary punishment, were being voiced by men like the Fieldings in the mid-eighteenth century. These concerns received a boost with the publication of two books: the first English translation of Cesare Beccaria's *Dei Delitti e delle Pene* appeared in 1767, and ten years later John Howard published *The State of the Prisons in England and Wales*.

Beccaria's treatise, originally appearing in Italy in 1764, was seized upon by progressive thinkers throughout Europe. It outlined a system of punishment that appeared in keeping with the ideas of the Enlightenment. Existing punishments, Beccaria insisted, were arbitrary and barbaric, and they did not diminish crime. Punishment should have aims which were explicable and rational; it should be the certain outcome of any lawbreaking; it should suit the offence, prevent the culprit from offending again, and deter potential offenders. Rather than relying upon the death penalty for many offences it would be more salutary, Beccaria believed, to deprive offenders of their liberty, and to compel them to recompense society for their transgressions with a period of hard labour visible to the public. In November 1770 Sir William Meredith, M.P. for Liverpool, urged the Commons to mount an enquiry into the criminal law; his speech was suffused with Beccarian ideas. He was concerned:

that a man, who has privately picked a pocket of a handkerchief worth thirteen pence, is punished with the same severity, as if he had murdered a whole family of benefactors.

Such punishment, Meredith maintained, only served to make the petty thief worse and more dangerous and, he went on:

none should be punished with death, but those who could not be made safely useful, except in cases of murder, where a capital punishment, as it would be less common, would operate more forcibly in terrorem, and consequently more effectually answer its end.[16]

The following year William Eden published the influential *Principles of Penal Law*, rejecting the existing system centred on capital punishment, querying the value of transportation and, on Beccarian lines, recommending some kind of continuing public display of useful punishment. Doubtful about the value of prison sentences, Eden believed that confinement often made offenders worse; however, within a decade he was helping to draft new penitentiary legislation. Eden's conversion to the idea of putting offenders into regulated, orderly prisons, like the similar conversion of other reformers, was largely through the work of John Howard.

Howard, a philanthropic, nonconformist gentleman with an estate at Cardington in Bedfordshire, had become county sheriff in 1773. He was appalled by the squalor of the county gaol which his new post led him to visit; he was also shocked by the plight of the prisoners, notably those who, although acquitted by the courts, were compelled to remain incarcerated because they could not pay the discharge fee required by the gaoler. These problems and abuses were not unique to Bedfordshire nor were they unknown before Howard's publications. The office of gaoler was typical of other petty offices during the eighteenth century; the holder was expected to be an entrepreneur who augmented such wage as he might receive with fees and the sale or rent of goods to those in his charge. What impressed the public about *The State of the Prisons* was certainly Howard's moral fervour but, perhaps more important, the systematic way in which he had gone about categorising every imaginable detail from diet to size of cell in every prison in England and Wales; more than this, he had contrasted the squalor of these gaols with, in particular, the Rasp Houses of Amsterdam and Rotterdam and the *Maison de Force* in Ghent. The book was an indictment of the administration of those local justices who rarely took seriously their responsibilities in supervising the local gaols and gaolers; yet, as Michael Ignatieff has emphasised, the book was not couched as an indictment but rather as 'a confrontation with Evil in the abstract'. Magistrates could therefore accept the conclusion without feeling that they themselves were being condemned.[17] Further editions of the book were brought out in 1780 and 1783, and Howard expanded his empirical research in Europe publishing, in 1789, *An Account of the Principal Lazarettos in Europe* which was itself reprinted in 1791, the year after his death.

Yet in spite of the enthusiastic reception given to the work of Beccaria and Howard and the boost which they gave to reformers, change remained slow and continued to depend on the zeal and initiative of private individuals rather than on government direction. In 1779 parliament passed the Penitentiary Act; drafted by Blackstone, Eden and Howard, this provided for the construction of two penitentiaries in the metropolis, one for 600 men, the other for 300 women. Here offenders, otherwise liable for transportation, could be imprisoned for up to two years. They were to be uniformed, kept to hard labour in association with each other by day and shut in solitary confinement by night. Section 5 of the act emphasised the reforming intention of the penitentiaries: inmates were to be inured 'to Habits of Industry'. But conscious of complaints that some of the poor might prefer the clothing, diet and lodging of the penitentiaries to their hard life outside, the legislators were determined to make confinement sufficiently hard, rigorous and disagreeable to deter any such preference. In the event, these penitentiaries were never built. Death and resignation broke up the board of commissioners established to oversee implementation of the act. There were problems over the purchase of land. But, probably most important, none of the ministries between 1779 and 1785, when the plans finally lapsed, had the building of the penitentiaries among their prime concerns even though at the end of the American War there was an increase in prosecutions. Ministers had to busy themselves with concluding the war and struggling for the continuance of their shaky administrations.[18] The hulks were accepted as 'temporary expedients' and for the government to take on the expense of permanent structures would not have been popular in years when economic reform and retrenchment were watchwords. Such a reform, even though it had passed through parliament, might also have been condemned as enlarging the patronage of the Crown and encroaching on the rights of local boroughs and counties to administer gaols. Furthermore the belief continued that prisons, and the hulks, by throwing first offenders together with recidivists, only served to make all offenders worse. Jonas Hanway, an advocate of solitary confinement from the early 1770s, branded the London Bridewell as 'a nursery for thieves and prostitutes'.[19] The House of Commons Committee on Transportation argued similarly in 1784 and went on to explain that, while prisoners released from the gaols and the hulks could get neither work nor parish relief and consequently returned to crime, transportation to America had 'tended directly to reclaim the Objects on which it was inflicted, and to render them good Citizens'.[20] The Transportation Act 1784 signalled a continuing preference in central government circles for removing offenders overseas, even though the site for a new penal colony was still to be found. Nor was it only among government circles that such sentiments existed. In March 1786 the Lord Mayor and Aldermen of the City of London petitioned George III about 'the rapid and alarming increase of crimes and depredations in this city and its neighbourhood, especially within the last three years'. The petitioners asserted that the end of transportation and the release of offenders back into English society was 'alone sufficient to account for all the evils that are so heavily felt and so justly complained of'. The only punishments mentioned in the petition were death and transportation, 'without which all other regulations must prove nugatory and abortive'.[21] In the closing decades of the eighteenth century it was influential figures in county administrations who organised the building of new gaols or the refurbishing of old ones, and who introduced new regimes of regular work, solitary confinement, and the separation of different classes of offender – men from women, first-time offenders from recidivists, those convicted from those awaiting trial. Notable among these reformers were the Duke of Richmond in Sussex, Sir George Onesiphorus Paul in Gloucestershire, and Thomas Butterworth Bayley in Salford.

By the decade of the French Revolution the exertions of local reformers together with the steady stream of printed propaganda were beginning to make the penitentiary a viable alternative punishment. Furthermore it was a punishment with the added advantage, according to its advocates, of reforming the prisoner for the benefit of English, as opposed to a colonial, society. Those released from the rigours of the penitentiary would be accustomed to hard work, instead of idleness, while religious teaching and periods of solitary confinement would have helped the offender to contemplate the evils of wrong-doing thus inculcating morality and virtue. But there was no steady triumph of a single penitentiary idea. Reformers themselves were divided about the kind of work and about the role and effect of solitary confinement. In 1791 Jeremy Bentham threw his intellectual weight behind prison reform with his own plan, *Panopticon*. The panopticon structure was to enable the constant supervision of convicts working, and thus reforming, for perhaps as many as sixteen hours a day; it also provided for the supervision of the prison guards, for here Bentham parted company with other reformers in suggesting that the custodians themselves might need watching. Bentham's principal gaoler – and Bentham had himself in mind for this role – was to be the entrepreneurial gaoler *par excellence* running the panopticon as a profitable commercial enterprise and selling the products of the convicts' labour. The need to have a fit and healthy workforce would, according to Bentham, ensure that the convicts were looked after. In 1794 legislation provided for the construction of the panopticon and Bentham acquired a site at Millbank, but the Treasury never released the money.

In addition to their differences over the best system, the prison reformers received setbacks from the criticisms levied at the realities even of new gaols by political radicals. The English Jacobins who spent time in prison for sedition or under the suspension of the Habeas Corpus Act were few in number, but they were articulate and able publicists. Paul's Gloucester Penitentiary and, more especially the House of Correction in Coldbath Fields, were the focus of this criticism. Coldbath Fields had been opened in 1794, designed with Howard's principles in mind, but it was unfortunate in acquiring as its first governor a former baker, Thomas Aris, who turned out to be precisely the kind of grasping gaoler of whom Howard was critical; the problem was compounded by the Middlesex justices giving Aris a free hand in the administration of the gaol.[22]

The wars against Revolutionary and Napoleonic France again involved government departments in the organisation and administration of large numbers of prisoners on British soil. The wars created problems in transportation, not the least of which was the higher cost of freight; this led to more and more convicts being incarcerated on the hulks, and while contemporaries did not really do the sums, those lodged in this way were less costly than those shipped to Botany Bay and their labour on public works, notably for military purposes, was valuable.[23] But prisoners in the government's charge during these years were not simply convicts; there were also prisoners of war in unprecedented numbers who, because of the duration and new style of war, were kept over a longer period than in previous conflicts. It is impossible to measure the precise impact on penal policy of keeping large numbers of convicts on the hulks and enemy servicemen in prisoner of war camps, but in 1816, the year following the battle of Waterloo, the first national penitentiary was opened at Millbank. This was the result of the report of a parliamentary committee appointed in 1810 under the chairmanship of George Holford. The committee, packed with keen advocates of the penitentiary idea, was primarily concerned with choosing between different forms of penal discipline: that exemplified by the Gloucester Penitentiary where solitary confinement was given a key role in an attempt to change the offender's character by bringing him, through religion, to an awareness of his wrong-doing; and that which gave offenders incentives to work in association with each other in the belief that instilling habits of work would drive out the bad habit of idleness which led to crime. Holford's committee came up with an amalgam of the two; the first part of a convict's sentence was to be spent in separation, the second part in association. It rejected Bentham's plans for running the prison like a factory as well as his elaborate panopticon structure, though elements of Bentham's structural ideas for supervision were incorporated into Millbank's seven massive pentagons. Bentham himself was compensated financially for his efforts spread over the preceding two decades. The construction of Millbank was begun in 1812 and eventually cost the enormous and quite unexpected sum of £450,000. It was the largest prison in Europe when it opened and marked a significant step in the state taking on the management of convicts in an institution on native soil.

A few years after the opening of Millbank the government became involved in funding another penal institution, but not as the result of any legislative initiative. In the opening decade of the nineteenth century judges at the Old Bailey began recording the sentence of 'judgment respited' against certain, usually very young, offenders. These offenders were then handed over to one of two charitable institutions, the Philanthropic Society or the London Refuge for the Destitute, which sought to reform them. A few magistrates began to follow suit and in 1814, in a tacit acknowledgement that the Refuge was saving money by dealing with offenders that otherwise could have been imprisoned or transported, the government gave it a grant of £1,500. Three years later the grant became annual and, in the early 1820s which became the peak years of the policy, the annual grant reached £5,000.[24]

But while the government was sucked more deeply into penal administration and reform, the running for the changes in penal policy continued to be made by a small group of M.P.s passionate in their philanthropy and politically tending towards the opposition Whigs. The Gaol Fees Abolition Act 1815 which signalled the beginning of the end for the entrepreneurial gaoler was introduced into parliament by one of these reformers, Henry Grey Bennet. But most notable among this group was Sir Samuel Romilly. Prison improvement was just one element of Romilly's campaign to mitigate and rationalise the Bloody Code. From the early years of the new century he campaigned vigorously for a reduction in the number of capital statutes. He protested that there was a 'lottery of justice' in that there was uncertainty about the punishment for different offences; even when a capital sentence was passed it was far from certain that it would be carried out and consequently there was no lesson for the public. Judges, he feared, had too much potentially tyrannical discretion; furthermore they responded to different offences in their own individual ways.

Romilly and reformers like him have been lionised by the Whig historians of criminal justice; they have been portrayed as far-sighted humanitarians beset on all sides by die-hard reaction. Humanitarians they certainly were, yet whether their achievements were as great and whether the issues were as clear-cut as Whig history would suggest, is a moot point. It was emphasised earlier that there were never 200 or so separate and completely different offences liable to a capital sentence and as Tables 10.1 through 10.4 reveal there was a proportional decline in the numbers executed for property crime. '[T]he legal massacres . . . when "the prisons of the metropolis are emptied into the grave"'[25] were being queried long before Romilly began his campaign. Put in the context of a growing unease about the Bloody Code and its ritual paraphernalia the role of Romilly as a courageous initiator of reform is less pronounced. Rather he, and other early nineteenth-century law reformers, were able to get things done because parliamentary opinion, across the political spectrum, was already beginning to accept some of the arguments that they deployed. In his *Memoirs* Romilly protested that the French Revolution had made it exceedingly difficult to get 'legislative reform on humane and liberal principles' and he cited the abuse which his 1808 bill to abolish the death penalty for pickpockets had prompted from the younger brother of a peer. What he does not mention is the fact that his bill went through parliament without a division and received the royal assent less than six weeks after its introduction.[26] Admittedly other bills were less successful: in 1810, 1811, 1813, 1816 and 1818 the Commons passed bills to abolish capital punishment for stealing from a shop to the value of five shillings; on each occasion the Lords rejected the bill. But the statistics collected by the government revealed that between 1805 and 1820, when the Stealing in Shops Act was passed, no-one was executed for the offence.[27]

As with the opponents of police reform, the early nineteenth-century opponents of reform of the criminal law had a coherent and logical case, though few historians have given them credit for such. Anti-reformers insisted that justice was not a lottery and that judicial discretion was sensibly and conscientiously practised. Just as the reformers could point to cases of injustice, so their opponents could point to examples which showed the system working with mercy and moderation. No-one, for example, was executed for stealing goods from a shop valued at less than five shillings, but the potential was there if someone with a particularly evil character did face such a charge or if it was considered that an example was required *pour décourager les autres*. Probably the strongest plank in the platform of the traditionalists was their doubt that there could ever be a significant measure of certainty in the way that a punishment was meted out to fit a particular crime. The Criminal Law Commissioners who were appointed in 1833 ran into major difficulties when they sought to establish a rational system of punishment. In their second report, in 1836, they specified four overall classes of crime, each with two alternative penalties; in their fourth report, three years later, there were fifteen overall classes of crime, each with a far greater range of penalties; by 1843, and their seventh report, the scale of penalties had reached forty-five, more than double the number of twenty which they had initially specified as the absolute maximum. The attempts of the commission to establish precise penalties for precise offences eventually foundered.[28] Randall McGowen has argued, persuasively, that the issue in dispute between traditionalists and legal reformers in the early nineteenth century:

was not how to secure the greater efficiency of the criminal justice system, but how to present a more pleasing image of justice. The desire was not just to reduce crime but to secure wider support for the legal order.[29]

The traditionalists were defending an aristocratic and paternalistic image of justice and focused on the practice of the courts and the use of mercy; the reformers focused on existing severities and called for impersonal justice with the law being above the suspicion of dependence on any personal discretion. The problem for the opponents of reform was that influential Tories like Peel were also pressing for change. It remains a matter of debate whether this was simply the result of a mixture of humanitarianism, rationalist ideas rooted in the Enlightenment larded with evangelicalism and Benthamite utilitarianism; whether, as McGowen argues, beneath this there were also structures of developing class alliances in a fast-changing society; or whether, as Gatrell maintains, Peel and his colleagues were seeking primarily to shore up and revitalise a system in danger of collapsing under the weight of increasing convictions and the corresponding necessity for more pardons. What needs to be acknowledged is the logic of the traditionalists' case; what needs to be rejected is the notion that the reformers had a far-sighted vision of nineteenth-century progress which would culminate in the modern legal system.[30]

It was under Peel's reformist regime at the Home Office during the 1820s that the first significant moves were made by a government to rationalise the criminal justice system. Urged on by the energetic philanthropists of the Prison Discipline Society, Peel sponsored a Gaol Act in 1823, and amending legislation in the following year, which sought to establish a measure of uniformity throughout the prisons of England and Wales. The legislation was informed by the idea of the penitentiary: it spelled out health regulations and religious regulations; it required the separation of different categories of prisoner and facilities for hard labour; it directed magistrates to inspect their local gaols three times a quarter, and demanded that annual reports be sent from each gaol to the secretary of state. Many local gaols ignored at least some of these regulations, including the requirement for an annual report. Peel was reluctant to antagonise local sensibilities over independence and consequently made no attempt to impose either sanctions or a national system of inspection. It was not until 1835 that the reforming Whig government of Melbourne, with Lord John Russell at the Home Office, established a prison inspectorate of five. Yet from Peel's time onward, home secretaries were interventionist and every government developed some sort of policy on the punishment of criminal offenders.

The death penalty began to lose its central role in the criminal justice system with Peel's rationalisation of the law even though the numbers capitally convicted continued to rise roughly in line with the rise in criminal statistics during the 1820s and early 1830s. Nevertheless, following on from Peel's reforms, the number of capital offences continued to be reduced throughout the 1830s and early 1840s.[31] By the late 1830s it was rare for anyone to be executed for any offence other than murder (Table 10.5), and by the mid-1840s a significant movement had developed for the total abolition of capital punishment.[32] With the decline in the use of the death penalty prisons acquired a more central role in the criminal justice system, but until the middle of the century transportation also remained an option for the courts when dealing with those deemed serious offenders.

The numbers transported began to increase from about 1,000 to about 2,500 a year with the perceived crime wave at the end of the Napoleonic Wars. They increased further during the 1820s and reached a peak in the early 1830s with about 5,000 convicts being shipped to Australia each year from Great Britain and Ireland; the numbers transported from England and Wales constituted roughly two-thirds of the total. From the beginning of the second decade of the nineteenth century until the mid-1830s, about one-third of all those convicted at assizes or quarter sessions were either sentenced, or had a death sentence commuted, to transportation. This fraction began to fall rapidly over the subsequent decade to about one-seventh. Except for the early years and the very last years of the system, between two-thirds and three-quarters of those sentenced to transportation were actually shipped to Australia.[33]

During the eighteenth century doubts had been expressed about the extent to which transportation was a punishment; one penal reformer, writing in the aftermath of the loss of the American colonies, suggested that those who had been transported had actually been given the opportunity to become 'profitable members of another state'.[34] Similar doubts were raised about conditions in Australia. The relatively liberal and reforming regime of Governor Lachlan Macquarie in New South Wales was criticised in J. T. Bigge's official enquiry into the conduct of the colony published

TABLE 10.5 *Capital sentences, number executed and number executed for murder, 1805–54*

Ten-year period	Average number capitally convicted per annum	Average number executed per annum	Average number executed for murder per annum
1805–14	443	66	13
1815–24	1,073	89	16
1825–34	1,218	53	12
1835–44	199	13	10
1845–54	57	9	9

Source: Based on figures given in Parliamentary Reports

in 1822. As a result of Bigge's report restrictions were put on the governors of the colonies and policies of greater severity were applied towards convicts. Even so in 1826 the Reverend Sydney Smith could write to Peel satirising a sentence of transportation as follows:

translated into common sense [it] is this: 'Because you have committed
this offence, the sentence of the Court is that you shall no longer
be burdened with the support of your wife and family. You shall be
immediately removed from a very bad climate and a country over
burdened with people to one of the finest regions of the earth, where
the demand for human labour is every hour increasing, and where it is
highly probable you may ultimately gain your character and improve
your future. The Court have been induced to pass this sentence upon you
in consequence of the many aggravating circumstances of your case, and
they hope your fate will be a warning to others.'[35]

Stories circulated of men committing crimes simply to get transported.[36] Yet as the Select Committee on Transportation which met between 1837 and 1838 under the chairmanship of Sir William Molesworth, the treatment of many convicts in Australia was appalling. The problem was that, as the committee rightly pointed out, the penal colonies were so far away that people in England were unaware of the severity of the life and, consequently, there was no deterrence.[37] The committee condemned the existing system of transportation and favoured the building of penitentiaries; the majority proposed penitentiaries in both Britain and the colonies but Molesworth himself opposed their establishment in the colonies on the grounds that this simply perpetuated transportation under another name. The report ultimately led to changes in the system of convict labour and to experiments aimed particularly at the reformation of convicts, but the practice of shipping abroad the more serious offenders was not abolished as a judicial sentence until 1857. A few offenders continued to be sent to Western Australia and in 1863 a Royal Commission advocated continuing transportation and using it as the climax of a convict's sentence,[38] but the proposal came to nothing. It was as much pressure from the colonists, increasingly proud of their new land, as any growing faith in prisons as the best means of punishment which finally brought about the demise of transportation in the British penal system.

As the wave of colonial opposition to transportation built up during the 1830s and 1840s so a particular concept of prison discipline began to dominate from Westminster. The Select Committee of the House of Lords whose report, in 1835, recommended the appointment of a government inspectorate of prisons, also advocated a system of prison discipline based on silence. Wakefield Gaol and Coldbath Fields had adopted the silent system the preceding year. Overnight, recalled the governor of the latter institution, 'all intercommunication by word, gesture or sign was prohibited'.[39] A different group of experts advocated the separate system in preference to silence; notable among these were William Crawford, a leading figure in the Prison Discipline Society, and the Reverend Whitworth Russell, a former chaplain at Millbank; both men were among the first five appointees to the prison inspectorate. Separation, or solitary confinement, had been central to the thought of many early advocates of the penitentiary. A visit to the United States by Crawford convinced him of the superiority of the separate over the silent system and on his return he published a massive study of American prisons explaining his conclusions. More importantly, while there was no unanimity among the prison inspectorate, both Crawford and Whitworth Russell took every opportunity to urge their preference in their inspectors' reports. Somewhat hesitantly Lord John Russell authorised the construction of a new national penitentiary in London and Captain Joshua Jebb of the Royal Engineers was entrusted with the design. Jebb, subsequently appointed Surveyor-General of Prisons, was favourable towards the separate system himself, but his evidence to a parliamentary committee in 1850 suggests that the leading advocates of the system were not averse to a bit of blackmail:

I was requested by . . . Mr Crawford and Mr Russell . . . to allow them to be associated with me in the consideration of the plans, and they urged this reason: they said, 'We do not wish to control your professional opinion; but if you erect a prison which we do not consider to be adapted for the enforcement of the system which we advocate, we will not certify the cells, and the prison will be useless.[40]

Pentonville, the end-product of Jebb's designs and Crawford's and Whitworth Russell's urgings, was opened in 1842.

The inmates of Pentonville were kept in solitary cells. Each wore a mask, the 'beak', when moved around the building so that anonymity was preserved. At the required church parades each convict was confined to a separate box so that communication with his fellows was all but impossible. The plan was for the solitary confinement and anonymity of Pentonville to last for eighteen months before a man was transported. It was believed that, thrown in upon themselves, in the quiet, contemplative state of the solitary cell, convicts, assisted by their bibles and the exhortations of the chaplain, would come to a realisation and repentance of their wrong-doing. The Reverend John Clay, another enthusiast for the separate system recorded how:

a few months in the solitary cell renders a prisoner strangely impressible. The chaplain can then make the brawny navvy cry like a child; he can work on his feelings in almost any way he pleases; he can, so to speak, photograph his thoughts, wishes and opinions on his patient's mind, and fill his mouth with his own phrases and language.[41]

The problem was that not every convict was quite as malleable; some abused and assaulted warders, others developed serious psychological disorders or attempted suicide. Before the end of the 1840s even the annual reports of the prison's commissioners were compelled to admit that there were difficulties with the system.[42]

The initial, optimistic logic of the separate system, together with increasing pressure from the Home Office for national uniformity, led to some county and borough authorities establishing a cellular system in existing or in purpose-built prisons. But, as with provincial policing, provincial gaols were always limited by cost. The Bedfordshire justices ruled out the construction of a miniature Pentonville for their county on the grounds that it could not be done for less than £25,000. When, in 1848, they did embark on a rebuilding programme on a tender of just over £17,000 they faced a vociferous protest from ratepayers. Northernhay Gaol in Exeter was completed in 1819; by the 1830s it was insufficient for the number of prisoners sent to it but, primarily because of the expense, there was no new gaol and no provision for the separate system. The Lancashire magistrates, partly at the prompting of Clay, were committed to the separate system by the middle of the century, but a ratepayers' revolt helped to put the brakes on any successful implementation.[43]

Religion was central to the convict's reformation in the eyes of advocates of the separate system. This led to the eclipse of the idea that useful and profitable labour could be an element in reformation. Preston Gaol had provided the model for the industrial prison with its inmates subcontracted by three local textile firms and being allowed a proportion of the monetary value of their work. The practice was vehemently condemned by Sydney Smith in a celebrated article for the *Edinburgh Review*. In Preston itself the practice received little support from Clay, while Crawford objected that prisons were not intended as training schools for artisans. Work had a place, but only as a privilege, and to prevent the convict from dwelling too much on his previous evil way of life.[44] As a consequence labour in prisons from the 1820s tended to be increasingly pointless marching on the treadmill, turning a handcrank or picking oakum in the solitude of a cell, or shifting cannonballs along a line of men from point A to point B and back.[45] But, again, whatever the theories of the influential experts some local gaols continued to go their own way. During the 1840s the inmates of Durham Gaol were producing cloth, mats, nets and rugs for sale in nearby markets; indeed one of the prison inspectors even suggested employing a tailor to teach his trade to the prisoners and replacing a treadmill with a smithy and a workshop.[46]

To a lesser extent the arguments over work in prisons were replicated in arguments over education. Moral reformation did not necessarily require the development of basic skills in literacy and numeracy; and, it was argued, prison should punish offenders, not reward them with educational advancement. Few seriously questioned the necessity of educating, and thus reforming and rescuing, juvenile offenders however, and some prisons offered educational opportunities to all inmates. From the early nineteenth century the central government committed itself to such education though, as in other matters, it was left to those in the localities to decide on how best to go about this. Education was initially linked to

Convicts picking oakum
A typical task for prisoners was to unpick old, tarred ships' rope (oakum). Men were normally expected to pick three pounds a day. The walls of the shed in the Clerkenwell House of Correction, where this drawing was made, were adorned with religious homilies; note 'The Eyes of the LORD are in every place'. © Illustrated London News Ltd/Mary Evans

religious teaching but, as the century wore on, religion and education were increasingly decoupled. Costs kept educational provision down as with other issues managed in the provinces, but exceptionally progressive magistrates, such as those in Berkshire could, and did, provide significant educational improvements.[47]

The need to separate young offenders and to prevent their corruption by hardened recidivists had been urged for generations. By 1818 magistrates in Birmingham, like those in London, were sentencing some juveniles to short periods in a local reformatory financed by private subscription.[48] Melbourne's government took a positive step towards separating the juvenile offender in 1838 when a former military hospital on the Isle of Wight, Parkhurst, was opened with a reformatory regime for convicts under the age of eighteen prior to their transportation. The experiment was short-lived. During the 1850s a band of indefatigable reformers including Mary Carpenter and Matthew Davenport Hill proselytised in favour of reformatories and industrial schools while private organisations, like the Philanthropic Society, established such institutions on an independent basis to reform and educate juvenile offenders. In 1853 a Select Committee on Criminal and Destitute Children recommended a degree of state assistance for reformatory schools and the Youthful Offenders Act 1854 provided for persons under sixteen years to be sent to such schools for from two to five years following a prison sentence. Three years later legislation sanctioned sending to industrial schools any children between seven and fourteen years who had been committed for vagrancy. A perceived decline in juvenile crime during the second half of the nineteenth century was often attributed by the reformers to the reformatory and industrial schools; though they also insisted that a lack of trained staff and a reluctance on the part of some magistrates to use the provisions limited the success of the schools.[49] It is, of course, unlikely that a decline in juvenile crime can be put down to one single element and taking the country as a whole it is clear that there was no common sentencing policy with reference to juveniles, the number of places available in these schools varied from locality to locality,[50] and the majority of convicted juveniles continued to be sent to ordinary gaols. Furthermore, locality and gender both appear to have influenced sentencing decisions: more urban than rural offenders were sent to prison, more boys than girls; also disproportionately more Irish children were incarcerated. All of which suggests sentencing practices in keeping with prejudices about crime and offenders.[51]

The deaths of both Crawford and Whitworth Russell in 1847 removed the two most ardent advocates of the separate system at the centre of national prison administration. The system had never been implemented across the nation with the uniformity and rigour that they had wished and, within a decade of their deaths, debates about the respective superiority of separation and silence gave way to other questions: how to handle convicts who, because of the end of transportation, were now released into the home community; and was the whole penal system sufficiently severe? Furthermore the deaths of Crawford and Whitworth Russell contributed to the balance of the system swinging away from the idea of religion as a central and significant aspect in the convict's reformation and towards a more rigorous application of the idea of prison as punishment.

The ticket-of-leave, introduced by the Penal Servitude Act 1853, was not entirely new.[52] Releasing convicts on licence following good behaviour had become a feature of the system in the penal colonies; moreover large numbers of persons sentenced to transportation were, for a variety of reasons, never shipped abroad and were released in Britain after a term in gaol. The virtual end of transportation in the early 1850s required that something be done for those convicts in the national penitentiaries who were expecting a release on licence at some stage after they reached Australia. Jebb warned the Home Office of a build-up of tension among frustrated convicts and while there were considerable qualms expressed by both the Home Secretary, Lord Palmerston, and his civil servants, the ticket-of-leave seemed to offer an answer. The ticket-of-leave was a conditional pardon with remission granted towards the end of a sentence to any convict not guilty of idleness or misconduct. Initially the press and members of parliament were reasonably sympathetic to convicts released in this way, particularly when they seemed unable to get work or seemed to be the objects of police harassment.[53] But the lack of an administrative bureaucracy organised and primed to cope with the ticket-of-leave system created major problems. Furthermore by the mid-1850s both sections of the press and some members of parliament had become vociferously hostile, linking an apparent rise in violent crime with ticket-of-leave men now prowling the English streets rather than those of the antipodes. Probably also these suspicions were linked with the perceptions of criminals as a group. While Mayhew himself was sympathetic to the plight of ticket-of-leave men, the picture that he, and others, sketched of criminals as a class apart brought up to their own, skilled criminal trades, was not conducive to the ex-convict being accepted and reassimilated as an unfortunate, *former* offender who had paid his debt to society. Amending legislation in 1857 tightened up the system and extended prison sentences so that seven, rather than four years' penal servitude in England, became the equivalent of seven years' transportation to Australia. Momentarily, the concerns subsided, but they erupted again with the garotting panic of 1862. Garotting was seen in many quarters as the work of ticket-of-leave men; like housebreaking it was defined in the press as a 'science'.[54] Parliament responded with the 'Garotters' Act', which authorised a flogging of up to fifty strokes in addition to any other punishment given to those found guilty of armed or violent robbery. A Royal Commission appointed to investigate the legislation relating to transportation and penal servitude resulted in the new Penal Servitude Act of 1864. This required police supervision of ticket-of-leave men and specified minimum sentences of penal servitude: five years for a first offence, seven years for any subsequent.

There was doubt about the precise meaning of the term 'penal servitude' when it was first enshrined in law in 1853; the doubt continued. Even though the Home Office was increasingly issuing directions and taking responsibility for prison administration, no government was prepared to commit itself as to whether the penal system as a whole, and penal servitude in particular, was designed to deter, to punish, or to reform. The Penal Servitude Acts were *ad hoc* legislation rather than the product of any consistent, reasoned policy. The initial legislation established 'penal servitude' (whatever it was) to balance the declining use of transportation, with those sentences which were served at home to be marginally less than those in the colonies. Amending legislation ironed out some problems but generally made penal servitude sentences longer in response to concerns about the end of transportation, the ticket-of-leave system and the garotting scares of 1856 and 1862.[55]

The year 1863 witnessed another round of increasing severity in the penal system. In addition to the Garotters' Act it was in that year that Joshua Jebb died. Knighted and promoted to a major-general, Jebb nevertheless died with the regime which he had administered as Director of Convict Prisons increasingly coming under attack for being too soft on dangerous men. That same year Edmund Du Cane, another officer of the Royal Engineers and a strict disciplinarian who was ultimately to take over the directorship, was appointed an Assistant Director of Convict Prisons. Finally, but by no means least, a Select Committee of the House of Lords, chaired by the Earl of Carnarvon, presented its report on Gaol Discipline. The Carnarvon Committee disputed the suggestion that moral reformation was more important than punishment and it extolled the virtues of the crank, the treadmill and shot drill. The Committee also urged the closure of small prisons and the withdrawal of Treasury support from any local gaol which did not conform to Home Office regulations. Many of the recommendations, particularly those advocating greater severity, were incorporated in the third Penal Servitude Act. The results were not always what was intended. While the crank and the treadmill were recommended for those sentenced to penal servitude, they seem to have been more likely the lot of the short-term prisoner confined to a local gaol for a petty, and often a first-time offence. After nine months of solitary confinement in Millbank or Pentonville, where they generally picked oakum or sewed, long-term penal servitude convicts were removed to the public works prisons of Chatham, Dartmoor, Portland or Portsmouth where, often at great risk to life and limb, they generally quarried stone or constructed fortifications and dockyard facilities.[56] Some of the smaller local prisons also continued to go their own way and it was not until 1877 that all prisons were brought under central control, which in practice then meant the strict supervision of Du Cane.

The hardening attitude towards prison discipline drew on the changing perception of the offender. There was little point in attempting the reformation and education of those identified by Social Darwinists and positivists as innately criminal and inferior.[57] Yet these emerging theories also coincided with further limitations on capital punishment, the final shift of physical punishment away from public view, and an increasing tendency to have decisions made by experts regarding the fate or treatment of offenders. While in practice since the 1840s no-one had been executed for any crime other than murder, it was not until the Offences Against the Person Act of 1861 that parliament finally abolished the death penalty for all crimes except murder and high treason. In 1856 a select committee recommended the ending of public executions. A royal commission made the same recommendation ten years later. The deterrent effect of a public execution was now perceived as negligible and far outweighed by the problems and dangers created by the large crowds which such executions attracted. The last public execution took place outside Newgate on 26 May 1868. Except for the occasional glimpse of a convict gang in the vicinity of a public works prison or the possible sight of a convict being escorted by guards on a train, the penal system was now closed to public view. After sentencing in court – justice as personified by the courts still had to be *seen* to be done – the convict was not seen again by the public until release; the capitally convicted convict was never seen again in public, unless subsequently reprieved and released. In the eighteenth and early nineteenth centuries the decision as to whether or not a felon should go to the gallows had been a royal prerogative; the decision was actually made in the King's Council. But by the mid-nineteenth century the prerogative of mercy was administered by the home secretary and his bureaucrats working to a series of loose guidelines that were not greatly different from those applied earlier – age, reputation, previous convictions and so forth.[58]

The removal of the convict and of punishment from public gaze robbed the felon of any moment of glory or martyrdom. This was also in keeping with notions of dignity and decorum so important to Victorian sensibility, but which were emerging before Victoria's reign.[59] Whether the mystery of punishment increased its deterrence is a moot point.[60] Whether the dramatic reduction of the number of capital offences together with the bringing down of the curtain on the theatre of public executions produced a qualitatively more humanitarian penal system is also open to debate. Of course convicted criminals were no longer executed, or at least sentenced to be executed, in large numbers. The early reformers like Howard and then the gaol inspectorate led to prisons being better regulated and cleaner; the chance of death from the variety of typhus known as gaol fever was all but removed. The replacement of the entrepreneurial gaoler with an increasingly centralised and regulated system also meant a common diet for all prisoners whatever their financial situation. Yet whatever the boasts of the experts the diet was not particularly nourishing and regularly brought on the most unpleasant and painful stomach complaints. If public spectacle had gone, brutal punishment still remained with the added variant of electric shock treatment – 'galvanising' – for convicts suspected of malingering. In addition to the official brutality of the birch, the crank, electric shock and the treadmill, there was the psychological suffering brought about by solitary confinement and enforced silence. Warders, like policemen, had discretion and were not always under the eyes of upright superiors; some showed kindness and generosity towards those in their charge; others were noted for lashing out unofficially with boot, club and fist. Convicts responded in kind.[61]

Entrepreneurial gaolers and the officials responsible for penal colonies could coerce their charges, but the notion of reformation required sanctions to make the recalcitrant conform even if they did not intend to reform. If one or two convicts were allowed to set bad examples the system would be undermined. Together with sanctions came the introduction of token rewards to encourage compliance and reward good behaviour. Ferocious abuse from a warder, a bread and water diet, solitary confinement, or a flogging provided the stick; gratuities for good conduct and industry among long-term prisoners, and the ability to work time off the end of a long sentence by collecting high 'marks', provided the carrot. The 'marks' system was finalised to mechanical perfection under Du Cane and, at the same time, different uniforms were designed to denote what stage a convict had reached in his sentence, and whether his behaviour had been good or bad.[62]

The increasing role of prison staff in deciding the treatment of convicts in their charge developed as arguments and unease continued about sentencing policy in the courts. While some late-eighteenth and early-nineteenth-century reformers had sought particular punishments to fit particular crimes, the improved bureaucracy and record-keeping at both the national and local level meant that previous convictions could more easily be brought to a court's attention before sentence was passed.[63] For some offenders a criminal record became a veritable millstone around their necks; being 'known to the police' and being found in suspicious circumstances in itself could lead to magistrates inflicting a short sentence as a suspicious person. As noted in the previous chapter there was insufficient evidence to convict the two ex-ticket-of-leave men charged with garotting James Pilkington M.P., but the police magistrate nevertheless sentenced them to three months' imprisonment as suspicious persons.[64] Liberal public concern centred on the discretion and veracity of the police. In 1866, following a burglary trial in which the police had given corrupt evidence and, initially the magistrate had refusal to hear evidence for the defence, *Fun* ridiculed the Metropolitan Police Courts with a cartoon of a magistrate rejecting a ragged boy while a smug policeman looked on (see the illustration 'Nupkins's Justice').

The sentence of penal servitude gave magistrates and judges the opportunity to inflict ferocious sentences on persons who, while undoubtedly pests in that they were continually being brought before different courts, never carried out any particularly serious offence. The prosecution and sentences of Crowsley, Hudson and Taverner offer examples of this (see Table 10.6 and the illustration 'Prisoner records: William Hudson'); and it is significant here that one of the sentences, imposed on Taverner (in March 1861) was three months for being a suspicious person. Yet the use of this legislation varied from place to place. The magistrates in the industrial districts of the north west used it more than those in London or in rural counties; and Gloucestershire and Hampshire stand out among the rural counties for their use of the Penal Servitude Acts, almost certainly because of the influence of T. B. Lloyd Baker and the Earl of Carnarvon on their respective county benches.[65]

Sentences of this sort on relatively minor, if persistent and infuriating offenders, brought forth criticism from liberal-minded reformers.[66] Concern was also expressed that sentences for property offences often seemed excessive in comparison to those meted out to violent offenders. But, as in the case of prison policy, no consensus could be reached on how to improve the sentencing system. There was a basic conservatism in the legal profession and especially among the judiciary which worked against proposals for a codification of the law. Codification was a foreign route; and while it was a last resort, Francophobia could always be enlisted to bolster arguments

NUPKINS'S JUSTICE.

Learned Magistrate :—" HEAR THE EVIDENCE FOR THE DEFENCE? NONSENSE! I WON'T HEAR A WORD OF IT! WHAT'S THE USE?——I COULD NOT THINK OF DOUBTING A POLICEMAN'S WORD."

'Nupkins's Justice'
(British Cartoon Archive, University of Kent, www.cartoons.ac.uk)

that, whatever the merits of the Code Napoleon, the reasons for its creation were not relevant to England, and the means by which it was established were alien to the English constitution. When even Du Cane criticised the system of sentencing, his comments served, not to foster change, but to reveal a division within the Home Office over whether government should appear to give directives to judges and magistrates. Throughout the century when judges and magistrates came to pass sentence they continued to use their discretion and to be swayed by influences external to the case before them; and while reformers and codifiers might lament it, others boasted, in contrast, that herein lay one of the strengths of the system. 'It seems to me', remarked Baron Alderson in 1854 (see Table 10.6).

a very unwise thing to abolish the common law principles of decision, which can accommodate themselves to the varying circumstances of the times, and thus, as it were, to stereotype them by Act of Parliament in verbal definitions, many of them inaccurate. This will leave the courts only to construe precise words, instead of adapting old principles to new cases as they arise.[67]

TABLE 10.6 *'Penal servitude' for petty recidivists*

(a) Prosecutions and convictions of William Henry Crousley, born c. 1849, labourer

Offence	Court	Date	Sentence
Stealing provisions	†	7 July 1862	1 calendar month
Stealing bread	Bedford Borough	Easter 1863	Acquitted
Stealing tares		1 June 1863	1 calendar month
Assault		4 July 1864	1 calendar month
Wilful damage		5 Sept. 1865	1 calendar month
Stealing potatoes	Bedford Borough	Midsummer 1866	12 calendar months
Stealing growing crops		4 May 1868	2 calendar months
Using insulting words		7 Jan. 1870	7 days
Riot	Bedford Borough	Epiphany 1871	acquitted
Stealing 2½ pecks potatoes	Bedford Borough	Easter 1872	7 years' penal servitude and 7 years' police supervision

(b) Prosecutions and convictions of William Hudson, born c. 1808, labourer

Offence	Court	Date	Sentence
Sheep-stealing	Beds Quarter Sessions	Midsummer 1838	Acquitted
Stealing a spade	Beds Quarter Sessions	Midsummer 1838	6 weeks
Stealing a fowl	Beds Assizes	Lent 1839	1 year
Game Laws		Feb. 1844	6 weeks
Stealing hen and chickens	Beds Quarter Sessions	Epiphany 1845	acquitted
Sheep-stealing	Beds Quarter Sessions	Epiphany 1845	Transported 15 years

(b) Prosecutions and convictions of William Hudson, born c. 1808, labourer

Offence	Court	Date	Sentence
Stealing potatoes		Aug. 1854	1 calendar month
Stealing hay	Beds Quarter Sessions	Midsummer 1860	7 days
Stealing meat	Beds Assizes	Lent 1876	3 calendar months
Stealing sickles, basket and other articles	Beds Quarter Sessions	Michaelmas 1868	7 years' penal servitude

(c) Prosecutions and Convictions of Samuel Taverner, born c. 1839, labourer

Offence	Court	Date	Sentence
Stealing fowls	Beds Quarter Sessions	Michaelmas 1855	3 calendar months
Stealing iron		25 Mar. 1856	3 calendar months
Wilful damage		17 Nov. 1857	6 weeks
Stealing barley	Beds Quarter Sessions	Epiphany 1858	No true bill
Assault		8 June 1858	1 calendar month
Wilful damage		14 Sep. 1858	21 days
Stealing barley		14 Sep. 1858	21 days
Stealing a rat trap		31 Jan. 1860	1 calendar month
Suspicious person		5 Mar. 1861	3 calendar months
Drunk and riotous		21 Oct. 1861	21 days
Stealing manure bags	Beds Quarter Sessions	Epiphany 1862	3 years' penal servitude
Drunk and riotous		27 Sep. 1864	7 days
Stealing cabbages		10 June 1865	1 calendar month
Game Laws		19 Dec. 1865	2 calendar months or £3 8s. fine
Game Laws		18 Sep. 1866	1 calendar month or £2 14s. fine
Stealing barrow wheel and some iron (value 3s.)	Beds Quarter Sessions	Michaelmas 1867	7 years' penal servitude
Stealing 5 pieces of lindsey (value £1)	Beds Quarter Sessions	Epiphany 1874	10 years' penal servitude and 7 years' police supervision

Source: Based on details in Beds. R.O. QGV 10/4†
† Where the court is unspecified in the records it was almost certainly petty sessions

Prisoner records: William Hudson
Note the missing left hand replaced by a hook. (Bedfordshire Archives)

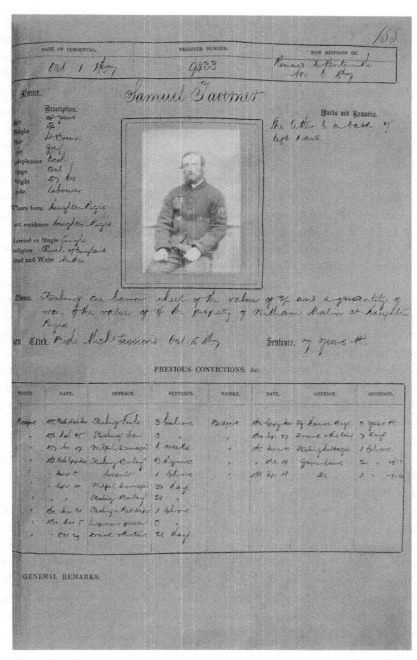

Prisoner records: Samuel Taverner
(Bedfordshire Archives)

Yet if controversy continued to remain about sentencing policy a significant change had taken place. In the space of one hundred years a custodial sentence had become virtually the only punishment that the courts could award; fines continued to be imposed for many petty offences, but with the proviso that failure to pay would lead to imprisonment. These changes in the system of punishment have been related to the great changes taking place in society. This was implicit in the writings of the Whig historians who thought in terms of progress and who saw British society as, essentially, consensual. Others, in contrast, have explained the development of the prison in terms of the control needs of bourgeois capitalism, or else have adopted the bleak vision of Foucault that society was geared increasingly towards categorising, controlling, measuring and imposing new levels of surveillance. The old notion of the 'truth' lying somewhere between the extremes will not do; why should the 'truth' necessarily be found between diametrically opposed world views?

Humanitarianism counted in the reform of punishment. Whatever the psychological make-up of late-eighteenth and early-nineteenth-century reformers which fostered their ideas of prison discipline,[68] they drew considerable inspiration from the humanitarian and rational elements within the Enlightenment. Brutal punishments, suffering in unregulated gaols, the apparent lottery of who was executed and who was not, all mattered to these reformers; they also convinced others that these things mattered, and notably they convinced men at the centre of government. The state played an important role in the changes in punishment. It was a capitalist state and, arguably, increasingly a bourgeois state. Anglo-Saxon historians have, perhaps, been too timid in acknowledging the role of the state in pushing ahead with many reforms in the nineteenth century. Albeit piecemeal and, at times, reluctantly governments sponsored legislation which reduced capital punishment and were prepared to become involved in the administration of convicts and prisons; once involved it was probably impossible for the state to extricate itself as bureaucratic machinery spawned and renewed itself. But, at the same time, it is difficult to detect a simple 'state' or a 'class' line on punishment developing consistently during these years.[69] Serious divisions remained and at the beginning of the twentieth century, Sir Robert Anderson lamented the way that punishment continued to swing between extremes:

Let anyone propose, for example, that a 'hooligan' shall receive the sort of punishment which at a public school would be meted out to the son of a duke for gross misconduct, and they will raise such an outcry as will stifle legislation to that end. Another minority, equally small in numbers, will always protest against any amelioration of the prisoner's lot. And thus the pendulum is kept swinging, while an easy going public remains perplexed and passive.[70]

Much of the legislation – the Penal Servitude Acts for example – was *ad hoc*; and when parliament legislated, or when the Home Office issued directives, many localities were reluctant to act promptly and thoroughly in accordance with the new law or the new directive, partly because of local pride but more often perhaps because of the expense. If the bourgeois capitalist state wanted a new system of punishment to help control the new and growing proletariat, the provincial bourgeois capitalists – even in the heartlands of the Industrial Revolution – may have been notably keen to see the Penal Servitude and Habitual Criminals legislation enforced, but they were most reluctant to pay increased rates and taxes to finance changes in policing and prisons. 'Prisons', according to one author:

like the workhouse under the New Poor Law, were not primarily for locking people up, but about disciplining those who were not in prison. So, although convicts might resist and obstruct prison discipline, their role in social control was assured simply by their existence.[71]

The fact that the new prison was developed at roughly the same time as the workhouse under the New Poor Law makes this equation appealing; the parallel with the control system of the new factory can also be drawn.[72] Clearly there are similarities: closed institutions are going to resemble each other from the very fact of being closed institutions, though this does not necessarily prove similar motives for their creation. Vagrancy and idleness were faults which reformers like Chadwick perceived as rampant in sections of the working class; these faults had to be eradicated and the threat of the workhouse was a means to this end. In this perception of the world vagrancy and idleness also led to crime, which gives further underpinning to the equation. But the equation requires some qualification; there were also considerable differences in intention between the two institutions, and considerable differences in perception which it would be difficult to put down simply to bourgeois hegemony. Provision for the very old, the very young, and the infirm was also supposed to be a part of the new workhouse; and the debate over whether prisons were meant to reform and inculcate good habits, or simply to punish, was never resolved. But perhaps most important is to look at the two institutions from the bottom up. There was no working-class sanction for the workhouse as the disorders of the

1830s and 1840s, and the continuing hostility throughout the nineteenth century, demonstrates. The workhouse hung over sections of the poorer working class like a sword of Damocles in a way that the prison never did. The workhouse was more visible; several of the great convict prisons were constructed well away from centres of population and what went on inside them was increasingly private – one reason perhaps for the apparent popularity of prison biographies which revealed this secret world for the vicarious pleasure of the nineteenth-century reader.[73] Groups of workers who profited from illegal fiddles and perks did not regard as 'criminals' those of their workmates who were caught, convicted and imprisoned for such offences. Yet other former convicts from the working class did find it hard to get accepted, not simply by employers, but also by some working-class communities after a prison sentence.[74] Since the working class were often the victims of crimes it is scarcely surprising if they had little time for many former offenders. The popular abuse heaped on certain unpopular offenders as they were conveyed to Tyburn Tree in the eighteenth century should warn against any notion of the working class automatically siding with convicted criminals against a common class enemy. There is no reason to suppose anything other than that, in the popular mind, the prison was accepted as being designed not as an encouragement to them to behave, but as a place where genuine offenders were to be punished.

Notes

1 The best of the Whig studies is **Leon Radzinowicz**, *A History of English Criminal Law*, vol. 1, Stevens, London, 1948 and (with **Roger Hood**) vol. 5, 1986; the latter volume has been re-published as *The Emergence of Penal Policy in Victorian and Edwardian England*, Clarendon Press, Oxford, 1990. For a Whig view of the abolition of the death penalty see **David D. Cooper**, *The Lesson of the Scaffold*, Allen Lane, London, 1974. **Michael Ignatieff**, *A Just Measure of Pain: The Penitentiary in the Industrial Revolution 1750–1850*, Macmillan, London, 1978, constitutes one of the most stimulating works of revision, though Ignatieff has backtracked to some degree, see his 'State, civil society and total institutions: a critique of recent social histories of punishment', in **S. Cohen** and **A. Scull** (eds), *Social Control and the State*, Oxford U.P., Oxford, 1983. There is a passionate study of the reality of the public execution, its cultural meanings, and the role of these meanings in the gradual repeal of the Bloody Code, in **V. A. C. Gatrell**, *The Hanging Tree: Execution and the English People, 1770–1868*, Clarendon Press, Oxford, 1994. **David Garland**, *Punishment and Modern Society: A Study in Social Theory*, Clarendon Press, Oxford, 1991 is a subtle and very readable analysis

of the theoretical literature with a thoughtful and stimulating approach
to assessing punishment as a cultural phenomenon which embodies and
expresses the cultural forms of a society.

2 *P.P.* 1833 (344) xiii, *Select Committee on Municipal Corporations*, pp. 2730,
3088–9 and 6388–90; **R. E. Swift**, 'Crime law and order in two English
towns during the early nineteenth century: The experience of Exeter and
Wolverhampton 1815–56', unpublished Ph.D., University of Birmingham,
1981, pp. 82–3.

3 For example at the Old Bailey Sessions in January 1801 George Mell was
convicted of stealing indigo from an East India Company warehouse in
Billiter Lane; he was sentenced to six months in Newgate and a public
whipping to be conducted for a distance of one hundred yards in Billiter
Lane. At the same sessions Richard Cain was convicted of stealing coal from
a barge at Queenhithe; he was sentenced to twelve months in Newgate and
a public whipping from Queenhithe to Queen Street. OBP t18010114–17
(Mell) and t18010114–18 (Cain).

4 For the use of the stocks in the mid-nineteenth century see **Clive Emsley**,
'The Bedfordshire Police 1840–56: A case study in the working of the Rural
Constabulary Act', *Midland History*, vii (1982), pp. 73–92 (at pp. 84–5);
B. J. Davey, *Lawless and Immoral: Policing a Country Town 1838–57*,
Leicester U.P., Leicester, 1983, pp. 44, 143, 147, 162 and 164.

5 The best survey of eighteenth-century punishment and the contemporary
debates is **J. M. Beattie**, *Crime and the Courts in England 1660–1800*,
Oxford U.P., Oxford, 1986, chapters 9 and 10. Beattie argues that the 1718
Transportation Act constituted a fundamental break with the practices and
intentions of the penal policy of the past, and that it was, in consequence, as
significant as the establishment of prisons in the last decades of the eighteenth
century. See also, **A. Roger Ekirch**, *Bound for America: The Transportation of
British Convicts to the Colonies, 1718–1775*, Clarendon Press, Oxford, 1987.

6 *Hansard*, new series, xiv, col. 1220.

7 **J. A. Sharpe**, *Crime in Early Modern England 1550–1750*, 2nd edn,
Longman, 1999, pp. 90–99; **Clive Emsley**, 'Repression, "terror" and the rule
of law in England during the decade of the French Revolution', *E.H.R.*, c
(1985), pp. 801–25 (at pp. 822–3).

8 Gatrell, *The Hanging Tree*, *passim*.

9 **Randall McGowen**, 'From pillory to gallows: The punishment of forgery in
the age of the Financial Revolution', *P and P*, **165** (1999), pp. 107–40; see
also, *idem*, 'Forgery discovered: Or the perils of circulation in eighteenth-
century England', *Angelaki*, **1** (1994), pp. 113–29.

10 **Robert Shoemaker**, 'Streets of shame? The crowd and public punishments
in London 1700–1820', in **Simon Devereaux** and **Paul Griffiths** (eds),

Penal Practice and Culture 1500–1900: Punishing the English, Palgrave, London, 2004.

11 *Northampton Mercury*, 12 August 1754.

12 *Ibid.*, 20 July 1752, quoting the *London Evening Post*.

13 *Ibid.* See also *Sussex Weekly Advertiser*, 30 August 1819, for the following: 'Upon arrival of the cart under the fatal tree the Rev Mr Noyce, the clergyman in attendance, ascended it and began to pray . . . requesting the unhappy man to join him, but this Piper refused to do, saying that he was a murdered man and that Pearce was perjured and that he never snapped a pistol at him . . . he went on to observe that there was no law for a poor man, and referred to a case last Assize wherein one prisoner was condemned to death and another, charged with a similar crime, was sentenced to two months imprisonment, and called down heavy vengeance on the heads of his prosecutors.'
Martin Madan reported 'the understanding and policy of a low thief to say to *Judge Burnett*, once, at *Hertford* Assizes – "My lord, it is very hard to hang me for *only* stealing a horse". It was worthy the good sense and wisdom of the learned Judge, to answer – "Man, thou art not to be hanged *only* for stealing a horse, but that horses might not be stolen".' **Martin Madan**, *Thoughts on Executive Justice*, London, 1785, p. 105.

14 **E. T. Hurren**, *Dissecting the Criminal Corpse: Staging Post-Execution Punishment in Early Modern Europe*, London, Palgrave Macmillan, 2006, http://link.springer.com/book/10.1057%2F978-1-137-58249-2

15 **J. S. Cockburn**, 'Punishment and brutalization in the English enlightenment', *Law and History Review*, **12** (1994), pp. 155–79.

16 *Gentleman's Magazine*, **xli** (1771), p. 147.

17 Ignatieff, *Just Measure of Pain*, p. 57.

18 Lord North's government finally collapsed in March 1782; the second Rockingham administration lasted only till July 1782 and Lord Shelburne's administration, which followed it, fell in April 1783. The Fox-North coalition lasted from April to December 1783, and while the younger Pitt ultimately brought stability, he had to fight a general election in December 1784.

19 **Jonas Hanway**, *The Defects of Police, the Cause of Immorality and the Continual Robberies Committed, Particularly in the Metropolis*, London, 1775, p. 72; for similar criticism of the hulks see Madan, *Thoughts on Executive Justice*, pp. 74–6.

20 *Journals of the House of Commons*, **xl**, pp. 1161–4.

21 *Gentleman's Magazine*, **lvi** (1786), pp. 263–4.

22 Ignatieff, *Just Measure of Pain*, pp. 128–42.

23 A. G. L. Shaw, *Convicts and the Colonies: A Study of Penal Transportation From Great Britain and Ireland to Australia and Other Parts of the British Empire*, Faber and Faber, London, 1966, p. 59.

24 Peter King, *Crime and Law in England, 1750–1840: Remaking Justice From the Margins*, Cambridge U.P., Cambridge, 2006, chapter 4.

25 *Gentleman's Magazine*, lvi (1786), p. 102.

26 John Cannon, *Parliamentary Reform 1640–1832*, Cambridge U.P., Cambridge, 1973, p. 140, note 3.

27 Cooper, *The Lesson of the Scaffold*, p. 33 states that the 1820 legislation failed, but see K. K. Macnab, 'Aspects of the history of crime in England and Wales between 1850–60', unpublished Ph.D., University of Sussex 1965, appendices pp. 22 and 24.

28 Sir Leon Radzinowicz and Roger Hood, 'Judicial discretion and sentencing standards: Victorian attempts to solve a perennial problem', *University of Pennsylvania Law Review*, 127 (1779), pp. 1288–349 (at pp. 1290–9).

29 Randall McGowen, 'The image of justice and reform of the criminal law in early nineteenth-century England', *Buffalo Law Review*, 32 (1983), pp. 89–125 (at p. 96).

30 No historian has argued simply and explicitly that Romilly, Mackintosh and other reformers had a contemporary legal system in mind as the model toward which they aspired; yet this view implicitly informs the work of the Whig historians. McGowen highlights this in his excellent critique of Radzinowicz: 'His volume on the death penalty is informed by one idea – that the gallows represented an inefficient and inhumane form of punishment. This observation is so obvious to him that he pauses to wonder before thinkers and politicians who for so long resisted the "truth". The opponents of change are portrayed as simple reactionaries, blinded by self-interest or prejudice from seeing the value of new institutional forms.' *Ibid.*, p. 94. Simon Devereaux recently has come to the defence of Peel against Gatrell by stressing that the real increase in executions came under Peel's predecessor at the Home Office, Lord Sidmouth. Peel, Devereaux argues, was more conscientious in his decisions over pardons and more sensitive to growing concerns about the number of executions. Simon Devereaux, 'Peel, pardon and punishment: The Recorder's report revisited', in Devereaux and Griffiths (eds), *Penal Practice and Culture 1500–1900*.

31 Macnab, 'Aspects of . . . crime', appendix 3, pp. 13–14 lists twenty-six acts of parliament removing capital punishment from particular offences between 1808 and 1835; subsequent legislation, in 1837, removed the death penalty from such offences as assembling with arms to assist smugglers, abortion, forging wills and power of attorney for the transfer of stock, attempted murder, burglary, piracy, arson of buildings or ships; and legislation of 1841

abolished the death penalty for rape, carnally abusing girls aged under ten, riot, and embezzlement by Bank of England servants. Following the Offences Against the Person Act 1861 the death penalty remained only for murder and high treason.

32 Cooper, *Lesson of the Scaffold*, pp. 45–53 and chapter 3 *passim*.

33 Shaw, *Convicts and the Colonies*, pp. 147–50; **L. L. Robson**, *The Convict Settlers of Australia*, Melbourne U.P., Melbourne, 1965, p. 9. Unless otherwise stated the discussion of transportation is based on the work of Robson and Shaw.

34 *Gentleman's Magazine*, lvi (1786), p. 103.

35 **Charles Stuart Parker** (ed.), *Sir Robert Peel: From His Private Papers*, 3 vols, London, 1891, i, pp. 400–1.

36 **J. J. Tobias**, *Crime and Industrial Society in the Nineteenth Century*, Penguin, Harmondsworth, 1972, p. 246.

37 P.P. 1837–38 (669) xxii, *Select Committee on Transportation*, p. 20.

38 P.P. 1863 (3190), *Report of the Royal Commission to Inquire into the Operation of Acts Relating to Transportation and Penal Servitude*.

39 Quoted in **Philip Priestley**, *Victorian Prison Lives: English Prison Biography 1830–1914*, Methuen, London, 1985, pp. 35–6.

40 Quoted in **Christopher Harding *et al.***, *Imprisonment in England and Wales: A Concise History*, Croom Helm, London, 1985, p. 152. There was little love lost between Jebb and these two inspectors, see **Eric Stockdale**, 'The Rise of Joshua Jebb, 1837–50', *British Journal of Criminology*, **16** (1976).

41 **W. L. Clay**, *The Prison Chaplain: A Memoir of the Rev John Clay*, London, 1861, p. 386.

42 Ignatieff, *Just Measure of Pain*, pp. 9–10; Priestley, *Victorian Prison Lives*, p. 38.

43 **Eric Stockdale**, *A Study of Bedford Prison 1660–1877*, Phillimore, London, 1977, pp. 165 and 176; Swift, 'Crime, law and order', pp. 87–8; **Margaret E. DeLacy**, 'Grinding men good? Lancashire's prisons at mid century', in **Victor Bailey** (ed.), *Policing and Punishment in Nineteenth-Century Britain*, Croom Helm, London, 1981, pp. 209–11.

44 **Sydney Smith**, 'Prisons', *Edinburgh Review*, **xxxvi** (1822); DeLacy, 'Grinding men good?', pp. 200–2.

45 Priestley, *Victorian Prison Lives*, pp. 121–31; Harding *et al.*, *Imprisonment*, appendix 3.

46 **James C. Burke**, 'Crime and criminality in County Durham 1840–55', unpublished M.A., University of Durham, 1980, p. 91.

47 Rosalind Crone, 'The great "Reading" experiment: An examination of the role of education in the nineteenth-century gaol', *CHS*, **16**, 1 (2012), pp. 47–74; see also, Priestley, *Victorian Prison Lives*, pp. 108–11; Burke, 'Crime and Criminality', pp. 93–6.

48 Barbara Weinberger, 'Law breakers and law Enforcers in the late Victorian city: Birmingham 1867–77', unpublished Ph.D., University of Birmingham, 1981, p. 116.

49 Jelinger C. Symons, *Special Report on Reformatories in Gloucs., Shropshire, Worcs., Herefordshire and Monmouthshire, and in Wales* (Printed in *P.P.* 1857–58 [2315] xlvi, *Minutes of the Committee of the Council on Education*); John Trevarthen, 'Hooliganism', *Nineteenth Century*, **xlix** (1901), pp. 84–9.

50 Stockdale, *Bedford Prison*, p. 153.

51 John A. Stack, 'Children, urbanization and the chances of imprisonment in mid-Victorian Britain', *C.J.H*, **13** (1992), pp. 113–39.

52 Unless otherwise stated what follows is drawn largely from Peter W. J. Bartrip, 'Public opinion and law enforcement: The ticket-of-leave scares in mid-Victorian Britain', in Bailey (ed.), *Policing and Punishment*.

53 Police harassment could be used as a defence in court by former convicts who insisted that because of the police they were unable to get a steady job. For example in November 1856 Charles Hunter, accused of robbery with violence at the Old Bailey protested: 'When I came home from transportation, I obtained a situation at a beer house in the Waterloo Road, where I was getting a comfortable living, and supporting my wife and aged mother; I had been there a few weeks when sergeant Broad came and told the landlord that I was a ticket-of-leave man, and if he allowed such characters in his house he should indict it; he told me to go; after that I drove a costermonger barrow, and he followed me about the streets, telling my customers to see that their change was good, for I was a ticket-of-leave man; I was compelled to give that up; I went to live with my parents, and worked at tailoring, and every time I came in or out of the court where I lived, he would stop and search me, if any of the neighbours or their children were about; so that at last I could get nobody to trust me with anything; what had I to do? I would work if they would let me, but they will not.' OBP t18561124–87. See pp. 182–3, this volume.

54 H. W. Holland, 'The science of garotting and housebreaking', *Cornhill Magazine*, **vii** (1863), pp. 79–92.

55 M. Heather Tomlinson, 'Penal servitude 1846–65: A system in evolution', in Bailey (ed.), *Policing and Punishment*; see also Bartrip, 'Public opinion and law enforcement'.

56 Priestley, *Victorian Prison Lives*, pp. 131–4. An exhaustive account of Carnarvon's ideas and how these fed into Du Cane's practice, is to be found

in **Sean McConville**, *English Local Prisons 1860–1900: Next Only to Death*, Routledge, London, 1995.

57 **W. J. Forsythe**, *The Reform of Prisoners, 1830–1900*, Croom Helm, London, 1987, chapter 8.

58 **Roger Chadwick**, *Bureaucratic Mercy: The Home Office and the Treatment of Capital Cases in Victorian Britain*, Garland Publishing, New York, 1992. See especially his discussion of the Home Office's Criminal Memoranda for decisions, pp. 382–83.

59 In March 1825, for example, during discussions on a bill dealing with the punishment for sending threatening letters and a Felonies Pardon Bill, Ralph Bernal condemned the 'most unbecoming' practice employed at some of the London Police Offices 'of passing the prisoners, many of whom stood charged with common assaults, manacled through the streets from the offices to the prison'. Peel agreed about the 'indecency' though he considered that it would be too expensive to provide transport; he had advised the magistrates to use hackney carriages. *Hansard*, new series xii (1825), col. 1167.

60 **Henry Fielding**, *An Enquiry Into the Causes of the Late Increase of Robbers*, 2nd edn, London, 1751, was critical of the Tyburn executions and urged privacy drawing a theatrical parallel. 'Foreigners have found fault with the Cruelty of the English Drama, in representing frequent Murders upon the Stage. In fact, this is not only cruel, but highly injudicious: A Murder behind the Scenes, if the Poet knows how to manage it, will affect the Audience with greater Terror than if it was acted before their eyes.' He instanced Macbeth's murder of Duncan as performed by David Garrick (p. 193).

61 Priestley, *Victorian Prison Lives*, especially chapters 7 and 9.

62 Harding *et al.*, *Imprisonment in England and Wales*, p. 229.

63 During the 1830s local gaolers kept the Bedfordshire Clerk of the Peace informed of men awaiting trial who had faced previous prosecutions. See, for example, Beds. R.O. 1834/634–5, 640 and 644–5.

64 See p. 250, this volume.

65 **S. J. Stevenson**, 'The "Criminal Class" in the mid-Victorian city: A study of policy conducted with special reference to the provision of 34 and 35 Vict., c. 112 (1871) in Birmingham and East London in the early years of registration and supervision', unpublished D.Phil., Oxford University, 1983.

66 Radzinowicz and Hood, 'Judicial discretion and sentencing standards', pp. 1310–11; *Sir James Fitzjames Stephen* argued in his *A History of the Criminal Law of England* (vol. 1, p. 479) that there could be some justification for bringing back the death penalty not only for brutal violence, but also for someone who, it was proved, was totally irredeemable. See the discussion in **Robert Anderson**, 'Our absurd system of punishing crime', *Nineteenth Century*, **xlix** (1901), pp. 268–84.

67 Quoted in *ibid.*, pp. 1302–3 (emphasis in original).

68 Ignatieff, *Just Measure of Pain*, is excellent on the psychology of reformers like John Howard.

69 Simon Stevenson suggests, persuasively, a pendulum effect in the final third of the nineteenth century with the authoritarian side of Benthamite liberalism dominant among legislators from the mid-1860s to the mid-1870s, a swing to a more liberal intellectual outlook during the 1880s, with a swing back towards coercive solutions in the 1890s. Stevenson, 'The "criminal class" in the mid-Victorian city', pp. 389–422.

70 Anderson, 'Our absurd system of punishing crime', p. 278.

71 **Philip Rawlings** in Harding *et al.*, *Imprisonment in England and Wales*, p. 179.

72 See, for example, **D. Melossi and M. Pavarini**, *The Prison and the Factory: Origins of the Penitentiary System*, Macmillan, London, 1980.

73 See the bibliography in Priestley, *Victorian Prison Lives*.

74 Weinberger, 'Law breakers and law enforcers', p. 156.

CHAPTER 11

Concluding remarks

Different contexts foster different areas for historical study. It is interesting to speculate why there has been a growth in academic interest in the history of crime and criminal justice in the last half-century or so. Anyone interested can now turn to Paul Knepper's book *Writing the History of Crime* which addresses this issue together with informative surveys of the different theoretical approaches and the use of evidence within a variety of historical fields.[1]

Many of the social historians who began the current wave of research into crime, and which led to the first edition of this book, had been nurtured in the heady political enthusiasm of universities during the 1960s. Their inspiration came from studying 'history from below' and particularly the work of Eric Hobsbawm, George Rudé and E. P. Thompson. Much of their interest was directed to the enormous economic and social changes of the eighteenth and nineteenth centuries. The criminal law and the courts were seen as one way into a deeper exploration of class relationships; after initial studies of crowds and rioting, they focused their attention on property crime. A later generation, much more gender sensitive, shifted towards studying crimes of violence – offences which might have been inter-class, but were rather more likely to be inter-gender. In this context the criminal law and the courts were seen as routes into the exploration of gender norms and shifting relationships. The growing interest in cultural history has fostered an interest in the ways that different forms of media constructed and reported crime and the criminal justice system, and how this inter-reacted with popular understanding and policy making. It might also be stressed that the growing availability of online resources like eighteenth- and nineteenth-century newspapers has greatly facilitated such cultural history research. The Old Bailey online has similarly assisted historians. For example, a name search in the Old Bailey online for George Frederick Field, the Metropolitan Police detective lionised by Charles Dickens, reveals that he made only five appearances at the court between 1847 and 1852. But a man who shared his name, John Field, Inspector of the Mint, appeared in no less than seventy-three Old Bailey trials in 1840 alone. Yet the warning on this website needs constant repetition: the Old Bailey did not hear all, or even a majority of cases brought in London. The Magistrates' or Police Court remained the forum for hearing lesser offences.

The historical study of crime underlines the fact that it is the law that defines crime, that it was, and remains, legislators who criminalised or decriminalised specific activities though sometimes pushed by the behaviour of the judiciary, of juries or of the population in general. The collective noun 'crime' encompasses vastly different activities from murder and rape to petty theft. Some of these activities are the result of careful planning and premeditation, and some are perpetrated largely because the opportunity presents itself. During the eighteenth and nineteenth centuries the small opportunist theft was, statistically, the most common form of offending. Yet the petty nature of most criminality was, and still is, often obscured by the vicarious appetite for violence fed by sections of the newspaper press as well as by much popular literature which implied that violence was part of crime *per se*. Violent crime was what worried people; it was central to the moral panics and crime waves; it provided good copy. Yet statistically the incidence of serious inter-personal violence committed by thieves in the process of robbery was rare. Crime waves did not centre on the fear of being murdered or assaulted by spouse, parent, child, other relation or acquaintance; but statistically, perhaps they should have done.

Monocausal explanations for property crime and for inter-personal violence both present difficulties. John Waldon's decision to sell his master's stool and the calm removal of 'over a million in sterling' from the strong room of Matheson and Jardine by a nephew of Matheson, were both thefts. Opportunity may provide part of an explanation, but whatever prompted the nephew's activities it can hardly have been real economic necessity. In contrast, there is some justification for accepting Waldon's plea of poverty. The murders of Jack the Ripper and of Thomas Neill Cream, and the drunken return home of Patrick Barry which resulted in his wife being kicked to death, may all help to illuminate gender relations in Victorian London, but it is something rather different to suggest that they had a common cause rooted in those gender relations. Murder, and especially serial murder, was not a common offence. Wife-beating was, though it was not always brought before the authorities. The incidence of such beatings can only be guessed at, but there is no reason to suppose that it was necessarily any greater than the percentage of relationships which never witnessed physical violence. Assaults on the police – for which prosecution rates were running at roughly sixty-six per thousand of the population in the mid-1860s and forty per thousand at the end of the century – illuminate some aspects of police-public relations, but do not tell the whole story. Furthermore, while assaults on policemen and assaults on women and wives were alike in being defined as assaults by the law, the term itself is of little value in understanding either motive or context.

Economic development during the eighteenth and nineteenth centuries brought increasing wealth, more goods in shops and warehouses, more moveable property in people's homes and at the workplace. All of these provided greater opportunities and greater temptations for property crime. The extension of the business and commercial worlds increased opportunities for embezzlement, fraud and corruption – offences which, generally, were far more difficult to uncover and prosecute than the straightforward theft of small, moveable property. Most such offences can be linked with the workplace, but their range makes workplace crime too complex and varied to be explained solely in terms of an employer's determination to maximise his profits and an employee's desire to hang on to customary practices and perks. Indeed it would seem that in some instances the employees preferred regular wage payments to old customary practices.

The increase in property crime recorded by the admittedly imperfect statistics during the serious economic slumps of the first period of industrialisation appears significant. But the equation of poverty leading to theft is too simple. Most offenders were young. There was, perhaps, a degree of alienation among them. Some suffered a marginal existence, they had no responsibilities, and no way of making their voice heard in society. In addition, there were the pressures of the peer group to enjoy communal leisure activities, activities which generally cost money. Any or all of these elements could combine, perhaps also with the thrill of breaking the law, to encourage criminal behaviour when an opportunity arose or was perceived. Economic hardship brought about by a slump worsened poverty and probably spread temptation. But if there is a correlation between the peaks of property crime and the troughs of the business cycle, it is also apparent that the steepest overall increase in the criminal statistics during the period 1750 to 1900 coincides with fear for the social order, fear of 'the mob', fear of revolution and, during the 'hungry forties', the identification of, and anxiety about, 'the dangerous classes'. J. A. Sharpe has identified a similar statistical peak in crime coinciding with fears for the social order two centuries before.[2] The problem is explaining why these issues should coincide. Was it that, in times of social tension, people were more aware of their vulnerability to thieves and therefore more inclined to report offences and to prosecute if an offender could be identified? Was it also that an apparently shaky social order encouraged more people to reject accepted morality and to steal when the opportunity presented itself?

In his lively study of the 'respectable fears' about street crime and disorder during the nineteenth and twentieth centuries, Geoffrey Pearson suggested that such fears seem 'to serve a specific ideological function within British public life, as a convenient metaphor for wider social tensions which attend the advance of democratisation'.[3] The difficulty here is that some of the short-term panics which he identifies are not well synchronised with concerns about the social order and democratisation. The mid-nineteenth-century garotting panic offers a good example. Chartism was scarcely perceived as a threat after 1848 and three years later the Great Exhibition ushered in a period of relative social peace and satisfaction. Yet it was precisely the ten years following the Great Exhibition that experienced the fears of 'garotting'.

Crime is rarely something that people experience regularly as victims, and perceptions of crime therefore depend largely on what people are told about it. When they are informed, authoritatively, that crime is a serious problem, and when this is reiterated and backed up with statistics and graphic instances, they will probably believe it. It seems that 'crime waves' and 'moral panics' could be accelerated, perhaps even generated, during the eighteenth and nineteenth centuries by newspapers eager to boost their sales or crusading for changes in the penal system.[4] The publication of national crime statistics, together with faith in the new science of statistics, the fearful example of European revolutions together with reports of riots and disorders at home, and the repetition of notions like the concept of the 'dangerous classes', possibly served to foster the perception of a longer-term crime wave in the first half of the nineteenth century. As people's concern about crime was heightened so, arguably, more crime was reported and prosecuted. This is not to deny that necessity and need prompted some people to steal simply to exist in the early nineteenth century, but rather to re-emphasise that an increase in statistics was not just the result of more crime. By the same token, the general stability of the Victorian social order in the second half of the nineteenth century, the faith in progress, and the belief that, in spite of one or two spectacular failures, the police and the courts were improving and winning the war against crime, may have contributed to a decline in the reporting and prosecution of minor offences. The greater regularity of employment in the second half of the nineteenth century may, similarly, have eased some of the pressures on those tempted to property crime.

Conceivably the belief in progress and civilisation might have contributed to the domestication of individuals prone to violence. Towards the end of the eighteenth century there appears to have been an increasing intolerance of violent behaviour. This was manifested in a greater conviction rate and a preference to punish with imprisonment rather than just a fine; and this was a trend that was continued by judges and magistrates throughout the nineteenth century. Such intolerance may have worked upon the incidence of violent offending though, as ever, the mechanism would be hard to prove. The statistics of crime only show a decline in violent offences during the second half of the nineteenth century; and there could be other elements at work here. As the century progressed it became a mark of respectability for the working-class man to be the sole breadwinner and for his wife to supervise the domestic sphere. This put much of the onus of establishing a family's respectability on the wife. It may be that a very positive side of the separate spheres came in the form of the exhortation and the moral influence of women on their menfolk to be 'respectable' and, as part and parcel of this, to eschew different forms of aggression.

It is probably true that the state has yet to be established in which the law treats those lacking power and influence in precisely the same way as those possessing power and influence. The law, the police and the courts tend to reinforce divisions and inequalities. Yet often they seek also to overcome divisions and inequalities. Both courts and legislators in the late eighteenth and early nineteenth centuries, recognising that poor victims were disadvantaged in prosecuting offenders, sought to remedy the situation. Possibly some of this was done out of self-interest and to bolster the notion of equality before the law. At the same time it would be arrogant to deny that, among members of the elite, there were sincerely held liberal beliefs in the value and existence of such equality as well as a determination to help the less well-to-do. Similarly legislators and the courts began very gradually to modify their attitude towards, and their treatment of, female victims. Feminist activism had a role in this, but so too did Victorian notions of progress and decency, and also the Victorian understanding of gender differences. Again it is impossible to quantify the impact of these shifting attitudes.

The main argument put forward for establishing the new police was that they would contribute significantly to the prevention of crime. Unfortunately the arguments presented by advocates of police reform were rarely challenged by the first historians of the police. New research, however, is demonstrating that the old system was far from useless and that much of the old co-existed with the new until well into the nineteenth century. Indeed, victims and others continued to track, apprehend and punish offenders with or without police assistance.

Yet however much the new police were involved with the prevention and detection of crime, from the moment that they took to the streets and country lanes they were also deployed to enforce new concepts of order among the working class. At the same time police aid was demanded by, and rendered to, working-class communities and individuals. There were, however, serious gaps in what the police could do. They were discouraged from getting involved in domestic disputes. In an idealised Victorian image the family and its dwelling were havens of safety and accord and the public force of the police was not expected to invade this private sphere. Yet however much police officers held back in instances of domestic arguments and spousal abuse, the social welfare roles undertaken by police in working-class districts has been ignored too often by historians.

If the arguments for establishing the police were firmly rooted in the problem of how to prevent crime, the arguments for a new system of punishment were rooted in an Enlightenment vision of humanitarianism and rationality. Of course hidden agendas can be identified; and sometimes it seems that public arguments become more influential when change is already happening. But emphasis on a hidden agenda can obscure and deny the significance of the public one. There was heightened concern about order in late-eighteenth and early-nineteenth-century England which contributed to the creation of the new police and which led to their deployment in enforcing particular concepts of decorum and respectability. Yet allowing the hidden agenda of 'order' to mask the public agenda of 'crime' results in a distorted picture of police development. The gospel of work was central to Victorian ideology. Instilling habits of work and morality in convicts, commonly perceived as having taken the short step from idleness to crime, was regarded as beneficial both to society and to the offenders. Yet to conclude from this that the prison system that developed in the late eighteenth and nineteenth centuries, together with the new police, stemmed essentially from the control requirements of new forms of capitalism or new notions of discipline and surveillance, is to short-cut a variety of processes and to obliterate many nuances in, and impediments to these new systems.

Changes in fashion and changes in technology have led to changes in forms of offending: the cutpurse metamorphosed into a pickpocket; the development of the internal combustion engine and the decline in horse-drawn transport made 'van-dragging', by which goods were lifted from a moving vehicle, an extremely hazardous occupation.[5] The growth of, and changes within the economy in the period 1750 to 1900 fostered new opportunities for criminal behaviour. As in other periods the statistical pattern of crime appears to follow concerns about social order, though the coincidence between the troughs of the business cycle and the peaks of crime in the first half of the nineteenth century also suggests some links between economic necessity and petty theft. The reorganisation and ratio-nalisation of the criminal law, the changes in punishment, and the creation of new organs of containment and control reflect, in a variety of ways, the changing economic and social order. These developments also needed, and benefited from, a state which was increasingly prepared to be inter-ventionist. But being prepared to intervene did not mean that there was a determination within government to take control and centralise. With respect to both provincial police and prisons, governments at Westmin-ster were keen to maintain the system in which local government played the key role. Policing remained under local control with the inspectorate ensuring some national conformity in return for the Treasury grant. It was only after forty years of inspection that it was decided that the only way to ensure uniformity in the prison system was to bring the whole under Home Office supervision. Yet the traditions of the past, together with the rhetoric of English rights and liberties continued to contribute to the shape of the criminal justice system and to constrain change. Finally, the extensive range of people who participated in this system, often with considerable discretion, militates against any simple equation of either a ruling class making and administering the law for its own benefit, or a sys-tem steadily ironing out problems and abuses and developing towards a modern system somehow legitimated by the concept of the rational march of progress.

Notes

1 Paul Knepper, *Writing the History of Crime*, Bloomsbury, London, 2016.

2 J. A. Sharpe, *Crime in Early Modern England 1550–1750*, 2nd edn, Longman, London, 1999, pp. 263–68.

3 Geoffrey Pearson, *Hooligan: A History of Respectable Fears*, Macmillan, London, 1983, p. 230.

4 **Peter King,** 'Newspaper reporting, prosecution practice and perceptions of urban crime: the Colchester crime wave of 1765', *Continuity and Change*, 2 (1987), pp. 423–54; **Rob Sindall,** *Street Violence in the Nineteenth Century: Media Panic or Real Danger?* Leicester U.P., Leicester, 1990, especially chapter 3.

5 For 'van-dragging' see **Raphael Samuel** (ed.), *East End Underworld: Chapters in the Life of Arthur Harding*, RKP, London, 1981, pp. 70–1 and 284. There is an example in OBP t1899109-106, the case of Michael William Hickey, aged twenty-one, who in January 1899 was sentenced to nine months' hard labour for endeavouring to pull a post packet and seventeen postal orders off the back of a mail van. He was apprehended by the driver of the following van.

Further reading: further research

I have endeavoured to make the notes to each chapter as detailed as possible, not to obviate the need for a bibliography, but rather to supply a guide to further reading and to current debates and controversies under the relevant headings. What follows here is simply an attempt to point, first, to the most significant and useful sources and texts and, second, to topics where new research might be undertaken.

The growth of the web and the digitisation of some sources has provided students of history with ready access to a variety of archives. Notable for the history of crime and criminal justice are the digitised Proceedings of the Old Bailey from 1674 to 1913. But these need to be researched in the knowledge that most criminal cases went before lower courts. Moreover, it must not be assumed that the kinds of trials that went before the Old Bailey were replicated in the county assize courts. Some of the group involved with the Old Bailey project have, more recently, produced www.digitalpanopticon.org containing information on 90,000 offenders and their families from the eighteenth to the early twentieth centuries and enabling work on both the offenders themselves and the impact of various forms of punishment. The British Library has made available a large number of eighteenth- and nineteenth-century newspapers which are useful for getting a feel of the lower courts and the different representations of offenders; a link between the Open University and the Metropolitan Police has led to the digitisation of a few London police archives.

Douglas Hay, Peter Linebaugh, E. P. Thompson *et al.*, *Albion's Fatal Tree: Crime and Society in Eighteenth-Century England* (Allen Lane, London, 1975) was the first significant text by social historians on the history of crime. It remains a valuable starting point for eighteenth-century crime, and is usefully supplemented by the rather different angle of vision taken in the essays in **John Brewer** and **John Styles** (eds), *An Ungovernable People: The English and Their Law in the Seventeenth and Eighteenth Centuries* (Hutchinson, London, 1980). The outstanding monographs on eighteenth-century crime and the courts are **J. M. Beattie**, *Crime and the Courts in England 1660–1800* (Oxford U.P., Oxford, 1986) which is based largely on material relating to Surrey; and **Peter King**, *Crime, Justice and Discretion in England 1740–1820* (Oxford U.P., Oxford, 2000) which works out from a detailed study of Essex. For an important northern study that balances Beattie and King see **Gwenda Morgan** and **Peter Rushton**, *Rogues, Thieves and the Rule of Law: The Problem of Law Enforcement in North-East England, 1718–1800* (U.C.L. Press, London, 1998). The minor courts are often omitted as the documentation tends to be fragmentary or difficult to locate. An excellent account of the summary courts of Georgian London is **Drew D. Gray**, *Crime, Prosecution and Social Relations: The Summary Courts of the City of London in the Late Eighteenth Century* (Palgrave Macmillan, Houndmills Basingstoke, 2009).

   J. J. Tobias, *Crime and Industrial Society in the Nineteenth Century* (Batsford, London, 1967; Penguin, Harmondsworth, 1972) was pioneering. It remains useful for its survey of the contemporary literature, but subsequent research has challenged many of the basic assumptions and conclusions. **V. A. C. Gatrell** has produced a cogent case for the use of nineteenth-century criminal statistics in 'The decline of theft and violence in Victorian and Edwardian England', in **V. A. C. Gatrell, Bruce Lenman** and **Geoffrey Parker** (eds), *Crime and the Law: The Social History of Crime in Western Europe Since 1500* (Europa, London, 1980). But this needs to be set alongside **Howard Taylor**, 'Rationing Crime: The political economy of criminal statistics since the 1850s', *Economic History Review*, **51** (1998), pp. 569–90. There are several nineteenth-century regional studies in thesis form, most of which show the influence of **David Philips**'s excellent study of the Black Country, *Crime and Authority in Victorian England: The Black Country 1835–60* (Croom Helm, London, 1977). More recent, valuable regional studies are **Carolyn A. Conley**, *The Unwritten Law: Criminal Justice in Victorian Kent* (Oxford U.P., New York, 1991) and **David J. V. Jones**, *Crime in Nineteenth-Century Wales* (University of Wales Press, Cardiff, 1992). Both of these touch significantly on questions of gender, but the outstanding monograph on women before the law is **Lucia Zedner**, *Women, Crime and Custody in Victorian England* (Clarendon Press, Oxford, 1991). Also important in this respect is **Dierdre Palk**, *Gender, Crime and Judicial Discretion, 1780–1830* (Royal Historical Society/Boydell Press, 2006). Juvenile crime excited passions among contemporaries; the best book remains **Heather Shore**, *Artful Dodgers: Youth and Crime in Early Nineteenth-Century London* (Royal Historical Society/Boydell Press, 1999). Shore has also published an important study of London's criminal groupings – sometimes families, sometimes people linked by offence, *London's Criminal Underworlds, c. 1720–c. 1930: A Social and Cultural History* (Palgrave Macmillan, Houndmills Basingstoke, 2015).

On rural crime, **John E. Archer**, *'By a Flash and a Scare,' Arson, Animal Maiming and Poaching in East Anglia 1815–1879* (Clarendon Press, Oxford, 1990) provides a valuable, level-headed account of what appears to have been peculiarly extreme violence in Norfolk and Suffolk. **Timothy Shakesheff**, *Rural Conflict, Crime and Protest: Herefordshire, 1800–1860* (Boydell, Woodbridge, 2003) addresses similar problems on the opposite side of England and draws significantly on the concept of social crime.

No-one interested in the legal, penal and police reforms of the eighteenth and early nineteenth centuries can afford to ignore **Michel Foucault**, *Discipline and Punish: The Birth of the Prison* (Allen Lane, London, 1977). While the bulk of the illustrative material here is French, the arguments range much wider. These reforms, as they occurred in England, provide the focus for **Sir Leon Radzinowicz's** exhaustive *A History of English Criminal Law* (Stevens, London, 5 vols, 1948–86). Alternative interpretations to Radzinowicz's fundamentally 'Whiggish' approach can be found in **Michael Ignatieff**, *A Just Measure of Pain: The Penitentiary in the Industrial Revolution 1750–1950* (Macmillan, London, 1978) and **V. A. C. Gatrell**, *The Hanging Tree: Execution and the English People, 1770–1868* (Clarendon Press, Oxford, 1994). The intellectual underpinning of penal policy is expertly described by **Martin J. Wiener**, *Reconstructing the Criminal: Culture, Law and Policy in England, 1830–1914* (Cambridge U.P., Cambridge, 1990). For broad surveys of developments in police see **Clive Emsley**, *The English Police: A Political and Social History* (2nd edn, Longman, London, 1996), *idem, The Great British Bobby: A History of British Policing From the 18th Century to the Present* (Quercus, London, 2009, revised edn. 2010) and **David Taylor**, *The New Police in Nineteenth-Century England: Crime, Conflict and Control* (Manchester U.P., Manchester, 1997). A detailed focus on the crucial developments in provincial policing in the early nineteenth century can be found in **David Philips** and **Robert D. Storch**, *Policing Provincial England 1829–1856: The Politics of Reform* (London: Leicester U.P., 1999).

Violence and sexual offending have become significant areas for research over the last decade. Important here are **Louise A. Jackson**, *Child Sexual Abuse in Victorian England* (Routledge, London, 2000) and **Shani D'Cruze**, *Crimes of Outrage: Sex, Violence and Victorian Working Women* (U.C.L. Press, London, 1998). The latter has also edited a useful set of introductory essays, *Everyday Violence in Britain, 1850–1950: Gender and Class* (Longman, London, 2000). **Martin J. Wiener**, *Men of Blood: Violence, Manliness, and Criminal Justice in Victorian England* (Cambridge U.P., Cambridge, 2004) provides an important and stimulating argument about the use of the law to curb violence and reformulate notions of masculinity during the nineteenth century. **John Carter Wood**, *Violence and Crime in Nineteenth-Century England: The Shadow of Our Refinement* (London, Routledge, 2004) describes the origins of violence as a 'problem' within English society while **Clive Emsley**, *Hard Men: Violence in England Since c. 1750* (London, Hambledon, 2005) links the understanding of violence with perceptions of Englishness. **James Sharpe**, *A Fiery and Furious People: A History of Violence in England* (London, Random House, 2016) usefully and importantly surveys the problem over a much longer time scale.

One of the most novel approaches to violence is **Rosalind Crone**, *Violent Victorians: Popular Entertainment in Nineteenth-Century London* (Manchester U.P., Manchester, 2012). This addresses how respectable Victorians, while determined to hide offenders and punishment from public gaze, positively revelled in violent media as well as representations in brutal melodramas and puppet plays. Indeed, the representation of crime through various forms of media – broadsheets, newspapers, novels, plays – is beginning to emerge as a significant area of research, but for the moment perhaps rather better served for the eighteenth than the nineteenth century.

Most journals concerned with cultural and social history now regularly carry articles on crime and criminal justice. There is also a specialist, bilingual (English/French) journal, *Crime, histoire et sociétés/Crime, history and societies* that anyone interested in the subject should consult; and a specialist online journal *Law, Crime and History* (www.pbs.plymouth.ac.uk/solon/hjournal).

The opportunities for archival research remain plentiful, especially now that there has been a shift away from property crime to gender differences in criminal behaviour and to inter-personal violence. Eighteenth- and nineteenth-century quarter sessions provide a rich mine; the county material is usually more detailed than that for the boroughs. Assize records in The National Archives and petty sessions records in local archives are rather more fragmentary, but the latter should prove particularly useful for the new direction of research. Perhaps the next generation of historians of crime should attempt more detailed studies based on depositions which are, as yet, a greatly under-used source. There also remains a range of issues about which it would be useful to know much more: first, the workings of the old system of police, especially in rural areas, and the extent to which it survived during the nineteenth century; second, the way in which police prosecution and the courts developed during the nineteenth century; third, the way in which the law was interpreted and acted upon by different individuals, and in different contexts, not least in the summary courts; and fourth, the extent to which the civil courts may have heard cases involving criminal behaviour, particularly instances of assault.

Index